Second Edition

The New Elementary Teacher's Handbook

Flourishing in Your First Year

Kathleen Feeney Jonson

CORWIN PRESS, INC.
A Sage Publications Company
Thousand Oaks, California

For information:

Corwin Press, Inc.
A Sage Publications Company
2455 Teller Road
Thousand Oaks, California 91320
E-mail: order@corwinpress.com

Sage Publications Ltd.
6 Bonhill Street
London EC2A 4PU
United Kingdom

Sage Publications India Pvt. Ltd.
M-32 Market
Greater Kailash I
New Delhi 110 048 India

Printed in the United States of America

Library of Congress Cataloging-in-Publication Data

Jonson, Kathleen Feeney.
    The new elementary teacher's handbook: Flourishing in your first
year / by Kathleen Feeney Jonson.— 2nd ed.
        p. cm.
    Includes bibliographical references.
    ISBN 0-7619-7872-0 (c) — ISBN 0-7619-7873-9 (p)
        1. First year teachers—United States—Handbooks, manuals, etc.
2. Elementary school teachers—United States—Handbooks, manuals, etc.
3. Elementary school teaching—United States—Handbooks, manuals, etc.
I. Title.
    LB2844.1.N4 J65 2002
    372.11—dc21
                                                        2001004494

This book is printed on acid-free paper.

01 02 03 04 05 06 07 7 6 5 4 3 2 1

Acquiring Editor:	Rachel Livsey
Corwin Editorial Assistant:	Phyllis Cappello
Production Editor:	Olivia Weber
Editorial Assistant:	Cindy Bear
Typesetter/Designer:	Denyse Dunn
Copy Editor:	Rachel Hile Bassett
Cover Designer:	Michael Dubowe

Contents

....

Chapter 4   Preparing Lesson Plans and Units That Engage Students   76

Preface to the Second Edition

$\textbf{H}$ere in the first year of the new millennium, there's a simple but unavoidable truth about improving our schools: We can't do it if we don't have qualified teachers in every U.S. classroom. As school enrollments grow and as more teachers retire, we face a huge challenge in training—and retaining—enough high-quality new teachers.

In my own state, California, some three hundred thousand new teachers will need to be hired during the next decade. In places like Los Angeles, the shortage has reached epic proportions: More than half of the new teachers hired this school year lack certificates. About one fourth of the district's teachers are working with emergency credentials, and not surprisingly, they are concentrated in schools with the most disadvantaged students.

If you are one of those new teachers, we need you! We are glad you have chosen teaching as a profession, and we want you to like it and to stay. This book has been written with you in mind.

I recently read a wonderful report about new teachers: *A Sense of Calling: Who Teaches and Why* (Farkas, Johnson, & Foleno, 2000). Based on an in-depth survey of 664 public school teachers and 250 private school teachers who have been in the classroom for less than five years, the researchers reported that far from feeling indifferent or disgruntled, new teachers are highly motivated professionals who bring a strong sense of commitment and high morale to their work. They see themselves as talented, hardworking professionals who have responded to a calling. They convey a love of and dedication to their craft.

The new teachers were quick to point out that theirs is a profession that requires a sense of mission and demands high levels of effort and energy. Yet enthusiasm for the job came up repeatedly in the interviews. What's more, the teachers surveyed overwhelmingly believe that the other new teachers with whom they work share their enthusiasm and commitment.

All agree that the job requires talent, judgment, and skill. Given the high priority of education in recent years and its centrality on the agendas of local, state, and national administrations, scrutiny of teacher effectiveness is likely to continue and intensify. The national discussion of standards, accountability, and high-stakes testing will put teachers' work in the limelight.

The second edition of *The New Elementary Teacher's Handbook* contains new material taking into account this changing context of education. The new edition highlights conditions that currently affect teaching and the challenges they raise for teachers. For instance, emerging demographics are significantly affecting classrooms across the country. The technological revolution has added to the challenges and opportunities teachers face. The press for standards and accountability, accompanied by increased testing, are based on the proposition that American schools are not meeting desired outcomes in terms of student achievement. All the demands have strong implications for teaching. The second edition of this *Handbook* discusses these new realities of teaching and their implications for classroom teachers. Additionally, twelve new resources have been added to the end of chapters to provide practical, ready-to-use ideas for busy beginners.

The growing pressure on teachers is manifest. Yet in the face of it all, new teachers believe in what they do, care about their students, and are deeply committed to their profession. I applaud you. Best wishes in your work to make a difference in students' lives.

A teacher affects eternity. He can never tell where his influence stops.

—Henry Brooks Adams, 1907

Acknowledgments

The contributions of the following reviewers are gratefully acknowledged:

Nancy Creech
Multiage Primary Teacher
Roseville Community Schools
Roseville, Michigan

Victor J. Ortiz
Associate Professor of Education
Kean University
Union, New Jersey

Rose H. Weiss
Principal
Cambridge Academy
Pembroke Pines, Florida

E. Ann Adams
Associate Director
Granite School District
Salt Lake City, Utah

Arlene R. Delloro
Principal
Montebello Elementary School
Suffern, New York

Preface to the First Edition

Phone calls to my office in August and September are often filled with exciting news. Another of our newly credentialed teachers has been offered a first teaching position! I smile as I listen to the animated description of job search, interview process, school district, and school. Then, the inevitable question, in some form, arises: "Dr. Jonson, do you have any advice to get me off to a good start? Help!" Anticipating the first year in their own classrooms can be breathtaking for new teachers.

I encourage them to think back on what they have done as student teachers and to build on their many successes, but no phone conversation is long enough to give them all the tips, hints, and caveats they truly need. My goal in writing this book is to provide practical advice, strategies, and resources to help new teachers succeed in their difficult first years.

Stories of beginning classroom experiences are part of teaching lore. Although some are heartwarming, many are heart-wrenching and filled with humiliation. Too many teachers have frustrating tales to tell about their first years on the job.

Of course, the beginner's experience is common to every profession; new physicians, lawyers, and architects all must apply the elements of their trade for the first of many thousands of times. All must learn to transfer what they were taught in university course work to what they must do as practitioners of their chosen profession.

Beginning teaching is no exception—or is it? What other professions physically isolate their newest members from daily contact with their colleagues? What other professions provide such low levels of supervision and role modeling or require newcomers to assume responsibility on a par with the most experienced veterans? Some of the most painful stories of beginning teachers result from this work environment. Many educators believe that the profession has hindered development of new teachers and has lost many of those with high potential.

My work in the Teacher Education Department at the University of San Francisco and as consultant for the Beginning Teacher Support and Assessment program in the San Francisco Unified School District made it clear to me that new teachers need extensive support and practical advice to

- Become better teachers
- Remain in the teaching profession
- Help their students become better learners

The California New Teacher Project (a research project of the Commission on Teaching Credentialing and California Department of Education, 1988-1992) found extensive problems confronting beginning teachers, leading to worrisome levels of stress and burnout.

> In recent years, 30% of new teachers left California's metropolitan schools and rural schools after just one year in the classroom. Nationwide, 30% leave teaching within the first two years, another 10% leave after three years, and more than half leave within five to seven years. Academically talented teachers are the most likely to leave the schools. After . . . the preparation of thousands of teachers each year, our schools lose most of this talent before our children realize many of the educational benefits. (Pearson & Honig, 1992, p. 205)

The challenge for education professionals is to alleviate the conditions that make this revolving door turn so fast.

The situation, fortunately, is changing. At this writing, more than half of the fifty states have begun systematically addressing the needs of beginning teachers by implementing formal programs of induction into the profession. Many of these induction programs feature experienced and accomplished teachers, often referred to as *mentors,* who provide assistance to new teachers. This book is designed and written to support both beginning teachers and the mentors who help them survive their first years on the job.

Among the great challenges of this profession are the loneliness of teaching and the presence of what, at times, can be an awful feeling of isolation. New teachers need to know that they are not alone, that others care, and that help is available.

The New Elementary Teacher's Handbook opens with a chapter devoted to building the professional relationships that will help new teachers succeed. Titled "You Are Not Alone," Chapter 1 details strategies to help the beginner fit in and seek assistance from a variety of sources. Chapter 2 contains classroom-tested ideas for setting up and organizing an effective elementary learning environment. It also discusses the importance of time and stress management and of finding balance in one's personal and professional life. The routine management of daily classroom life is the subject of Chapter 3. It encourages beginning teachers to set clear expectations and develop learner-friendly procedures to keep their classrooms running smoothly. Teaching requires good management before good instruction is possible. Chapter 4 describes effective lesson and unit planning and guidelines for using various instructional approaches. This chapter also discusses why *time on task* is essential for student learning. The importance of planning instruction and designing learning experiences for *all* children is emphasized.

Chapter 5 illustrates how to manage and monitor student behavior, one of the chief concerns of many new teachers. The chapter focuses on establishing clear standards of conduct; maintaining them consistently; using preventive discipline approaches; and demonstrating genuine warmth, caring, and respect in teacher-student interactions. In Chapter 6, various approaches to the assessment of student learning are described, especially performance-based and authentic assessments. Guidelines for portfolio development are provided. An overview of typical learning objectives for elementary students is supplied for easy reference. Chapter 7 is devoted to developing partnerships with parents. Educators have long recognized that the participation of students' families in the educational process enhances student learning. The chapter offers suggestions for communicating with families and keeping them informed of events in class, as well as tips for successful parent conferences, back-to-school nights, and open houses. Suggestions for class newsletters and sample parent letters are provided.

Chapter 8 presents answers to common problems and frequently asked questions, many of which deal with classroom management and student behavior issues. Novice teachers realize instinctively that learning cannot occur when student behavior is out of control, yet sometimes what appears to be misbehavior is actually a result of other causes. This chapter reemphasizes a key to efficient and respectful management of students: agreed-on standards of conduct and clear consequences for overstepping the bounds. The chapter also notes how in responding to classroom problems, it is also important to be sensitive to students' individual needs. Chapter 9 concludes the book by stressing the importance of continuing professional development, even for busy beginning teachers. Reflecting on teaching experiences is strongly recommended: Through reflection, real growth and therefore excellence are possible. Development of a teaching portfolio is advised as a guide for reflection and self-analysis and as a support for mentoring relationships.

Written in a practical, easy-to-understand manner, *The New Elementary Teacher's Handbook* contains a multitude of classroom-tested ideas. It can be used as a reference to the various skills and knowledge needed to become an effective teacher. The descriptions and examples of a wide variety of instructional and management issues should save the new teacher immense time and energy in planning and implementing an effective classroom program.

Although this book focuses on elementary classroom experiences, secondary teachers will also find much of value here. School principals, mentors, district supervisors, and college faculty can use this guidebook in working with new teachers. Ideally, the book will stimulate all sorts of mentor-protégé teams to create mutually beneficial and rewarding relationships.

For the new teachers I know, and all the many others, my heartfelt wish for them is to feel welcomed and comfortable in their crucial first year of teaching. I hope that this book will be a small part of the professional and social support system that helps them endure the uncertainties and emotional hardships of their tentative first year. Bright, capable, and newly certified, they have just begun the really significant learning that will happen as they close their classroom doors and begin teaching. This book is intended to help them approach their first year with courage, confidence, and self-assurance.

About the Author

Kathleen Feeney Jonson, EdD, has taught at the elementary and secondary levels and has served as a remedial reading specialist and as a teacher of students who are gifted. In her thirty-one years as an educator, she has also been a director of staff development, a principal, and a director of curriculum and instruction. She has conducted numerous workshops for teachers and administrators on such topics as integrating the curriculum, the writing process, portfolio assessment, peer coaching, and beginning teacher assistance programs. She has authored extensive handbooks, training syllabi, and curriculum guides for educators and parents. Since 1993, she has served as full-time faculty member and elementary credential program coordinator in the Teacher Education Department of the University of San Francisco, where she is currently an Associate Professor. As the oldest of nine children, she says she was "raised to teach and to mentor!"

With love to Jer, who is always there for me
even when the going gets tough,
and to Kevin, who keeps me clear
about what's really important in school and in life.

You Are Not Alone

Welcome to the teaching profession! Often named the noblest of all professions, teaching is certainly among the most important jobs in the world. No one can doubt that teachers have broad, long-lasting impact on the lives of children. People who choose teaching for a career are special. They often want to make the world a better place, to make a contribution to the future. Few become teachers for money or prestige—both should be greater. A deeper purpose, a larger vision of service, motivates most new teachers. The work is indeed rewarding. Nothing quite compares to a student's face lighting up to learning. Teaching is about learning, growing, and changing. It grants the opportunity to make a difference in the lives of children as they acquire the skills and knowledge to live and learn effectively.

As you interact with students during your hectic beginning years, stay in touch with the reasons that brought you to teaching in the first place. You, too, have only begun to learn and grow. Much of the time, you will be working alone in your classroom, with little opportunity to pause and reflect on your new role as a teacher. You may at times feel isolated and unsure. Few people will ever see you actually instructing your class. Although you may occasionally receive a compliment or an encouraging word, few adults will know the fine job you do behind the closed classroom door. Even your caring, compassion, and concern for children, the core reasons you became a teacher, are apt to go unnoticed. But keep smiling. Don't be discouraged. It is important to guard against becoming disheartened during the frenzied pace of the first year. Continue your good work. You are on your way to actualizing an important mission, a claim few in other professions can make.

After the scrutiny of a lengthy student teaching and credentialing process, you may, as many new teachers report, feel suddenly adrift. You are on your own. No university faculty or supervisors are there to provide a safety net. No friendly, familiar faces can be counted on for advice. In the months ahead, you need to find new sources of support from people who can help you survive and prosper as a teacher. These mentors and colleagues will show you how to navigate the complexities of the school system. They will welcome you personally and professionally and will provide a social and emotional support system. You are not alone. As you become better acquainted with the teachers, staff, and community of your new school, you will gradually learn what you need to know. You will refine your image or vision of what it means to be a teacher. You will move toward teacher efficacy, that confident feeling when you say to yourself, "I know I can teach any and all of these kids!" You will grow as a professional. You will also grow as an individual and begin to feel personally "at home," comfortable with your identity, safe to establish your own professional personality, and more able to explore existing options as well as to create new ones. During this process, you will become an increasingly better teacher for the children entrusted to your care.

In your beginning year, it is normal to feel overwhelmed, with little time and much to do. Establish priorities and focus on important tasks first, such as fitting into your assigned school. This chapter will help you do just that.

Basic Employee Information

Make sure you have the following basic employee information:

- Copy of your contract
- School and district rosters
- Benefit forms
- District calendar
- Current résumé

Start a special file folder for your key professional documents. Keep it handy. Update it each year.

Fitting In

Visit your assigned school at least one or two weeks before classes begin. It is important to learn about the social and cultural climate of your school and the surrounding neighborhood. Get to know the community. Subscribe to a local newspaper. Familiarize yourself with the attendance boundaries of this particular school and then walk through the neighborhood. Eat lunch in a nearby restaurant. Think about the backgrounds and values of your students, the ethnic and cultural groups represented in the neighborhood, and the economic base of the community. Perhaps your school draws from several neighborhoods. How do these neighborhoods contrast?

Now, take a walk around the school, both inside and out. You will sense your school's climate the minute you enter it. Is the atmosphere conducive to learning? Does it feel like a caring, student-friendly place? Tour the halls and look into classrooms. Locate the library or learning center, the teachers' workroom, the cafeteria, the teachers' and students' rest rooms, and the main office. You will see many new faces. Stop in to say hello to the principal. Introduce yourself to staff members you happen to meet. Visiting your new school as often as possible before the opening day provides you with an excellent opportunity to meet your new colleagues before they are faced with their own day-to-day teaching demands. Use the School Roster form (Resource 1.1) to make notes. Allow yourself some unstructured time to get a feel for the school before you're engulfed in opening week staff meetings, orientation sessions, and classroom preparation.

As you meet colleagues, you will begin to learn not only names and roles but also the informal norms and expectations of your new workplace. In some schools, beginning teachers find an open, welcoming atmosphere. In others, staff members act toward one another in a more formal, reserved manner. Some schools encourage fresh ideas and experimentation, whereas others strive to maintain tradition. Some feel that newcomers should "learn the ropes" and not "rock the boat." The social context of the school—its subtle web of unwritten rules, values, expectations, and personal backgrounds—will directly influence your teaching and your interactions with colleagues and students.

In the beginning, you will be learning how you fit into this established mini–social system. Pay close attention to the communication and relationships among staff members, students, and parents. All these relationships will take time to understand. Even with the help of a mentor or other colleague, this process involves trial and error. Take time to observe, and refrain from making snap judgments. As you listen and learn, continue to get along with everyone, and do not expect to fit in at once.

Strategies to Help You Fit In

- Learn names immediately—study the staff roster and practice pronouncing each name aloud.

- Use good manners.

- Become acquainted with one or more teachers in neighboring classrooms and with those who teach the same grade level as you do. Enjoy their company, and find something similar in your backgrounds. Ask about regular grade-level meetings. Bring cookies.

- Compliment a teacher who has an especially attractive, well-arranged classroom. Ask for tips. Be generous with compliments, but be sure you're sincere.

- Make it a point to hand in requested paperwork to the office on time. Make sure you know your duty assignment schedule (recess-playground, bus, and lunchroom duty). Be there promptly, without complaint.

- Visit the faculty room and eat lunch with the other teachers as often as you can—don't get in the habit of eating lunch isolated in your classroom to catch up on paperwork.

- Share a new teaching aid or software program, or perhaps offer to help one of the teachers master the computer or Internet.

- When you are assigned to recess duty, chat informally at least part of the time with the other teacher(s) on duty.

- Make sure your students do not roam the halls distracting others—avoid excusing them from your classroom unnecessarily with bathroom passes, library passes, or various errands.

- Join your local teachers' association, even if your district doesn't require it. Begin learning about association bargaining and politics, but don't get involved your first year.

- Contribute money cheerfully for faculty birthday gifts, cards, flowers, and new baby or hospital remembrances.

- Avoid cliques. Don't repeat rumors or spread gossip.

- Avoid taking sides on issues until you have had a chance to think them through carefully.

- Be an "upper"—not a "downer." "Up" teachers always find something positive to talk about. "Up" teachers are the bearers of good news about their students. "Up" teachers always leave a little margin for human error.

- Establish excellent rapport with your school administrator(s) early in the school year. If you say you will do something, do it.

- Find out who's who in the district administration. You may not see these people often, but you should know their names and roles. See Resource 1.2, School District Roster.

- Keep your sense of humor—smile!

- Strive to do a good job—give it your all. Your efforts will eventually be noticed, and you will become known as a conscientious worker and a positive addition to your school community.

Getting to Know Your School

Observe how staff members interact with each other, with students, and with parents. Use the following questions to guide your understanding of attitudes and relationships:

1. How do teachers interact with each other?
   a. What do teachers talk about in the lounge? In the office?
   b. Are there cliques within the staff?
   c. What are the teachers' attitudes toward students, parents, and the community?
2. How do teachers interact with the principal?
3. How do students interact with each other? What is the informal norm for student behavior in the halls, at recess, and at lunch?
4. How do teachers dress for work? Conservative or casual?
5. Who in the building really has the power to get things done?
6. Does the principal follow through? To which teachers does he or she seem to listen?
7. What other positions in the community are held by staff members?
8. How much input do parents have into the program of the school?
9. To what extent do teachers criticize policies and practices of the school or central office administration?
10. Is your school involved with an educational reform or improvement project? How are teachers reacting to the change?

As you answer these questions, you will get a better understanding of your school's inner workings and with whom you do and do not feel comfortable. You will also discover which teachers your principal often calls on for assistance and what is expected from them in return. Do you feel an easy camaraderie with these teachers? If so, consider yourself fortunate. At the same time, be careful. You do not know these teachers well yet. If they disagree with the way you conduct your class, for example, these teachers can easily report their observations to the principal without your knowledge. Make sure you allow enough time to find out who is who on your school's staff before you confide in, complain to, or criticize anyone.

Norms and Expectations

Learning what is expected, both formally and informally, is a crucial part of fitting into your new workplace. Start by making sure you learn your school's formal norms and expectations. Some of these formal norms are spelled out in your contract, handbooks, and school policies. Pay careful attention to the following items, areas in which new teachers often make their first social faux pas:

- Dress code for students and teachers
- Procedures for student discipline and student records
- Expectations regarding hall duty, lunch duty, student late passes, and fire-disaster procedures

In addition, be aware of two important, more subtle norms: the "autonomy norm" and the "hands-off norm." In the first norm, schools accord teachers informal autonomy to do almost anything they like in their individual classrooms, with the understanding that they are ultimately responsible for giving their students a good education. Teachers may not feel they have much power over decisions in the school district as a whole, but they do have a great deal of it in their own classes. Once their classroom doors are closed, teachers (even beginning teachers) do basically what they please and make almost all day-to-day curriculum and instructional decisions. This autonomy is part of the workplace culture of schools.

In addition to experiencing a great deal of autonomy in their individual classrooms, teachers also tend to have a hands-off norm that sanctions against interfering with each other's teaching. It is considered inappropriate, for instance, to suggest to colleagues that they handle student discipline issues or teach something differently.

In the hands-off norm, you are asking for problems if you interfere with the way in which veteran colleagues teach. Simply avoid discussing how these teachers provide instruction. Teachers can still be friendly and emotionally supportive, however. Teachers often talk with each other, but much informal discussion with colleagues tends to include only "safe" topics, such as students' personalities, backgrounds, social events, family affairs, and so on.

The autonomy and hands-off norms describe what typically is the case in education, not what is sound or desirable. These norms, however, will operate to some degree in your school. Many recent reform movements are trying to eliminate these norms by encouraging teachers to work together more closely.

Establishing Relationships to Help You Succeed

New teachers may seek help from many sources, including the principal, mentors, other classroom teachers, classified staff (secretaries, custodians, and teacher aides), volunteers, certified specialists, and substitute teachers. Most often, your mentor will be able to guide you. But if you do not have a mentor or if your mentor is unavailable, feel free to turn to the teacher in a neighboring classroom or to any other friendly colleague. In most cases, you can get needed information or suggestions by asking someone directly. Although strapped for time and overcommitted to a variety of projects, most teachers will be genuinely interested in helping whenever possible. Ironically, during their first shaky months, many new teachers sometimes act as if colleagues are unwelcome in their classrooms. Ask yourself if you are seeking out visitors and conversations. Are you making the time to talk? By your friendly, open approach, you are inviting your colleagues to be part of your safety net. If colleagues are unavailable, turn to an administrator, supervisor, or secretary.

Here are some general guidelines to follow when seeking help. Determine the best time of day to approach staff members or others. In emergencies, of course, it must be immediately. In other cases, you may choose to wait until lunch or break times, the end of the school day, or maybe even the following morning. When you are sensitive to others' schedules, you will find they have more time and appear more relaxed and ready to answer questions. If you feel uncomfortable, preface your inquiry with an opener such as

"I've been wondering . . ."

"Would you know . . ."

"I still don't understand . . ."

"I haven't seen anything about . . ."

"Have you received . . ."

"I've noticed that . . ."

The following sections provide information on how to establish good working relationships with the principal, staff members, and others who can help you succeed.

The Principal

The principal has a strong influence on the climate of the school. Most principals are effective, competent instructional leaders who will be able to help you with student management issues as well as with a myriad of other concerns. Think of your principal as your ally. You can expect your principal to be fair and supportive of teachers and to have students' best interests in mind.

Traditionally, it has been the role and responsibility of the principal to guide and assist the new teachers in the school. Growing demands on principals, however, have made it increasingly difficult for many of them to monitor carefully the needs and concerns of their beginning teachers. Many new teachers are first employed in schools that are large and crowded, with many students who are at risk and many students from diverse backgrounds. Thus, your principal may not have time to support you and offer needed and useful information.

Find out if you are required to make an appointment to see the principal or if you can approach the principal in the hallway, send notes, or meet before or after school. Ask your principal what types of situations he or she needs to know about. Become familiar with your school's policies regarding injuries and other emergencies. You are typically required to inform the principal immediately about injuries, emergencies, or other urgent situations.

Your principal is responsible for everything that goes on in the school. You must ask your principal about bringing outsiders into the building or taking students out for field trips and other school functions.

Usually, the principal or assistant principal evaluates teachers. Find out which administrator is responsible for your evaluations, what assessment instrument is used, and when you will be evaluated.

During your orientation meeting, the principal will usually review many of the items on the School Information Checklist (see Resource 1.3). Ask questions—do not rely on assumptions. Using the information obtained at this meeting, develop your own "To Do" list, consisting of forms to complete, dates for ordering supplies, after-hours building use, lesson plan and scheduling requirements, and so forth. Post the checklist and supporting information and memos near your desk.

Mentors

Experienced teachers are logical sources of assistance, support, and feedback for beginning teachers. Many school systems are now providing all their new teachers with mentors. Busy administrators recognize that mentoring is an effective way to support and retain capable new teachers, as well as to assist them in improving their teaching abilities. One of the most important staff relationships you will develop will be with your mentor. Typically, mentors are teachers with several years' experience at your school and grade level. Even if your mentor happens to now teach a lower or higher grade, he or she will still be familiar with your students' age level and perhaps with many of your students' families. Feel fortunate if you are employed in a school in which you can count on help from an experienced colleague assigned to provide professional advice and assistance. Such a mentor is a tremendous technical and emotional support as you deal with the concerns and problems of beginning teaching.

Asking Someone to Be Your Mentor

In a perfect world, every school and school district would have instituted a formal mentoring support program for new teachers—or a friendly, professionally savvy veteran colleague would tap you as his or her informal protégé without your having to ask. Unfortunately, in the real world of financially strapped school systems, you may not be assigned a mentor. Many experienced colleagues seem pressed for time and too busy to consider mentoring anyone. Yet you are likely to have a number of concerns and questions, for instance, about discipline and classroom management, that you feel uncomfortable asking an administrator to discuss with you. In the meantime, you are becoming friendly with one or more experienced colleagues who could help. Any of these colleagues might make a good mentor. But how do you approach them?

You and these colleagues often share the same recess or lunch periods. As you relax with them, mention that you could use some suggestions on grouping certain students, for instance, or ideas about how to handle a recent classroom management problem. When someone expresses interest in helping, you may have found a mentor. Explore the possibility by thanking this teacher for the assistance, then asking if he or she would be willing to occasionally talk with you about classroom issues. Assure this colleague that you will not need a great deal of time. Be clear about what you are asking for—that you could learn a lot about teaching reading from the colleague, for example, or that you would love to hear more about his or her students' successful work with math manipulatives. Find common ground. Be genuine and gracious. Remark that you are hoping for a chance to work more closely with someone and that you will truly appreciate any time he or she is able to spare.

If your colleague agrees, you may have found an invaluable support. On the other hand, he or she may politely decline, citing other commitments that make it difficult to consult with you. In that case, go ahead and approach other colleagues. Your respectful inquiries will be rewarded eventually.

A Good Mentor-Protégé Relationship

Working with a mentor is like having a friend who understands anxieties and concerns about teaching. Your mentor is also familiar with all those subtle nuances of your school and its informal and formal norms. In return, you must establish a good relationship with your mentor. Much will depend on the respect the two of you develop for each other.

Research on mentor-protégé relationships has found that the success of these associations is generally based on two major factors: (1) whether the protégé respects the mentor as a person, and (2) whether the protégé admires the mentor's knowledge, experience, and style. By the same token, a mentor must feel comfortable working with a new teacher. Ideally, a new teacher and mentor will get along both personally and professionally.

The following traits characterize the sort of person who becomes a good new teacher protégé. Check off all those traits you already possess.

_____ Has a "can-do" attitude
_____ Is complimentary more often than critical in interactions
       with others
_____ Has a "thick skin"
_____ Can laugh at self
_____ Is perceptive about self and others
_____ Is conscientious, well-organized, and hardworking
_____ Is ambitious
_____ Is loyal

_____ Has desire and ability to accept risk
_____ Accepts responsibility

Other Classroom Teachers

As a new teacher, you will find that faculty attitudes and interactions help set the climate of the school. Some schools will, as a whole, be more receptive to newcomers than others. Most often, you will find a supportive faculty willing to share materials and serve as informal mentors. Look for collegiality with teachers who are positive and helpful while avoiding those who seem negative. As you demonstrate your competence and willingness to learn, you will gradually gain acceptance.

Do offer to help with schoolwide projects, but also learn to say no, refusing to allow too many extras to be added to your assignment. Most of the time, you can refuse gracefully, saying that you are trying to complete a classroom project. You might also be tutoring students after school or may already have volunteered to help out in a community event. In other cases, you may be taking graduate courses one or two nights a week. Any of these reasons and excuses are perfectly acceptable. Remember also that some of the extras you may be asked to do are things no one else wants to do. Avoid overextending yourself in your first years.

On the other hand, it is important to spend some time and energy making a positive impact on your school as a whole. Pick one significant project that interests you and that will allow you to network with professional colleagues and win their regard. Devote energy to making this project a success. Your contribution will be noticed. Remember, you are launching your professional career, not just your first class.

Classified Staff Members

All classified staff members in the building have roles that directly or indirectly affect students' learning and the climate of the school. It is important to treat classified staff members with the utmost courtesy and to respect their important roles. They often know much about their school and community and can be wonderful resources for a new teacher.

School Secretaries. These invaluable staff members have a great deal of informal authority and often have the last word on how things need to be done. They can provide you with details such as phone use policies, attendance procedures, reduced-price lunches, information needed from students the first day, and accompanying forms. Learn the rules pertaining to the use of office equipment, such as the photocopy machine, and the use and location of cumulative record ("cum files"). Find out from the secretaries if there is anything else you should know about, such as due dates for progress reports, report cards, and other required material.

Custodians. Do not overlook the importance of these staff members. Custodians hold positions with potential for informal power. Establish a positive relationship with custodians by letting them know you want to co-operate. Find out what they do and how they want to have things done:

- How do custodians want the classroom to look at the end of the school day? Should chairs be placed on the desks? Should chalkboards and erasers be cleaned by students?

- What are the procedures for dealing with spills? Would custodians rather have students clean spills or deal with spills themselves?

- What is the procedure for making needed repairs? Will custodians be available to make repairs, such as fixing a broken window, window shade, desk, or chair? Or is a separate maintenance department responsible for these tasks?

- What is the procedure for getting new equipment in the room?

- Are items such as desks, tables, and old overhead projectors stored away that might be useful to you—and how can you get them?

- Is it possible to obtain such items as sponges and buckets to clean desks and table surfaces? If so, who provides these items?

Teacher Aides. These important paraprofessionals work under your direction, assisting with clerical work and noninstructional duties (everything from field trip permission slips to milk and lunch money collections, inventories, and ordering of supplies), as well as maintaining accurate records of student progress in learning and completion of assignments. More important, "para-pros" can help with certain types of instruction, such as working with individual children or small groups of students. Teacher aides are adult assistants you will soon find invaluable. Activities you might assign to teacher aides include the following:

- Tutoring individual students in specific subjects
- Helping students who were absent catch up on missed work
- Helping students find reference materials
- Helping struggling students with assignments
- Checking work and responding in writing to student journals
- Working with a small group directing an activity
- Helping with record keeping, profiles, and charts
- Preparing bulletin boards and other instructional materials and collecting and arranging displays for teaching purposes
- Duplicating, gathering, and distributing materials
- Helping with routine chores, such as attendance and lunch and milk counts

- Escorting individual students to the office, nurse, or specialist

Here are some tips for working with teacher aides:

- Allow time for you and your aide to meet and exchange introductions, to share your educational philosophy and teaching priorities, and to establish good rapport.

- As you train your aide for tasks, feel free to model as well as explain.

- Introduce your aide to the class and make him or her feel welcome. Give your aide stature as your "assistant teacher."

- Create a positive and cooperative classroom atmosphere. Your students need to see you and your para-pro working together as a team. Remember also that teacher aides observe what goes on in the classroom and interact with parents and other school staff.

- Always provide specific, helpful feedback that acknowledges good efforts and successful approaches, even when suggesting strategies for improvement.

Volunteers

Volunteers may include parents, high school and college students, and community members. Like aides, volunteers can help with individual tutoring and with clerical tasks such as worksheet grading, record keeping, preparing bulletin boards, and duplicating instructional materials for your class. Volunteers can provide valuable extra assistance and attention to students who have learning difficulties. Many teachers also invite volunteers to share special talents, such as teaching art or discussing careers. Some teachers use volunteers only for short times or special projects, such as orchestrating school talent shows and chaperoning field trips. In addition to providing assistance, volunteers often promote good public relations in the community, with other parents, and with school personnel.

Your school is likely to have policies or informal norms regarding the use of volunteers. Find out what these expectations are. Then consider the following strategies for working successfully with volunteers:

1. Discuss with a mentor or colleague whether you and your students would be likely to benefit from volunteers in your classroom. For instance, would volunteers be especially helpful for certain subjects or times of the day?
2. Find out if your school district has a well-established volunteer program and, if so, how it works and how you can use it. Inform your principal about your interest in using volunteers in your classroom.
3. If permitted, actively recruit volunteers: parents, community members, students, or senior citizens.

4. Decide early on which tasks you will have volunteers do. If you have time early in September, hold a volunteer orientation meeting.

5. Screen potential volunteers. Are they good role models for students? Are they reliable? Are they available when you need them? If they are parents of children in your class, how will students react? Can volunteers be trusted with confidential information about students? It is important that potential volunteers keep confidential any personal information about students they might observe in the classroom. It is your job to tell them what you expect.

6. Make volunteers feel welcome in your class. Get them involved in class activities as soon as possible after they have expressed an interest in helping. Whenever possible, give them a regular schedule.

7. Reward and recognize the work volunteers do. Never criticize volunteers in front of individual children or the class. (This admonition applies to aides, parents, and other staff as well.)

8. Monitor the work volunteers are doing and how they feel about their work. Troubleshoot when necessary.

9. Set up a schedule to discuss how the volunteers are doing in meeting established goals and to clarify any misinterpretations or misunderstandings that may occur.

Specialists Who Work With the Entire Class or Grade Level

Another source of help is the various specialists who may be available to work with your class. Specialists are usually itinerant staff members, including physical education, music, technology, and media teachers. With today's tight finances in typical school districts, specialists must often divide their time between two or more schools. Some specialists meet with a whole class or grade level once or twice a week. You may be expected to escort your class to the gym and art or music room. Check your school's policies and schedules for these special classes.

Here are some guidelines for working with specialists:

- Many schools have established schedules for specialists. If so, you will usually receive a printed schedule of specialists serving your students. Use a highlighting pen to mark each specialist's day, review the schedule with your students, and post this schedule in your room.

- If specialists complete their own schedules, work with these teachers in planning days and times that are acceptable to you both.

- Whether specialists take your entire class to another area or work in your room, be sure to have your students ready on time, and be understanding if the previous class runs a few minutes late.

- All your students should know the rules for behavior in and out of the classroom. Setting up consistent expectations—and sticking to them—is much more effective than threatening or implementing punitive measures later. See Chapter 5 for more on discipline.

Specialists Who Work With Individuals or Small Groups

This group of staff members includes teachers who work in remedial programs, special education, migrant education, English as a Second Language (ESL), and gifted and talented programs. Some of your students may be pulled out for remedial reading or math or for ESL classes. Although students may be pulled out during social studies, science, health, and art, in most school districts they are required to be in their regular classes for reading and math. You will be expected to work cooperatively with specialists in setting up schedules.

Discuss with a mentor or colleague ways to enable students who attend extra classes to make up missed work on returning to your room. Think about concepts children may have missed, rather than simply whether assignments were completed. Perhaps not all missed class work needs to be made up.

Substitute Teachers

Remember that substitute teachers are professional colleagues, too. Most substitutes are competent and well prepared, but they need your help and your students' cooperation. From time to time, remind your students how you expect them to behave for substitute teachers. The following suggestions will help your substitutes do a better job in your classroom:

- Prepare a folder for the substitute teacher ahead of time and place it in an accessible location. Your sub folder should include

    Lesson plan(s)
    Seating chart
    Attendance list or attendance report forms
    Bell schedule and recess and lunch times
    Copies of procedures for fire and disaster drills
    Information about students who require special services and
        those who are assigned duties
    Names and room numbers of helpful teachers
    Notes about school and classroom policies and procedures
        for discipline, attendance, and dismissal

See Resources 1.6 and 1.7 for a sample cover letter and feedback form to include in your sub folder.

- Avoid scheduling a test or a quiz that your substitute would have to monitor without knowing students' names well.

- Leave complete and specific instructions. The substitute may not be knowledgeable about your specific grade level or the content areas you want taught in your absence.

- When planning lessons, avoid incorporating manipulative materials, laboratory supplies, or objects that your substitute would have to inventory at the end of the day.

- Leave one day's activities as a special emergency plan in case your regular lessons (e.g., a complicated writer's workshop) might be difficult for the substitute to follow. Include sufficient worksheets for your students to complete.

- Ask colleagues for recommendations on requesting particular substitutes. Remember that the substitute you request may not be able to work in your classroom that day.

- Try not to be absent on Mondays and Fridays. Such absences tend to be viewed with skepticism by colleagues and administrators: "Is that teacher really ill—or just trying to extend the weekend?"

- Have a "buddy" teacher who can welcome your substitute and offer help. When you return, check with your buddy to see how effective the sub was in the classroom. This arrangement can be reciprocal.

- Remember, you do not have control over what the substitute does or does not do during the day. When you return, ask the children how the day went, and then put the day behind you and begin anew.

- Remember when you were a sub and felt alone. Substitutes are people, too. Make them feel welcome. Call them by their names. Do not refer to them as, "Oh, you must be Mr. Roberts today."

- If possible, inform the children ahead of time that you will be absent and preview the coming day's assignments. This preparation demonstrates to students your confidence that they can handle your absence.

Key Terminology and Special Programs

Educators use many terms, acronyms, and buzzwords for various programs and organizations. This "educationese" is important for newcomers to know. Understanding the jargon enables you to converse with the other insiders and helps you build working relationships with them. For a list of common terms and programs, see Education Terms (Resource 1.4) and Programs for Students With Special Needs (Resource 1.5).

Taking Initiative and Reaching Out

Your school, like all others, is a complex social organization with history, culture, values, beliefs, and expectations. You will be working not only with students but also with colleagues, administrators, and parents. Although your teaching effectiveness in the classroom is important, your interactions in the professional culture of your school are crucial to surviving and flourishing in your first year and beyond.

Do not become isolated. Because schools are organized so that each teacher is solely responsible for his or her own classroom, and because you will be so intensely busy, it is easy to withdraw. You must consciously make time in the school day to consult professionally with experienced colleagues. No one expects you to be perfect. You cannot have learned everything you need to know about teaching from your university preparation program, no matter how effective that program may have been. No one is ever totally prepared for the myriad day-to-day challenges of the classroom. Becoming a good teacher takes initiative and direction. As with any skill, you will become better with practice and coaching.

Yes, major challenges lie ahead—but you are not alone. Help is available. Many avenues of assistance, formal and informal, will be provided by experienced colleagues. So take the initiative, ask the right questions, and jump in with a smile!

In addition to the list of classroom teachers that you will obtain from your school office, make sure you also know these people in your building:

Principal: _____

Assistant Principal: _____

Secretary: _____

Custodian: _____

Cook and Assistant Cook: _____

Nurse: _____

Counselor: _____

Social Worker: _____

Gym: _____

Music/Band: _____

Art: _____

Library/Media Person: _____

Latchkey: _____

Aides (Para-Pros): _____

Room Parents: _____

PTA President and Vice President: _____

Speech Therapist/CDS: _____

Title I (or Resource Room): _____

Special Education: _____

1.2 RESOURCE
School District Roster

··

These are district-level people you may need to contact.

Superintendent _____ Phone _____

    Superintendent's Secretary _____ Phone _____

Assistant Superintendent _____ Phone _____

    Assistant Superintendent's Secretary _____ Phone _____

Curriculum Director _____ Phone _____

    Curriculum Director's Secretary _____ Phone _____

Personnel Director _____ Phone _____

    Personnel Director's Secretary _____ Phone _____

Business Office/Personnel:

    Secretary for Benefits _____ Phone _____

    Secretary for Payroll _____ Phone _____

Transportation Office _____ Phone _____

Instructional Materials Center (IMC) _____ Phone _____

Substitute Number _____ Phone _____

Credit Union _____ Phone _____

School Information Checklist

Here are some questions to ask your school principal before school begins to help you organize your first days:

_____ 1. How do I get the keys to my classroom or other rooms to which I may need access?

_____ 2. If necessary furniture is not in my room, how can I get additional tables, student desks, and so on?

_____ 3. What children are included in my class roster? Do I have any special education or resource students? Do they, or any other students, leave my room during the day? If so, what are their schedules?

_____ 4. Will a teacher aide be assigned to work with me and, if so, on what schedule?

_____ 5. What are the school rules and policies I will need to present to students?

_____ 6. What are the procedures for obtaining classroom books and for checking them out to students?

_____ 7. What expendable supplies are available, and what are the procedures for obtaining them?

_____ 8. What audiovisual materials and equipment are available, and what are the procedures for obtaining them?

_____ 9. What is the required paperwork for the first day of school, everyday attendance, and the lunch program?

_____ 10. What is the procedure for the arrival of students on the first day of school and for every day after that? (See also #13 and #17.)

_____ 11. What time will my class have music, recess, PE, lunch, computer lab, or library?

_____ 12. Are there any special events or assemblies I need to be aware of in the first week(s) of school?

_____ 13. How do students leave at the end of the day? Do I have any bus riders, and do they leave a few minutes early?

_____ 14. What are school policies about rules and consequences, suspensions, and keeping students after school for either makeup work or detention? Do parents need to be notified?

_____ 15. What duplication equipment is available, and are there specific procedures regarding its use?

_____ 16. How do I get assistance from the office for emergencies, illness, or discipline problems?

_____   17. What are the office procedures for early dismissal and late arrivals?

_____   18. Is a school nurse available? What are appropriate reasons for making a referral?

_____   19. Is a counselor available? What types of referrals does he or she want?

_____   20. What district resources are available for help in diagnosing and working with students with severe learning or behavior problems?

_____   21. What janitorial services are available for my room, and what should I do if there is an emergency cleanup need?

_____   22. To what parts of the building may I send students (library, rest room, etc.), and what procedures do I follow to send them?

_____   23. Do any of my students have some disabling condition that should be accommodated in my room arrangement or instruction?

_____   24. What is the bell schedule? (Are there bells?)

_____   25. How can I get a district and school calendar?

_____   26. Where are student cum files kept? What are the procedures to access them?

_____   27. Will I be assigned a mentor or a buddy teacher?

_____   28. When are you (the principal) available, and about what should you be consulted?

_____   29. _____

_____   30. _____

Education Terms

4th Friday Count	Attendance records on which state aid is based in some states
ACT	American College of Testing
ADA	Average Daily Attendance—a count of students in attendance, on which state funding amounts are based
ADD	Attention Deficit Disorder
ADHD	Attention Deficit Hyperactivity Disorder
()AEYC	(State) Association for the Education of Young Children
AFT	American Federation of Teachers
AI	Autistically Impaired
()ASCD	(State) Association for Supervision and Curriculum Development
ASCD	Association for Supervision and Curriculum Development
At-Risk	Students who are low achieving because of a number of factors
CAT	California Achievement Test
CTBS	Comprehensive Tests of Basic Skills
()CTM	(State) Council of Teachers of Mathematics
Cum files	Cumulative records for students
()EA	(State) Education Association
()EAP	(State) Education Assessment Program
ECE	Early Childhood Education
EDY	Educationally Disadvantaged Youth
EI	Emotionally Impaired
ELD	English Language Development
EMI	Emotionally and Mentally Impaired
ERIC	Educational Resource Information Center
ESD	Educational Service District
ESEA	Elementary and Secondary Education Act of 1988, which provides funds to districts to meet needs of EDY
ESL	English as a Second Language

FEP	Fluent English Proficient
GATE	Gifted and Talented Education
HI	Hearing Impaired
IEP	Individualized Education Plan
IRA	International Reading Association
ISD	Intermediate School District
ITBS	Iowa Tests of Basic Skills
ITIP	Instructional Theory Into Practice
LD	Learning Disabled
LEP	Limited English Proficient
LRE	Least Restrictive Environment
NAEYC	National Association for the Education of Young Children
NCSS	National Council of Social Studies
NCTE	National Council of Teachers of English
NCTM	National Council of Teachers of Mathematics
NEA	National Education Association
NEP	Non-English Proficient
Para-Pro	Paraprofessional
PET	Parent Effectiveness Training
POHI	Physically and Otherwise Health Impaired
()RA	(State) Reading Association
SAT	Scholastic Aptitude Test
SCE	State Compensatory Education
SMI	Severely Mentally Impaired
SXI	Severely Multiply Impaired
TBS	Test of Basic Skills
TC	Teacher Consultant
TET	Teacher Effectiveness Training
TMI	Trainable Mentally Impaired
VI	Visually Impaired

Programs for Students With Special Needs

....

Students with specific educational needs have the opportunity to participate in specifically funded programs. These programs are designed to provide additional assistance for identified students. Some of the specifically funded projects that may be available at your school site are included here.

Title I. Students who score below the 40th percentile in reading and/or mathematics on a standardized achievement test such as the Comprehensive Tests of Basic Skills (CTBS) are identified as educationally disadvantaged youth (EDY). EDY is a federal designation for students whose educational attainment is below the level appropriate for their age, on the basis of a nationally norm-referenced test. If your school is a Title I school, identified students are eligible to receive extra help in reading, mathematics, and language arts. Federal funds are allocated for this purpose. How students receive this service varies.

State Compensatory Education. State Compensatory Education (SCE) funds are allocated by most states to provide extra service and support for students who fall below the 40th percentile on standardized achievement tests.

Limited English Proficient/Title VII. Some students are identified as limited English proficient (LEP) or non-English proficient (NEP). Federal funds are allocated for the purpose of providing extra service and support for these students until they reach the level of fluent English proficient (FEP).

Special Education Programs. Students who are eligible for special education programs have been referred, identified, assessed, and placed in the most suitable programs. Individualized education plans (IEPs) will recommend the extent to which such students should be mainstreamed into regular classrooms. Placement follows the convention of the least restrictive environment (LRE).

Gifted and Talented Education Program. Students in gifted and talented education (GATE) programs are provided supplementary services that usually include an emphasis on reasoning skills, creative problem solving, and evaluative thinking. Some gifted and talented programs also address spatial intelligences and artistic and leadership abilities. A variety of teaching styles and materials are used to support and challenge students while developing their abilities.

Sample Cover Letter for a Substitute Folder

Dear Substitute:

I've prepared the information in this folder to provide you with a good deal of general information about my class and schedule. Whenever possible, I'll furnish specific daily lesson plans in addition to the enclosed materials. I hope this folder is useful and that you have a good day with my group.

When you finish the day, please complete the feedback sheet and return it to the office with the folder. Thanks for your help.

Sincerely,

Teacher _____ Room _____ Grade ____

Home Phone Number _____

Inside this folder you will find:

- Schedules (classroom and building)
- Emergency procedures
- Classroom rules
- Building and playground rules
- Attendance forms
- Class list
- Time schedule
- Seating chart

	Time Schedule	Routine
Doors open at	_____	_____
School begins at	_____	_____
Recess is scheduled for	_____	_____
Lunch time is	_____	_____
Noon recess is	_____	_____
Dismissal time is	_____	_____

Feedback Form for a Substitute Folder

From Your Substitute

Name _____ Date_____

The day went . . .

About the lesson plan(s) . . .

Students who were helpful . . .

Students who were absent or tardy . . .

Any problems . . .

Comments . . .

2 CHAPTER

Organizing Your Classroom and Yourself

What to Do and Think About Before the Children Arrive

A cheerful, well-organized classroom motivates students and augments your instruction. It sends the message that you care and that you are planning an exciting year. Sit down at one of the desks in your quiet, empty room and daydream a little. How will you transform stark walls and naked bulletin boards into an attractive, inviting, effective learning environment? Ponder the physical design of the room, as well as class routines, procedures, and groupings. List all your great ideas for the coming year. Then, to be realistic, eliminate 50 percent of them. Circle the key remaining items that truly resonate with you, and start with these. Ideas for which you feel a passion are easiest to implement.

Function is the most important aspect of any classroom environment. A well-organized room not only keeps materials ordered and accessible to students but also allows for a variety of learning styles and learning situations. As you arrange your room, decide where groups will meet, where supplies will be kept, and how students will move around the classroom. Survey and note any repair needs and report them immediately to the office. Request additional furniture or adjustments in desk heights to meet students' needs. Rooms that are properly cared for send a powerful message about the stimulating learning that will take place there.

Clarify that mental image of what you want your classroom to be like. What is the feeling? How does it look (ordered or relaxed)? How does it sound (low buzz or quiet)? What does it say to your students? Can every student learn here? The key to good classroom management is to be proactive. This means organizing the classroom to maximize learning time. It is based on your ability to foresee any impediments to instruction.

Setting Up Your Classroom

To make your classroom a positive environment for learning, make sure that all necessary items are in place before the children arrive.

Physical Equipment

- Enough desks or tables with chairs for each student
- Teacher desk and additional desk or table for teacher aide and/or parent volunteers
- Storage space for students' personal belongings (coats, hats, shoes, lunches, etc.): cubbies, shelves, and closets
- Storage space for supplies: shelves, filing cabinets, and tote trays (Label storage containers so you know what is inside.)
- Table and chairs for meetings of small instructional groups
- Pencil sharpeners that work, trash cans (at least two), clock
- Electrical outlets, projection screens, overhead projector

Supplies

- Lesson plan book
- Grade book and attendance register
- Sets of texts or instructional materials for each content area you will teach and related teacher guides
- Reference books, maps, charts, globe, calendar, number line, and alphabet (manuscript display or cursive)
- Chalkboard or whiteboard erasers, pencils, crayons, markers, rulers, paper, tape, and staplers
- Classroom library books and magazines
- Art paper, arts and crafts materials, and easel
- Manipulative materials for science and math activities
- Cleaning supplies, paper towels, and dustpan and brush

Teaching Tip

If you choose a cluster seating arrangement, assign a student "supplies coordinator" for each table group. Change coordinators every week or so using a random drawing. Assign each group a number or color. Fill a basket of supplies (scissors, markers, rulers, glue, staplers, etc.) for each table group. Leave labeled baskets on a special shelf to be picked up when needed. Then ask supplies coordinators to get baskets for their tables.

Organizing Room Space

Consider seating arrangements. Do you plan to begin the year with students sitting in rows or in small groups? Arrange the desks or tables accordingly. (See "Desk Placement" section later in this chapter.) As the year progresses, change these seating arrangements to suit the needs of your students and of the instructional activities. Be flexible. For example, you may add an additional learning center or put student desks in a U shape for oral sharing of completed projects.

Consider how you will provide room for one or more students who are unable to cope behaviorally or academically in class. These pupils may at times work better alone. Some teachers set up a three-sided study carrel in a quiet corner of the room.

Do you have room for a rug? Especially if you teach primary children, set aside open space for a large rug or carpet on which children can sit in a semicircle for calendar/morning meeting activities and story time.

Provide a library corner and, especially for primary children, a place for oral activities such as puppet theater. If your room is small and you must choose between a library corner and a space for dramatics, opt for the library corner. A well-stocked library corner (including children's magazines and student-authored books) is inviting to children and is a fine place for a couple of soft chairs. When you are ready to have your students participate in a whole-class dramatic activity, you can always move aside desks, adjusting the amount of space needed for a given activity. Such arrangements are temporary. You can replace desks in their original positions, leaving the general structure of the room intact.

A dramatics corner is popular with primary students. Provide plenty of intriguing materials for students' creative use, such as a box of hats and clothes for dressing up, "junk" jewelry, old neckties, and a mirror. One teacher gathered pairs of high-interest adult-size shoes such as cowboy boots, ballet slippers, high heels, snowshoes, fishing boots, ski boots, army boots, tap shoes, high-top sneakers, and corporate wing tips. She placed the shoes with a supply of story paper and markers. Children could slip their stocking feet into a pair of shoes, imagine their lives as adults in these shoes, then write and illustrate a story about one of their adventures.

For young primary students, provide a construction area, if space permits. You will need unit blocks, Lego sets, or other building materials appropriate for your grade level. An art area with easel and paints and a crafts table are excellent centers in a primary classroom.

Consider a permanent listening center with tape player, earphones, and recorded books—fiction and nonfiction. You can purchase commercially prepared audio/book packets of dramatic readings with actors portraying the characters and with entertaining sound effects and music. Or ask parent volunteers to record stories for children to "read-along" with the corresponding book in the listening center. Audiocassette stories provide excellent read-aloud models for children gaining reading fluency.

If you have classroom computer(s), be sure to organize a computer corner. To minimize questions about who has or has not taken a turn at the computer, write each student's name on a craft stick/tongue depressor and store the sticks in a container labeled "Next." Place the container of sticks (a frozen juice can works well) and a second container labeled "Finished" near the computer. When all the sticks are in the "Finished" container, you will know that each child has taken a turn.

Creating a Classroom Library

Sometimes busy new teachers (on tight budgets and paying off student loans) ask if they really need a classroom library. The answer is yes! Every teacher and every student deserves a classroom library. A collection of books—"real books," not textbooks—is essential. Even if you teach in a school with a wonderful central library/media center, your classroom should have an attractive collection of paperbacks displayed in a corner that invites browsing and reading. A colorful collection of books right in your room not only livens up the atmosphere and shows that books are important to learning, but also makes finding and sharing sustained silent reading (SSR) books a smooth and comfortable process. The classroom library is your most powerful tool for convincing children that you value reading.

Create a library corner that everyone uses, not just the kids who finish their work early. Depending on your personality, you may want to allow students to read on a rug, pillows, an upholstered chair or couch, or other "homey" furniture in the library corner. In any case, make sure your place is inviting.

Make books a central part of your classroom's decoration. Send e-mails to publishers to ask for their bright, fun, free materials—posters, bookmarks, and so forth. Use book jackets on bulletin boards. Staple up children's drawings inspired by books. Display books on chalk trays. Make sure all types of books are *visible;* don't hide them from the children behind locked cabinet doors.

Yes, it takes time to fill empty bookshelves. Start now! One way to get going is to ask your students if they have books at home that they are willing to share for the year. Check garage sales for kids' "outgrown" books. Enroll your class in a book club (Trumpet and Scholastic are good ones), and put the bonus titles in the classroom library. If the school has an annual book fair—as many do—teachers can provide "wish lists" to be posted at the sale for any families who would like to purchase a book to donate. Start a "Birthday Book" program in which the birthday child brings a favorite book (rather than cupcakes) as a gift for the class. Inscribe that book specially with the child's name and birthday. Many school districts and PTAs give beginning teachers a stipend for purchasing "supplementary" materials—an excellent way to fund a core of classroom library books. Be persistent, and over time you'll build a classroom collection with the titles and types of books you want.

See Resources 2.3 through 2.5 for suggestions on how to introduce library corner rules, book checkout procedures, and record keeping.

Suggested Materials for the Classroom Library

- "Library Corner" sign
- Open-faced bookshelves
- Approximately 100 books, fiction and nonfiction, displayed face forward, if possible (use plate stands or chalk tray to display at least some books)
- A rug or carpet section
- Pillows
- A rocking chair
- Beanbag chairs
- Table and chairs
- Special quiet places for reading (e.g., cushions in a large box, beneath a counter or table)
- Posters that advertise reading or that stimulate interest in specific books
- Stuffed animals and props associated with books
- Plastic baskets or tubs of books labeled by author, series, theme, topic, or genre (e.g., animals, humor, fantasy, fables, history, biography, poetry, riddles, etc.); for younger students, tubs with wordless books, fairy tales, alphabet books, number books, and color books
- Plastic tubs or baskets of high-quality magazines for children (e.g., *Zoobooks, Cobblestone, Cricket, Boy's Life, American Girl, Highlights*)
- For kindergarten and first grade, Big Books used previously in Shared Reading
- Plastic tub or basket labeled "Books Our Class Has Written"
- Plastic tub or basket containing audiotaped stories and tape recorder with headsets
- Library book check-in/check-out materials (see Resource 2.4)

Bulletin Boards

If possible, have bulletin boards and displays completed before school starts. If you are doing child-initiated boards, have ideas and samples ready. Background for bulletin boards may be done with neutral colors, fadeless paper, fabric, or wallpaper. Take a photo of your bulletin boards for your portfolio and for future reference. Try to use reusable or laminated letters. Bulletin board letters and decorations can be made with an Ellison die machine at most school district instructional media centers or can be purchased ready-made at teacher supply stores. If you need bulletin board ideas, ask to look at other classrooms around your school.

A favorite fall bulletin board topic is "What we'll know in June that we don't know in September," featuring drawings, photos, and tagboard designs of thematic units that you will cover in the coming year. You can put up the same bulletin board again in May as an end-of-year review. It will give both you and your students a sense of accomplishment.

A time-saving tip for the busy teacher is to use permanent bulletin board captions, such as "Student of the Week," "Quote of the Week," and "Word of the Week." Another bulletin board that can remain the same throughout the year is a display of each student's work. Post student names with a blank 12-inch-by-12-inch space under each name. Arrange a checkerboard pattern with construction paper stapled on a butcher paper background. Allow students to showcase a favorite or best work sample by posting it below their name whenever they choose. A growing "bookworm" is another fun and easy permanent display. Put up the worm's head in September, and invite students to add a worm segment (paper plate) each time they finish a book. Write the book title on each plate. Students enjoy watching how far the bookworm stretches around their room. Below is a list of bulletin board ideas to get you started.

Bulletin Board Themes

- Welcome
- Alphabet (manuscript or cursive)
- Assignments
- Birthdays
- Calendar
- Classroom rules and consequences
- Daily or weekly schedule
- Fall (and other seasons later)
- Guess who? (baby pictures)
- Number line
- Reading "book covers"
- Reading "bookworm"
- Safety (school bus, walking home, etc.)
- School information and announcements
- Student names and photos
- Student work display
- Student(s) of the week
- Student-created bulletin boards by project or topic/theme (e.g., oceans, heroes and heroines, favorite story, places visited, amusement parks, our state, our city, seasons, our families, our friends, our school)
- Things done over the summer (photos)

Desk Placement

One of the biggest decisions that most teachers (veterans as well as beginners) make at the start of each school year relates to furniture arrangement—a more complicated decision-making process than it may at first appear. Start by doing an inventory of not only the number but also the type of seats available. Have you been assigned to a classroom full of student desks with attached seats? Or do you have tables and separate chairs? Several large tables are handy for meeting with small groups or setting up activity centers. In primary classrooms, a curved reading table is especially useful.

An important next step is to reflect on your personal educational philosophy and style of teaching. How often will you use small-group or cooperative learning activities? Will you use whole-group instruction, lecture with recitation, demonstrations, or audiovisual presentations much of the time? Do you like to use the overhead projector? Will you set up centers? Do you like to see all the students' faces at the same time? The physical arrangement of the classroom must accommodate your teaching style. Depending on the space available, you may use several types of arrangements concurrently. For instance, you may set up several learning centers for students to work alone or in dyads, a carpet in one area for students to gather sitting on the floor, and a corner with a table and chairs to accommodate small learning groups.

To plan the physical layout of your classroom, consider the three most often used arrangements: linear rows, hollow circles or squares, and clusters or groups. A linear arrangement in rows with all desks facing the front of the classroom is the most traditional (Figure 2.1). It is a good arrangement for the beginning teacher who wants to ensure a conservative, orderly start of the school year. With desks in rows, students do not have face-to-face access to one another for unnecessary talking. This arrangement is best if you want attention focused in one direction (e.g., on you and the chalkboard) or during independent seat work. Arranging desks in rows, however, does not encourage interactive learning and a feeling of "we-ness" in the class.

Many teachers like to arrange desks in hollow circles or squares (U shapes) to promote whole-class discussion (Figure 2.2). This arrangement enables all students to see and hear one another easily. For primary classrooms with a rug space, ask children to sit in a semicircle rather than randomly. Some teachers write children's names on masking tape to label the rug spot, or the desk location, of each.

Seating groups or clusters of four to six are increasingly common in elementary classrooms (Figure 2.3). Cluster arrangements are useful for group discussions, cooperative learning, team games and contests, and various small-group tasks.

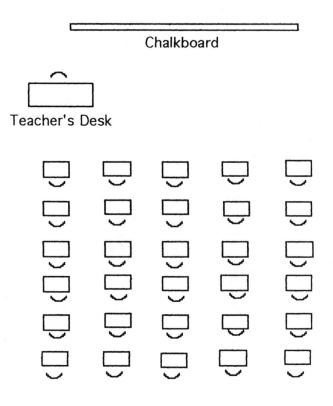

Figure 2.1. Traditional Seating Arrangement

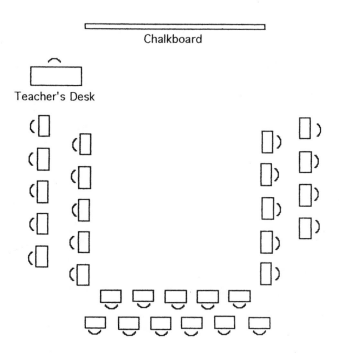

Figure 2.2. U-Shaped Seating Arrangement

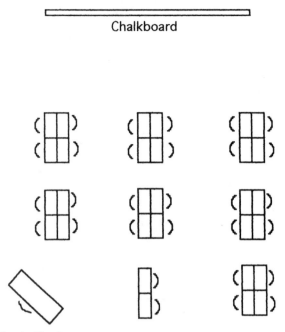

Chalkboard

Teacher's Desk

Figure 2.3.   Group Seating Arrangement

A number of variations of these basic three formations exist (Figures 2.4 and 2.5). For instance, instead of linear columns, you might arrange horizontal rows with desks quite close to each other and students facing forward. Or you could pair up every two rows with the students' desks facing inward toward each other. Such an arrangement allows students to work easily in pairs or groups of four, with no movement of furniture, while maintaining the advantages of traditional rows of desks.

Many new teachers are advised to begin the school year with a traditional room arrangement and to experiment later with different desk formations as their classroom management, control, and confidence increase. Too much experimentation, however, may confuse your students. If, for example, you have taught students to hand in papers by passing them up rows, you will need to teach a new procedure with each new desk arrangement. Each arrangement has its own rules and procedures. These relate to your own preferred teaching style. Do you expect students to raise their hands before commenting on a question? If so, would you expect students to speak out without raising their hands in a circle or small-group arrangement? Procedures and expectations must be taught and reinforced. Do not let frequent changes in room arrangement undermine your overall classroom management.

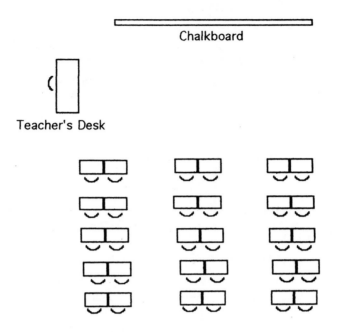

Figure 2.4. Paired Seating Arrangement

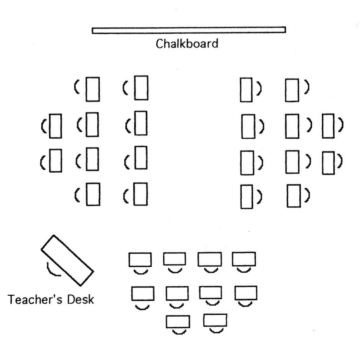

Figure 2.5. Y-Shaped Seating Arrangement

Students will often be cheerful and exuberant desk movers. When guidelines are carefully delineated ahead of time, your students can be energized by physically moving themselves and their desks to form groups or meet with partners or tutors. On the other hand, movement can lead to disruption and cause management problems. In smoothly managed classrooms, movement provides a quick break, after which students are ready to work. As you consider flexibility in seating arrangements, think carefully about how you will prepare students for movement and transitions between groups or activities. Regardless of what seating arrangement you use, always keep a seating chart in your lesson book in case a substitute needs to take over your class.

Seating Strategies: Who Sits Next to Whom?

Beginning teachers often have the most success with teacher-determined seat assignments at the start of the school year. This allows for the least confusion on opening day. If you choose to begin with assigned seats, place name tags on each desk before students arrive. Integrate sexes, abilities, and racial and cultural groups. Consider seating limited-English-proficient (LEP) students near the chalkboard, where they can see and hear you clearly. Before the opening day, review your class roster with your mentor or check with experienced teachers in your building to determine a successful seating arrangement. Younger children have fun on the first day finding "their" desks with their colorful, personalized nameplates.

After the first month, you may allow students to choose new seats, with the condition that you might change their seating if necessary. "Free choice" self-selection gives students the opportunity to make responsible decisions. Older students can discuss their selection process, for instance, "Should I sit near my best friend knowing we'll talk a lot, or at the front of the room where I'll pay good attention?"

Another seating method is random drawings. For example, have students pick numbered index cards that correspond to numbers on the desks. Show the numbers on an overhead transparency of your seating chart projected on a screen. Regardless of your method, have students change their seats throughout the year so they have the opportunity to mix with many other students.

Obtaining Teacher Manuals and Materials

Teacher editions of student textbooks will never substitute for your own specific planning, but they make the process immensely easier for your beginning year. Using the teacher guide does not negate your personal convictions and skills or your knowledge of your students' differences, interests, and abilities. Your final decisions about what to teach are guided by all of these.

Make sure, at the least, that you start the school year with reference copies of the basic teacher guide for each text or instructional program you will use with your students. In most schools, teacher manuals accompany each classroom set of student textbooks that are issued to you. Textbook publishers provide extensive teaching suggestions in the teacher guides, as well as resource materials to help you enlarge the learning beyond the student text.

You have probably discovered that many teacher editions are accompanied by sequentially designed resource units from which you can select and build specific lessons and teaching units. Typically, a resource unit consists of a comprehensive list of objectives, a large number and variety of activities, suggested materials, and extensive bibliographies for teachers as well as students. You can select those that best fit your needs and style to build an actual classroom instructional unit.

Sometimes, a beginning teacher asks, "How closely must I follow the school's or school district's curriculum guide or the course of study outlined in the officially adopted textbooks?" The answer to this important question varies widely. Certainly, you will want an answer before you start teaching. Discuss this with your principal and mentor or colleagues at your particular school.

Sometimes new teachers find that although they have enough copies of student textbooks, an accompanying teacher manual is missing. Perhaps a teacher at the grade level below or above yours kept a copy for reference. Occasionally, a teacher takes an extra copy home for weekend lesson planning. Some manuals have been used so long that they are tattered, torn, and ready to be replaced. Check storage areas for old copies. Most colleagues will readily agree that as a beginning teacher, you deserve the appropriate teacher editions for each subject's textbook. Perhaps you can locate missing manuals by tactfully asking neighboring teachers or the school secretary about spare copies. If you still can't locate copies, try checking with one of the administrators or even with the custodian. The key is persistence.

Additional support materials are available from the publishers of most textbook series. These components include

Blackline masters of practice materials/worksheets

Student workbooks

Overhead transparencies

Diagnostic and assessment materials

Record-keeping materials

Your school may have purchased additional supplementary "extras" that you will find useful, such as kits, charts, cards, audiocassettes, games, computer software, and videos. If you teach primary children, inquire about "big books" that may be a component of the district reading series.

Try to locate the textbook series' placement tests, blackline masters, and overhead transparencies well before the opening day of school. These extras may not always be available when you need them. Other teachers might be using them, or they may be in a storage area. At the start of the school year, it is especially helpful to have copies of diagnostic tests for reading and math to help you assess your students' instructional levels, strengths, and needs.

In the end, you will have to decide if your time is better spent searching for supplementary materials or seeking other suitable resources. If your time is limited, seriously consider other resources, such as trade books and previous lessons, for ideas and direction. When you find materials that appear to be suitable, decide if your students will be able to use them effectively and how much preparation time you will need before introducing them to your class.

Using the Teacher Manuals

Most teacher editions provide a reduced version of the student text reproduced, along with answers and related notes. Accompanying this material are suggestions for presenting, implementing, and enriching each lesson. At first glance, you may feel that you have everything you need, perhaps even too much.

You may not wish to follow the guide exactly or use all its many suggestions—nor are you expected to. Instead, identify the material that supports your lesson objectives. If one of your objectives is reinforcing multiplication facts, for instance, choose only those activities that will help you and your students do just that.

On the other hand, teacher guides may not include material you want to use or enough variety to accommodate the various abilities of your students. Expect this to happen. If you are short on time, check other pages of the manual for suggestions. Sometimes, you will be able to modify this material to suit your particular needs by making it simpler or more difficult.

Setting Up a Literacy-Rich Classroom

If you are planning an effective language arts program for emerging readers, you are not done yet. In addition to the basics of seating arrangements, supplies, bulletin boards, student texts, and teacher manuals, you need to design a "print-rich" classroom environment. Print-rich classrooms immerse children in an environment that serves as a ready reference for understanding written language. For instance, one suggestion is to label the classroom fixtures, furniture, and objects. For this type of teaching, you must view the classroom environment as more than merely a backdrop for learning. Failure to carefully plan the classroom context may result in *setting deprivation.*

The goal is to make your classroom full of print. Songs, poems, jokes, riddles, recipes, dictation, and so on should be enlarged and written on charts. Place these charts around the room for children to read alone or with peers. Classroom walls can be covered with many lists: a sign-in board for attendance, color chart, words we know list, songs we know

---

**Setting Up a Literacy-Rich Classroom
for Emerging Readers**

Materials You Will Need:

- Lots of books—three to five books for each student in the room, so if you have twenty-five students you should aim for 125 books. It's also helpful to have multiple copies of the most popular titles so more than one child can read the most sought-after books (this eliminates quarrels over books).
- Lots of magazines—both those considered to be for adults and those for children
- Two or three pocket charts (Vinyl, see-through pocket charts are recommended. These charts can be ordered from most school supply stores or catalogs.)
- Lots of blank sentence strips and word cards
- Sufficient number of black felt-tip pens for all your students
- Sheets of chart paper or a roll of butcher paper
- Overhead projector, screen, and blank transparencies

Examples of Literacy-Rich Activities:

- Every day, read to the children, usually from a chapter book. Read a book that you enjoy and that challenges the students to listen. Demand attention, but do not check comprehension.
- Every day, have SSR.
- Every day, sing a song.
- Every day, have the children write.
- Every day, chant a familiar poem.
- Every day, make sure that the students have time for individual or small-group work in which they read and write without your direct instruction.
- Almost every day, teach the children together from a shared text.
- At least once a week, teach the students a new poem and do a choral reading of it.

list, favorite books list, and favorite TV shows list. Post the daily schedule, calendar, lunch menu, and classroom helpers and jobs. Write out displays of classroom rules, directions for use of centers, activities directions, sign-up boards for conferences, and all management schemes. A message board can be placed in a prominent location in the classroom for you and the children to write messages to each other. Make a display of color words and number words that children can consult during writing. Magnetic letters, rubber stamps of letters, and stencils are fun to have available. And, of course, you will want many, many books and stories: commercially published trade books, big books, reference books, and informational books, as well as group-authored big books, chart stories, and informational charts. Set up a special bookshelf for individually authored child stories, including shape books, minibooks, big books, and accordion books. Create the right conditions in your classroom for children to learn to read and write as naturally and easily as they learn to speak.

Finding Time and Balance in Your Personal and Professional Life

As you begin your teaching career, you will find that you have more things to do and more details to remember than ever before. At the same time, it seems as if there is less time to get everything done. Occasionally, you may have extra minutes left after eating lunch, writing plans, or correcting papers. But even these snippets of time disappear quickly as you find yourself moving from one area or activity to another. During the day, there's no way to get a breather from your classroom responsibilities. Required paperwork takes more time than a few minutes here and there. So how do you find the time and balance that you need?

Using time well is a key to enhancing your effectiveness. Focus on the *really* important activities by clarifying your priorities. Use focused procrastination. Decide which tasks may be completed at a later date. Do those tasks last. Give priority to items that are due now or in the next few days. Mark all tasks on a calendar, along with times and dates of present and future commitments. This will allow you, for example, to see immediately which afternoons you are free after work. See Resource 2.1 for a "Things to Do Today" time management form.

Get unpleasant tasks done first. Break especially large or difficult jobs into manageable pieces, and start making progress right away. Schedule activities into your lesson plan book, using markers or brightly colored ink to remind you of priorities and deadlines.

As a new teacher, you have to learn to deal with paperwork efficiently. Paperwork can seem endless. A teacher's life is filled with forms, evaluations, notices, student papers, report cards, progress reports, cumulative record files, memos, letters, junk mail, reading material, lesson plans, and files of curriculum materials and instructional activities. Unless you develop effective ways of reducing the paperwork load and keeping it from hampering your overall performance, you will soon fall behind. Your principal and office staff will not appreciate having to remind you to turn in forms and reports.

You will find yourself faced for the most part with two types of school paperwork tasks:

1. Those tasks that are not directly related to teaching, for example, district forms, cumulative record cards, memos, and meeting agendas and minutes
2. Those tasks that are related to your classroom and teaching, for example, lesson planning, grading, and recording

To organize more efficiently, consider keeping separate folders for different types of paperwork, such as student papers and office notices. Label each folder.

Huge stacks of student papers to correct can be overwhelming. Student work must be corrected quickly, recorded, and passed back to your students. Feedback is important to students, and you need to monitor their progress.

Have your students correct as much of their own work as possible. Sometimes individual children will enjoy coming in at recess to help correct a class set of papers. If you teach at the primary level, ask the teachers of the fourth-, fifth-, or sixth-grade classes for student volunteers for help in correcting, collating, cutting, and stapling these materials. Older students often enjoy helping the "little kids' teacher."

Many teachers set up a file crate box with hanging files and folders for each student. Throughout the week, after students have reviewed their corrected papers, they are filed in the proper folder. On Friday, all the week's work is sent home to parents in a Friday Folder, usually with the class newsletter (see Chapter 7) and any memoranda from the office. This efficient, once-a-week system is well organized, saves time for busy teachers, and keeps parents up to date on their child's progress.

Use parents' help. You may be reluctant to ask for such help, feeling that you should be able to do it all and not impose on parents. Yet many parents are pleased to type, correct practice worksheets, produce cutouts for classroom bulletin boards, and so forth. (See Chapter 7 for a discussion of parent participation.)

Use your students to provide regular assistance in keeping the room tidy, counting out and distributing certain materials, and doing other routine chores. All children need to be taught to clean up after themselves. Remember that distributing papers is a coveted task that may be reserved for elected monitors or rotated so that everyone gets a turn.

Establish your own personal goals and priorities. It is easy to allow professional priorities to eat up even your nonschool hours. What time do you normally spend to meet personal and family needs? If this time has been shortened, consider extending it with more efficient planning. See additional planning suggestions in the next section.

Set Priorities and Find Shortcuts

1. List the routine things you need to do—plan, correct papers, record grades, put up bulletin boards, duplicate materials at the copy machine, and so forth.

2. Look at the time you have available: before and after school and during music, physical education, and library. Estimate how long it will take you to complete your planning and other tasks. To find the time you need, look at your schedule in school, but more important, consider how you spend your time before and after work. For example, is it possible to shorten certain routine activities just once? Find additional time by jotting down lesson and activity ideas from your present lessons for future use. Keep your ideas in a place where you will find them easily. Also consider the time frame outlined in your teacher manuals for reading, math, social studies, science, and other subjects. How much time is suggested for a unit of related concepts?

3. Use other teachers' ideas (OTI). Listen to other teachers. You may hear something that will work for you. Better yet, ask other teachers, including your mentor, how they find time to do things. Then thank them and see if one or more of their ideas will work for you.

4. Decide if the time spent looking for a certain book or resource is worthwhile. Perhaps an alternative would be even more effective.

5. Consider outside factors (e.g., the copy machine is always crowded in the morning but not during your prep period; parents come to visit unannounced).

6. Write a prioritized Must-Do list containing what must be done first, second, third, and so on. See Resource 2.1 for a handy list format and additional ideas.

7. Keep a log of what you actually do for two weeks to find out where your time-wasters occur. Then watch out for typical time-wasters (excessive chatting with your teacher aide, errands, getting coffee, trips to the school office or supply closet, idle telephone conversations, cluttered desk, inadequate filing system, inability to say no, etc.).

8. Plan ahead for times that will involve extra work (e.g., before report cards, parent-teacher conferences, back-to-school night, and open house). Don't procrastinate.

9. Use all those good classroom management ideas you have learned to organize your room and your routines so that as a

whole, your classroom runs smoothly. See Resource 2.2 for a sample of how one teacher organizes her school day.

10. Avoid taking on anything extra unless the reasons for taking it on balance out the time that is involved.

Sources of Stress

As a beginning teacher, you must expect to experience some stress. Following are common sources of stress frequently cited by teachers:

- Students
- Parents of students
- Loneliness and isolation
- Too little time and too much to do
- Managing the classroom and instruction
- Dealing with paperwork
- Coping with the workload: planning instruction for at least five subject areas, teaching outside your area of expertise, being assigned more "difficult" students, and too many extracurricular responsibilities
- Seeking support from colleagues and administrators
- Self: allowing paperwork to pile up (planning to do it later, but uncertain as to when it must be completed); not developing good rapport with parents, administrators, colleagues, and students

Adjusting to the work environment found in a typical elementary school is not easy, particularly when "reality shock" first sets in. Stress can become a problem if you let it. Stress can be either positive, keeping you "on your toes," or negative, increasing your fatigue.

Tips for Relieving Stress

The first step is to figure out what things cause you stress. Analyze the stressor. If stress is caused by something you can control, say, completing paperwork on time, change your routine by dealing with paperwork as you get it. Do not wait until the last minute. On the other hand, some stress is caused by factors you cannot control, such as the weather or even the school calendar. Use stress management techniques such as meditation or other relaxation methods, deep muscle massage, exercise, and a healthy diet. Explore alternatives to help minimize stress and to deal with it in a way that fits your lifestyle. Throughout the process, focus on your strengths, and celebrate and share your successes. Here are some ways to handle different types of stress.

School Stress

Begin with aspects you can control, such as how you manage your classroom and relate to students. If work feels dull, for example, break your routine. If you teach young children, take time to play ball and jump rope with them. Older children might enjoy a new art or science project or a backward schedule, in which you reverse the usual sequence of activities.

While you are at it, take another look at your classroom's physical appearance, such as bulletin boards and arrangement of desks and other furniture. Can you add an item, such as a lamp, new chair, or live plant, to change and enhance your room's appearance? When was the last time you displayed your students' latest artwork or used that pile of old magazines? From time to time, renew the landscape of the room.

Remember your students. Sometimes you are all feeling stressed. Make sure that your expectations for them are realistic and clear. For example, are your students really ready to master division or write critiques of stories? Sometimes stress is caused by pushing to "cover" (rather than *teach*) all the required curriculum for your grade level. You might need to slow down to meet your students where they are. Discuss with your mentor or principal covering the curriculum scope and sequence.

Have you also set realistic expectations and allowed a few minutes for yourself? Do you stretch, relax, and breathe deeply every day?

Personal Stress

Much of the stress you experience is the result of coping with the demands of a busy schedule at school and home. Think about it. When you arrive home from work, do you try to take at least a few minutes to sit down for a break? Or do you rush madly from one chore to another? Your mental health is just as important as your physical health. Plan now to do something special for yourself.

Buy yourself a special treat (such as a book), go to a movie or sporting event, or take yourself out to dinner. A fun suggestion that works for busy teachers is to purchase season tickets to your favorite cultural or sporting events *before* the school year begins. You will then have something special to look forward to and no excuse not to treat yourself. Or consider doing all your day's paperwork at school, and enjoy some free, unstructured time at home for a change. You will be pleasantly surprised at how good you will feel! You will be more productive in school as well.

A Day in a Third-Grade Classroom

Morning

8:25-8:35	Attendance/lunch count
8:35-8:55	Current event, newspapers: "Lake Residents Seek Weed Killer Controls." Brainstorm effects of weed killer. Introduce vocabulary: defoliants, eco-system, chemicals, herbicide. Discuss article. Put words in word bank for the week.
8:55-9:05	Children write in journals.
9:05-10:05	Guided reading: red and yellow groups today (blue and green tomorrow on alternating schedule). When not with teacher at guided reading table, children work with partners to complete follow-up worksheet on story characters, then rotate to Writing Center or Computer Center. At the end of the hour, children can share what they wrote.
10:05-10:25	Recess
10:25-10:45	Spelling: Children use spelling words for the week in an original sentence.
10:45-11:05	Read-aloud
11:05-11:15	Cleanup/dismissal for lunch

Afternoon

12:15-12:20	Attendance/announcements
12:20-12:40	Read-aloud
12:40-12:55	Class plays a bingo game with multiplication facts.
12:55-1:30	Using manipulatives (place value cubes), children demonstrate the concept of multiplication, for example, "4 × 2" is 4 sets of 2.
1:30-2:00	Science: Pollution/litter. Divide class into groups of three to four children. Ask each group to predict the contents of the class wastebasket. One group member records the predictions (10 minutes). When complete, put items predicted on blackboard. Check contents of basket. Discuss how everyone contributes to litter and waste and what can be done to minimize classroom waste and litter.
2:00-2:30	PE today
2:30-2:55	Community circle: "Being a Friend." Have children think of at least one attribute that makes them a good friend. Share. Use self as a model first.
2:55-3:00	Cleanup/dismissal

Time Management for the Busy Teacher:
Things to Do Today

As a successful beginning teacher, you are doing careful and complete lesson planning. In addition, make sure you do some personal planning for the other important activities in your life. You may feel you don't have enough time to plan, but you won't have any more time available for your activities until you *do* plan effectively!

Successful time managers organize their in-school and out-of-school activities in a thought-out, systematic manner. Just as in lesson planning, start by clarifying your objectives. Exactly what do you need to get done? Then ask yourself what activities must take place to achieve your personal objectives by the end of the week. After you identify activities, set priorities and estimate the time needed to complete them. Many busy teachers find it best to spend a few minutes at the end of each day preparing a daily to-do list for the coming day. Keep focused on your personal objectives and priorities when writing your "Things to Do Today" list (see following sample).

Things to Do Today

Date

Item	Priority	Done

Notes

Scheduled Events	
7:00	
8:00	
9:00	
10:00	
11:00	
12:00	
1:00	
2:00	
3:00	
4:00	
5:00	
6:00	
7:00	
8:00	

2.3 RESOURCE
Library Corner Introduction: Sample Lesson Plan

Introduction to the Classroom Library

Objectives

- To introduce materials in the library corner
- To establish rules for the use of the library corner

Materials

See box, "Suggested Materials for the Classroom Library," page 30.

Step-by-Step Plan

1. Bring children into the classroom library. Ask them to sit on the rug. Explain that they will have a daily opportunity to use the many books and materials available. Discuss when during the day they may come to the library corner (e.g., after their guided reading group, after they have completed other assignments, during SSR time, and perhaps during recess or lunch).

2. Show and discuss the variety of materials they can use during classroom library time. Explain that they can work alone or with others. Buddy reading in quiet voices is OK.

3. Discuss and demonstrate the following rules:

   - Handle books and materials carefully.

   - Select only one item at a time.

   - Put a completed book away in the proper place (bookshelf or tub) before selecting another.

   - Treat each other with courtesy and respect.

4. Allow time for students to explore the books and audiobooks. If necessary, assist children in looking for "just right" books. Be prepared to closely supervise children's use of the library corner during the first week. When the class has mastered selecting and checking out books (Resource 2.4), introduce the idea of SSR at a specific time each day, and explain how to keep a record of books read (Resource 2.5).

Introduction to Checking Out Books:
Sample Lesson Plan

How to Check Books Out of the Classroom Library

Objectives

- To explain the system for checking books out and back into the classroom library
- To encourage reading at home

Materials

Two plastic index card file boxes, in two different colors, for five-by-eight-inch index cards. Clearly label the boxes, one for "Books Out" and one for "Books In."

Colored five-by-eight-inch index cards: two cards per student. Write the names of the children on the tops of their two cards, and then place one set of cards in alphabetical order in each of the two file boxes. *NOTE: If you wish, keep the colored cards blank for now and ask the children to write their own names on them before beginning the demonstration of the book check-out procedure.*

White five-by-eight-inch index cards: approximately ten per student. Put cards in the "Books Out" box, per Step 2a in the step-by-step plan.

Sample filled-in card to be posted by the boxes.

Step-by-Step Plan

1. Bring children into the classroom library. Ask them to sit on the rug. Review rules about the use of the classroom library and the location of materials in it (e.g., ask, "Who can show us where the tub of fantasy books is?" "Humor?" "Harry Potter?" etc.).

2. Explain that books can be checked out of the classroom library to be read at home. Show the two index card boxes. Explain and demonstrate the procedures for checking books out and returning them.

    a. To check a book out, children take a blank white card from the "Books Out" box and write on it their name, the title of the book they are borrowing, and the date. Then they put this card behind the colored card that has their name on it in the "Books Out" box.

    b. To check the book back in when it is returned, children take the card from the "Books Out" box, write the date they're returning it and a short comment about how they liked the book, and then place it in the "Books In" box behind the colored index card with their name on it.

3. Allow time for students to browse and discuss the books and to choose one to check out. Be available to monitor the check-out procedure and to assist with book selection as necessary.

RESOURCE
Introduction to Book Records: Sample Lesson Plan

How to Keep a Record of Books Read

NOTE: Do this lesson after several weeks of school, when students have had time to complete at least one book.

Objectives

- To motivate students to read during SSR and at home
- To provide the teacher and student with a means of keeping track of books completed during the year

Materials

White five-by-eight-inch index cards, lined on front, blank on back: at least ten per student to start

Colored fine-tip markers or colored pencils

One set of index cards and one plastic Ziploc bag per student

NOTE: If you are implementing the book check-out procedure described in Resource 2.4, you can eliminate the plastic bags and incorporate this activity as part of the check-in procedure.

Step-by-Step Plan

1. Invite children to come to the library corner with the book they have finished reading. Ask them to sit on the rug. Review the procedures learned in Resources 2.3 and 2.4. Explain that today you will discuss keeping track of the books they read throughout the year, why this activity is important and fun, and how to do it.

2. Show the "Books In" box. Tell the children that now that they know how to check books out and in, they will have one more thing to do to the book card. Show the basket of colored markers and pencils next to the "Books In" box. Explain that when the children finish their books, they will write the book's title and the date completed on the front of the card (as explained in Resource 2.4) and then flip the card over to write about and illustrate their favorite part of the story or their favorite character. Children should place the index card back in the box (or in their plastic bag) when completed.

3. Allow time for students to share a favorite part or character of the book they have read with the whole group or a partner. Then distribute cards and markers/pencils to write and illustrate. When done, ask volunteers to read their remarks aloud. (If students have read only part of a book, have them put the card in their book as a bookmark and remind them to finish the book and date the card before putting the card back in the file box.)

4. Review the students' cards on a regular basis. If you conduct reading conferences with the children, ask individuals to bring their cards to you for the conference discussion. This system can serve as an authentic assessment of literacy development.

As an alternative to the index card system described, see the Reading Log in Resource 6.2.

3 CHAPTER

Learner-Friendly Classroom Management

When twenty-five to thirty children are placed in a room at the same time with one teacher, some sense of order must exist. Classroom management means classroom organization. It also refers to the emotional climate, atmosphere, and ambiance you create while managing your classroom effectively. A positive climate conducive to learning evolves from students' sense of belonging to a classroom community and their involvement, whenever appropriate, in decision making. Your attitude, fairness, and clear communication to students will affect the atmosphere of your classroom. Classroom management is what you do when the school term starts and throughout the year to organize and manage students, space, time, and materials to create an orderly, friendly, and well-functioning classroom.

Think again about the classroom you worked in as a student teacher. Consider the daily and weekly management routines and procedures your cooperating teacher used and reinforced. What expectations did the students follow? How organized was the classroom? Would you have done anything differently? What systemized routines would you like to use again?

What Is Your Classroom Management Style?

Your classroom management style refers to the ways you work with students and routines to make the whole classroom environment support your instructional goals. For example, do you feel comfortable allowing students to talk during seat work? How much talking is too much? How much student out-of-seat movement around the room is appropriate? Do you prefer having students line up according to a specified order? How important is it for your students to move quickly, quietly, and efficiently from one activity to another? How do you feel about dealing with inevitable problems, such as late assignments? Sloppy, careless errors?

Incomplete work? Messy desks? Calling out answers or not raising hands? Not listening carefully or not following directions? How much group work do you feel is appropriate for students at your grade level? How much independent seat work? How teacher centered should the classroom be? In what type of classroom are you personally most comfortable? Preferences such as these will influence the types and number of management expectations you outline for your students.

Whatever procedures and routines you feel are appropriate for students at your grade level will determine how organized, structured, and predictable life in your classroom will be. Think about the classroom you are setting up. Write about it here, or draw a picture or mind map if you prefer.

Reflection: What Is My Personal Classroom Management Style?

Describe the type of classroom in which you feel most comfortable. What is it like, physically and psychologically?

Now take a few minutes to think about the items mentioned in the previous chapter, such as your room's size, desk arrangements, activities, and your philosophy of education. Together, all these considerations inform your personal classroom management style.

The key to effective classroom management is to be *proactive.* This means organizing your classroom to maximize students' engagement. Being proactive is based on your ability to foresee instruction—to think through what organizational structures must be in place for lesson plans to go smoothly for you and the students. Avoid being in a position in which you must constantly react to procedures that are confusing or to students who are unhappy or out of control. Good classroom management helps prevent problems before they occur.

In laying out your blueprint for the year, plan to be flexible. Hang on to those things that work for you, but don't be afraid to stop doing those things that don't work. Few teachers use only one model or approach to classroom organization. They borrow from several models, such as mastery learning, direct instruction, and cooperative learning, to create the learning environment they want for their students.

Conversely, don't give up on a new idea too quickly. Give a new idea a fair chance, which means allowing time to practice, make mistakes, observe effects, and adjust.

Students need continuity and stability. Avoid making frequent drastic changes, for example, in seating order or morning routines. Make changes only when appropriate or necessary. If procedures are constantly revised or improperly followed, then you and your students will experience considerable frustration from interrupted tasks, lost time, and the interference of continually adapting to modified expectations and procedures. If, on the other hand, you establish a workable system, the year's progress will be much smoother.

Develop a resource file for classroom management ideas from conferences, books, workshops, and other teachers. You should eventually have on file several ways to carry out every routine task.

Some teachers decide to ask students to help generate classroom rules. Getting students involved helps make them feel responsible for what happens in the classroom. For instance, some teachers raise students' awareness of the classroom structure by asking them to draw the traffic patterns in the room. What are the paths students should take to get to the learning centers, to the reading circle, and to the pencil sharpener? Students can often think of ways to improve congested areas. Nevertheless, even if you want students to share in the responsibility of deciding on classroom management routines and procedures, keep in mind that it is ultimately *your* task to make certain that the rules are adequate and appropriate. To do so, you must first consider your own bottom-line expectations regarding routines and procedures. A number of key decisions should be made before the first day of school. Here are several essential questions to consider in establishing classroom routines and procedures:

- How will students get to know each other and enjoy each other's company? How much socializing is all right with you?

- Should students raise their hands if they want to ask or answer a question? Under what conditions?

- May students move around the room without permission? If so, when? What are your expectations for student rotation in and out of learning centers?

- How should students get help when you are busy?

- How should students enter and leave the classroom for recess, lunch, library, PE, and final dismissal?

- What are your homework expectations? How often will you give homework in each subject?

- What should students do if they finish an assignment early? What are your "free-time" expectations?

Routines

A well-managed classroom enables you to provide exciting and dynamic learning experiences for everyone. When children are confused or unsure of what to do or how to do it, the emotional climate in the classroom suffers. Routines provide needed safety and security.

Beginning with the first day of school, setting a specific procedure for every routine activity saves time and aggravation for everyone. By establishing these procedures early, then reinforcing them often, you will improve your chances of surviving your first year with energy and optimism. Decide in advance which procedures you will establish, and communicate these carefully to your students so they will know what you expect. Here are important routines and accompanying questions for you to consider.

Daily Routines for the Start and End of the School Day

These routines tend to remain the same throughout the year, such as having the children hang up their coats as soon as they arrive, then go immediately to their desks to write in their journals or complete a quiet seat-work activity (sometimes called a "sponge" or "bell activity") while you take attendance. Start-up routines include how and when students should enter the classroom, where lunches should be stored, what to do with lunch money, and how the roll will be taken. Think about how homework will be collected so that class time for this organizational task is kept at a minimum. At the end of the school day, will students line up at the classroom door, or will you dismiss them from the class by row or table group (e.g., clean and quiet tables first)?

Interruptions

Common interruptions include student requests to use the rest room or the pencil sharpener, to go to the nurse's office, or to leave for a special pullout class. When do you expect your students to sharpen their pencils—before or after lessons? When may they go to the rest room, to the water fountain, and to the wastepaper basket? Most teachers implement a pass system for students needing to leave the classroom. Allow no more than one or two students at a time, who must wait until the pass (a permanent wooden or plastic one) is available and then leave quietly.

Other Routines During the School Day

It is important that children have a sense of the daily class schedule and structure. Students should know from the beginning of the school year what is routinely expected of them during the school day. Some teachers develop a schedule in which each day of the week, Monday through Friday, has its unique activities. Students soon learn this routine and know the activities for the day before even entering the room.

Begin establishing routines the first day of class. For elementary students, it is not enough to post rules on the bulletin board or even to read the rules together: Rules, routines, and procedures must be taught, demonstrated, and modeled. If the classroom management structure begins right away, it is much easier to maintain it than to attempt to establish it later in the school year. Research indicates that teachers who make it clear in the first weeks of school what is expected in daily routines have more smoothly running classrooms and spend less time on organization or behavior problems throughout the year.

Students need to know how to succeed in your classroom. Help them be successful by making it clear what is expected of them in typical daily situations. When may they get out of their seats? How should they get materials and supplies? When can they use the learning centers? Routines must be specific and detailed. For example, it is not enough to decide when students may use the learning centers—you must also specify items such as how many students can be in one learning center, when students may change from one center to another, and what behavior is expected in learning centers (voice level, sharing, use of materials, completing projects, cleanup, etc.).

Another important routine during the school day includes how to line up quietly for recess, PE, library, assembly programs, and fire/disaster drills. Make sure, for instance, that your students understand that they must remain in their seats until *you* dismiss them—they do not jump up to leave when the school bell rings or when the emergency signal sounds.

Student Movement as You Vary Teaching Activities

Will you break up your class into smaller groups only for certain subjects, such as reading, or do you plan small-group instruction in other subjects, such as math and spelling, too? In what sorts of hands-on, constructivist activities (e.g., science experiments and math manipulatives) will you engage students? How will you incorporate student oral reports, presentations, demonstrations, and simulations? What lesson topics are suitable for inquiry teaching and discovery learning? Are any of your lesson ideas suitable for independent investigation or projects? Will educational games or learning centers enhance your instruction? *You will need to think through a routine or procedure for each of your teaching activities.* As an effective elementary teacher, you will vary classroom activities and pace. Teach a management procedure for each new activity to prevent confusion and to help students proceed successfully.

Transitions—the time before, after, and between lessons and other organized activities—are often the acid test of your ability as a classroom manager. Down time causes problems. For some students, time not scheduled in a classroom is an open invitation to disruptive behavior. To effectively manage time and student movement during transition periods, it is essential to develop clear procedures and expectations. Your goal is to organize and supervise transition periods that maintain a smooth and brisk instructional pace and that allow no dead time. Your classroom management procedures should keep children lively, alert, and busy with no time to stand or sit around with "nothing to do." In general, student movement during transition times should be restricted to the purpose of your lesson activities.

You can save time in the following ways:

- Be ready yourself! Make sure you clearly know what the next step is. Teachers who have the most trouble with transitions are often those who are not well organized themselves.

- Have all materials ready, and remind your students what you expect from them as they move from one lesson to the next, such as having pencils and journals ready. Encourage your students to clear their tables or desks of unnecessary supplies or books to prepare for the next activity.

- When giving verbal instructions to your class, be succinct. If you talk too much or give too much detail, children will get bored and restless to move on.

- Arrange the classroom so that your students will not always need to leave their tables or desks to start a new activity or so that they use the most direct route in moving from one table or desk to the other. For instance, request that students walk toward the *closest* aisle or group of chairs instead of walking all the way around the room. Or appoint monitors. These students will be the designated "materials getters" from each row or table group, the only students allowed out of their seats at transition time. Rotate monitors regularly.

- Begin your lesson as soon as possible. True, some of your students may not be quite ready, but a prompt, decisive start will encourage the slower ones to pick up the pace. By beginning your lesson efficiently and in an organized manner, you are discouraging the fooling around and time wasting that might otherwise occur. This is important for both whole-group and small-group lessons.

- Before starting a new activity, be sure most of the children have had an opportunity to complete the present one. Then, end it definitively with a summary and bridge it to the next activity.

- Have trays, envelopes, or other holders available for completed papers from the previous lesson. Bulky projects may require larger containers or additional space. Students should know beforehand where they should place their completed work— labeled with their names and/or a proper heading on written work, of course.

- Early in the school year, teach a short lesson on how you want students to head their papers. Most teachers prefer headings in the top right corner, beginning on the first line. A heading includes student name (first and last), date, and subject. Model writing a correct heading on the chalkboard or an overhead transparency. Post it on a chart.

- If the transition involves moving from a seated academic activity, such as reading, to a nonacademic or outside activity, such as recess, lunch, or PE, your students must understand how they are to behave and what they are to do as they leave the classroom.

- To prevent noisy lines exiting the room, consider assigning each student to a specified place in line. You may need to occasionally separate students who talk loudly or shove.

- Ease your students into the next lesson or activity by providing a short written activity. Especially after breaks such as recess or lunch, the transition is eased if students have something to do as soon as they come into the room. Place the question, sponge activity, or brainteaser on the chalkboard or overhead projector for students to see so they can begin work on it immediately. This also gives you a few minutes to collect your thoughts or finish clerical tasks from the previous activity. See pages 63-64 for a suggested list of sponge activities.

- A frequently overlooked item, and a potential time-waster, is how students' work is stored between collection and marking. Too often, such work is merely stacked, one pile on top of another, in danger of tumbling to the floor. To avoid this, use separate storage bins for work from each subject or project. Later, you will feel less overwhelmed in organizing student work, checking it, and recording grades.

Procedures During Small-Group Instruction

- The students should know when their group is to come to the teacher. Place a schedule on the bulletin board or chalkboard along with each group's assignment. Icons and colors help younger children keep track of the schedule chart and proceed to the correct center. Try using a pocket chart to create an easily changed display of names and schedule cards.

- Do not call or signal for a new group until the previous one is seated and working at desks or centers. If students are to bring special materials to the instructional group, let them know before they move.

- Before meeting with a small group, give clear instructions for work and behavior to the rest of the class. If you expect children to rotate through several centers (e.g., writing, art, class library, or science), make sure you've demonstrated the specific tasks in each center for that given day or week, and set a limit to the number of participants. You may wish to assign groups to centers on specific days.

- Decide on your policy toward interruptions to the group. If students are to go on to the next question or assignment when they have a problem, state that clearly and allow no interruptions. If your room is arranged in collaborative table groups, you can encourage students to ask each other. A successful policy in such classrooms is "Ask three, then me." Do not respond to individual questions until the child has first asked peers, and then only *after* the small-group time is completed and you are cruising the room to answer questions and monitor class work.

- Assignments completed by children not in the group with you may be collected by monitors or put into students' personal work folders. Whatever you decide, be sure that the procedure is clear and that students know the location of the folders and who the monitor is.

- Make sure students understand what to do if assignments are finished early. They might help each other, sit at the listening center with headphones, read a book, or work at the class computer, for instance. Establish guidelines for free-time activities. Decide how you will monitor the proper use of free-time materials such as games and puzzles.

Implementing a Pattern for a Smooth Start Each Day

Like all good teachers, you will want to start the day on a positive note. A pattern or routine for beginning each day gives children a warm, comfortable welcome. Greet your children at the classroom door when they arrive in the morning, and say something personally to each child. Then try one of the following suggestions for morning rituals:

- Conduct a daily class meeting. Sit in a semicircle in which everyone can see one another's face.

- Share birthday celebrations, news, calendar, weather observations, and the highlights planned for the day.
- Sing a song together (primary grades).
- Teach students a greeting that they memorize to chant or sing each morning.
- Read and discuss a "Quote of the Day" or discuss a current event (intermediate grades).
- Read aloud a poem. Then do a choral reading of it.
- Do the flag salute. Let a different child lead it each morning or each week.
- Have your students write in journals. Interactive dialogue journals in which you have written back to individual students are eagerly read at the start of each day.

The morning ritual for the intermediate grades is more flexible than the primary pattern. Intermediate teachers tend to change the order of the morning routines and vary how they are done. But students and teachers at both grade levels find that a morning routine is a worthwhile way to start the school day.

Daily Schedule

As your day begins, it is often reassuring to point out the daily schedule so students know what to anticipate. Discussing the schedule helps primary children begin to get some feeling for the passing of time. For the first month of the school year, start by showing the activity sequence without times (or clock faces indicating times).

Questions to help children become aware of the daily sequence of events include these:

1. What will we be doing first this morning?
2. What happens right before lunch?
3. What are the second and third things planned for the morning?
4. What is the final activity for this day?

As you introduce time allotments to your daily schedule, you can teach primary children facts about the clock—minutes can be counted by ones or fives (then practice it), clock hands go clockwise, the hour hand is shorter, and so on. Telling time with confidence and accuracy requires years of practice. These activities help children develop an awareness of time. Questions to help your students relate the daily schedule to time could include the following:

1. Who knows what time we'll go to PE today?
2. What will our class be doing at 10:30?

3. How much time will we have for science today?
4. What is the second thing that will happen after lunch today?

You can write the daily schedule on the chalkboard. Many primary teachers make a permanent schedule display with a pocket chart (especially good if your schedule is flexible), writing time cards/clock faces and activity cards on tagboard strips. A sample daily class schedule in an elementary self-contained classroom is shown in Resource 3.1.

Increasing Your Efficiency With Class Monitors

Students can be a wonderful help in maintaining classroom order and routines. Delegate as many chores to students as their age and ability will allow. Assigning students to various classroom jobs gives them a chance to assume responsibility, feel independent and worthwhile, and acquire a sense of contributing and belonging. It also saves you considerable time and effort.

Depending on your management style, you may assign jobs according to the sequence of your class list or by a random lottery system. If you let children volunteer for jobs, make sure that everyone participates, including second-language learners and shy children. Especially in intermediate classrooms, teachers hold elections for class monitor positions, often calling monitors "officers," such as "class president," "vice president," "secretary," and "chairpersons" of the bulletin board committee, art committee, class library/book order council, and recreational equipment committee.

Do not use classroom monitor positions as a reward for good behavior or A grades. Make sure that no one is discriminated against—all students should get a chance to contribute to the smooth operation of their classroom. Rotate students assigned to tasks on a regular basis (weekly or semimonthly) to involve all students throughout the year. For tasks requiring students to leave the room, plan on designating two students as monitors. A sample list of monitors' duties follows:

- Animal cages (keeps clean)
- Animals (feeds)
- Art (keeps supplies organized and refills materials)
- Attendance (takes attendance cards to the office)
- Ball distribution
- Boards (erases and washes boards and cleans chalk trays)
- Collection (collects completed assignments)
- Computer (sets up computer program)

- Door (makes sure door is locked and holds it open)
- Erasers (takes to cleaning location)
- Errands
- Library (keeps room library in order)
- Lights (turns lights on and off)
- Lunch (takes lunch count and money to the office)
- Lunch cards (passes out lunch cards)
- Notices (gives out)
- Paper distribution
- Pencil sharpener (cleans)
- Plants (waters)
- Sink (keeps clean)
- Tape players and listening center (keeps audiotapes, accompanying books, headphones, etc., organized)
- Teacher's desk assistant (puts papers in order at the end of the day)
- Teacher's mailbox monitor
- Windows (opens and closes windows and drapes)

Whichever monitor positions you use, review the procedures and model the correct way of performing each task with the entire class. Keep a written description of all jobs in a binder for students' reference.

Tips for Moving Ahead With Clear Communications

Classroom Signal

Effective teachers have a procedure to quiet their class and gain students' undivided attention. It is often called a "freeze and listen" signal. For example, you might flick the lights, ring a bell, or stand quietly with your hand raised high. The students "freeze" (stop whatever they're doing), turn, and look at you. Demonstrate and practice this procedure until all your students understand the "stop, look, and listen" expectations.

You might create a classroom signal to call the class to order that all the students *imitate*. Many teachers use a simple gesture such as a raised hand with "peace sign" fingers or a series of rhythmic claps. One successful teacher instructs her children, "Put your finger on your nose when you hear me." When she needs their attention, she places the tip of her index finger on the tip of her nose, and her students follow suit. Another teacher uses an effective "Gimme 5" signal (see Resource 3.2). Whatever signal you use, be consistent and praise children who respond immediately with an imitation of the signal.

Giving Directions

- Limit yourself, when possible, to only two directions at a time for any given activity. This will help your students listen and implement the activity more effectively. For example, you might say, "Please clear your desks. Then take out your snacks."

- Give directions immediately before the activity.

- Remove distractions.

- Get the attention of every student before giving directions.

- Use both oral and written directions if they are complicated.

- Keep your voice low.

- Get feedback from students. Ask them what they understand the directions to be.

Before students proceed with independent activities, be sure they know

- Where to get materials
- What to do if they have a question
- Where to work
- Where to put finished work
- When and why the teacher is "off limits"

Keep Your Classroom Running Smoothly While You Are Busy

Sometimes, before school or during the day, you may be asked to complete additional paperwork from the office, speak to a parent or other visitor, remain on hall duty, or become involved in activities that divert your attention from class, but that does not mean that your students should be idle. To help focus their attention while you are occupied, have ready one or two short, interesting activities on the board or chart paper. Some of these sponge activities are suggested here. Also see Resource 3.3 for additional sponge activities.

Sponges

- Make up three names for musical groups.
- Take a number. Write it. Make a face out of it.
- Name as many teachers in this school as you can.
- List as many states as you can.

- List as many countries and their capitals as you can.
- Write down as many cartoon characters as you can.
- Draw and label as many kinds of flowers as you can.
- List all the things in your living room.
- List as many nouns in this room as you can.
- Draw and label five things you do after school.
- List one proper noun for each letter of the alphabet.
- List as many U.S. presidents as you can.
- Draw and label as many kinds of trees as you can.
- Write as many homonyms as you can.
- Name and draw as many breeds of dogs as you can.
- Solve a puzzle or a brainteaser.
- Write cursive handwriting sentences (for humor and interest, use students' names in examples to be copied).
- Learn a word of the day. Pronounce it correctly to a partner.
- Write a riddle (provide a funny example).
- Add to an art journal.
- Correct your homework (answers can be placed on board or overhead).

Reviewing Classroom Management Routines

A major point of this chapter is the importance of planning for routines and procedures that happen daily or frequently in the classroom. These procedures should be not only explained but also *taught* just like any content material. The following checklist can help you determine procedures for your classroom. This list includes common problem areas to plan for ahead of time.

_____ Taking attendance procedures
_____ Late-to-class procedures
_____ Absences/makeup work policy
_____ Getting papers and other supplies
_____ Talking (or not) during seat work
_____ What to do when class work is complete
_____ Putting away materials
_____ Lining up
_____ Dismissal
_____ Getting attention ("stop, look, listen" or "freeze and listen" signal)
_____ Fire/disaster drills

_____ Lunch
_____ Interruptions, such as intercom announcements
_____ Transitions to small groups or learning centers

In establishing procedures and routines, effective classroom managers take into account a number of factors, including the school's policies and informal norms. For example, your principal may allow you to excuse students from class to use the rest room, provided that you give these students a pass. You might choose to excuse these students only *after* you have presented your lesson. The procedures and routines you select will vary, depending on the building and its principal, room size and location, students (grade level, maturity, and cliques), activities, time of year, and, most important, your philosophy of education. Other points to consider in establishing classroom routines are shown below.

Tips for Making Your Classroom Learner-Friendly

- Keep high-traffic areas free of congestion:
    Pencil sharpener
    Trash cans
    Supply areas
    Teacher's desk
    Learning centers
- Be sure that you can see all the students and that they can see and hear you.
- Keep frequently used materials and student supplies readily accessible.
- Be sure that all students can see instructional displays and presentations.
- Provide a designated area for students' personal belongings (hats, coats, lunches, etc.).
- Make students responsible for keeping the classroom clean and in order.

Setting Expectations: Your Goals for the First Days of School

As you look forward to the first days of school, set goals regarding classroom management. Your success during the entire school year is often determined by what you do during the opening days of school. Overwhelming evidence from research and practical experience shows that the first two or three weeks of school are critical in determining how well students will behave and achieve for the remainder of the year. It is essential to set expectations and establish classroom procedures during the first weeks you spend with your students.

When establishing classroom expectations, your main goal is to help students become more responsible. Routines and procedures should help children learn appropriate and productive life skills within a comfortable environment. Also, keep in mind that your teaching accountability goes beyond content information. Teaching and developing student behavior are also critical parts of your job.

The activities of the first days of school (examples listed below) should lead to specific goals. These goals fit into three categories:

1. Getting to know your students
2. Students' getting to know you and each other
3. Classroom organization and management

Getting to Know Your Students

- Plan mostly review and diagnostic activities, both formal (e.g., testing) and informal. Do not introduce new content during the first week of school.

- Maintain a whole-group focus in instruction and review.

- Monitor student activities, both academic and social.

- Actively engage all students in learning activities.

Students' Getting to Know You and Each Other

- Greet students at the door each day; demonstrate warmth, caring, and personal interest.

- Plan activities to help students introduce themselves to each other. See Resources 3.4, 3.5, 3.6, and 3.7 for good "start-of-year" activities.

- Design lessons to ensure that all students feel successful. Keep activities simple but significant. Hands-on activities resulting in a product or a sense of productivity are especially beneficial.

- Establish an accepting climate.

- Have students do self-assessment activities.

Classroom Organization and Management

- Acquaint students with room and materials they will use (supplies, books, building).

- Teach appropriate behavior, rules, procedures, consequences, and attention signal (see Chapter 5 for more on behavior management). Practice each routine.
- Explain homework policies.
- Demonstrate that you are well prepared and purposeful and are looking forward to the year together.
- Provide an overview of curriculum to be studied (see Chapter 4 for information about planning lessons and units).
- Preview curriculum highlights as a motivational device. Do something fun within the first month!

On the Opening Day

- Wear *comfortable* shoes!
- Wear clothes with *pockets.*
- Pack a "pick-me-up" snack for recess or break time.
- Be at school at least one hour early.
- Make sure your name is posted outside your classroom door.
- Spend time with anxious parents (especially at primary level) who will accompany children to school.
- Help direct traffic in the hallways and assist excited students in finding their correct rooms.
- Stand by the door to greet each student with a welcoming smile.
- Know how to pronounce correctly the name of each student on your class roster.
- Place a fun, easy-to-do activity sheet on each desk for students to complete while you greet latecomers and say good-byes to parents at the door.

Sample Daily Class Schedule

	Monday	Tuesday	Wednesday	Thursday	Friday
9:00-9:15	Opening (Community Circle), Attendance, Lunch Count				
9:15-10:30	Reading/Language Arts Journal Writing (first ten minutes) Spelling (Monday, Wednesday, Friday)				
10:30-10:45	Recess and Snack				
10:45-11:00	Read Aloud to Class				
11:00-12:00	Math				
12:00-12:45	Lunch and Recess				
12:45-1:00	SSR, Reading Log, Reading Conferences with Teacher				
1:00-2:15	Writing (prewriting and draft)	Science/ Social Studies	Writing (finish drafting and authors' circle)	Science/ Social Studies	Writing (revise, edit, share)
2:15-3:15	PE	Science/ Social Studies	PE	Science/ Social Studies	Art
3:15-3:30	Announcements, Homework Reminders, Cleanup, Dismissal				

Sample "Freeze and Listen" Signal

When students in one teacher's third-grade class get too noisy, she announces "Gimme 5!" and holds up her arm with fingers of her hand spread wide. Students stop and raise their hands, too, knowing that each finger represents a class rule they must remember to abide by.

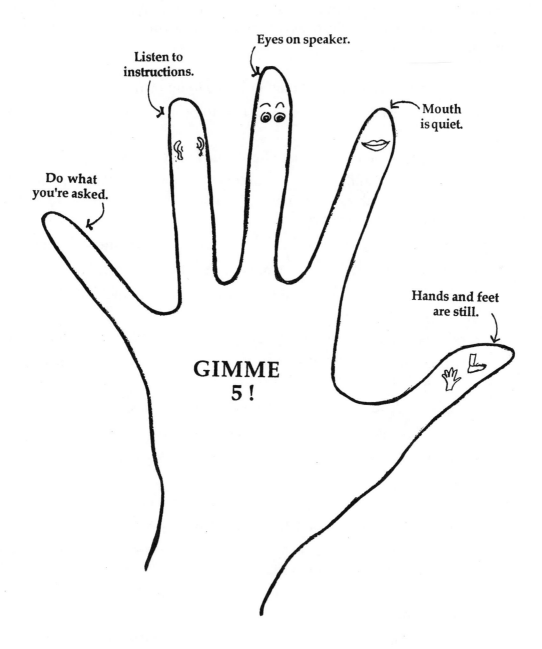

Eyes on speaker.

Listen to instructions.

Mouth is quiet.

Do what you're asked.

Hands and feet are still.

GIMME 5!

3.3 RESOURCE
Sponge Activities

....

More "Sponge" Activities

During a typical day in any classroom, many moments are lost while waiting in line for the bell to ring, waiting for intercom announcements, changing from one subject to another, waiting to go to recess or home at the end of the day, and so on. These extra minutes can be used for quick review and practice activities called "sponges." Often oral, sometimes written, the objective here is to keep the kids occupied as you squeeze in a bit of learning.

- Have children be ready to tell one playground rule.

- Ask, "What comes between these two numbers?" For example, 31 and 33, 45 and 47, and so forth.

- Ask, "What number comes before/after 46 (53, 32, etc.)?"

- Ask, "What month of the year has the most syllables? What city in our state has the most syllables in its name? Which student's name in our class? Which teacher's name in our school?"

- Write a word on the board and have students make a list of words that rhyme.

- Have students put spelling words in alphabetical order.

- Have students count to 100 (or as far as they can) by twos, fives, tens—either orally or in writing.

- Have students say the sevens table in multiplication. Then eights. Then nines.

- Have students think of animals that live on a farm, in the jungle, in the water, and so forth.

- Have students give names of fruits, vegetables, meats, and so forth.

- Play Hangman using spelling or vocabulary words.

- Have students list things you can touch, things you can smell, big things, small things, and so forth.

- Have students list the colors you (or they) are wearing.

- Have students draw something using only circles.

- Tell students, "Be ready to tell the names of children in our class that begin with 'J,' 'M,' and so forth."

- Write a word on the board. Have children list words with the same long or short vowel sound.

- Write a color word on the board. Have students draw something in or with that color.

- Tell students, "Take a number. Write it down, filling a whole page. Now make a face on it."
- Have children make a list of five things they do after school.
- Have students scramble five spelling or vocabulary words, trade with someone, and unscramble the words.
- Tell students, "Write a dialogue between _____ and _____."
- Have children name historical people (or story characters) with these initials: AL, AH, AJ, NK, IG, VC.
- Have students write a question that would check the understanding of a story.
- Have students write synonyms for vocabulary words on the board.
- Have students list the continents of the world.
- Have students name as many baseball teams as they can.
- Have children list five parts of the body *above the neck* that have three letters.

3.4 RESOURCE
Start-of-Year Activities

....

Activities for Starting the Year

Inheritance Fantasy

This activity gives you a writing sample and often reveals interesting facets of a student's personality.

Students write a paragraph telling what they would do if they won $10,000 with the restriction that they could keep only half and must give the other half away. They explain who would get the other half and why.

Guess Who I Am

This is a great "getting to know you" activity for the first week.

Students write autobiographical information on index cards and give them to you. You write one out, too. Then read one card aloud each day and have the students guess who the person is.

Forced Choice

This is a fun activity for any age group. It works anytime during the year but is especially worthwhile during the first few days. The kids feel comfortable doing this activity and get to know each other in the process. The activity can be written or done orally with younger children.

Students are given two choices (see suggestions below). They must choose one and give a reason for doing so. One effective way to work this activity is to use the space in your classroom. After giving the two options, ask the children to go to the side of the room identified for that option. There they can talk to other students who share their choice. (In the upper grades, the kids could start by writing out their reasons and then grouping together by choice afterward.) Following are some suggestions for choice options:

Are you a/an:			
	kite string	or	clothesline?
	addition sign	or	multiplication sign?
	Goofy	or	Mickey?
	ALF	or	Batman?
	president	or	captain?
	Hershey's Kiss	or	Snickers?
	skateboard	or	roller skates?
	Reebok	or	Nike?
	rock-n-roller	or	rapper?
	banana split	or	milkshake?
	roller coaster	or	Ferris wheel?

All About Me

Write your answers now in the first column. Then we will do it again in the spring in the second column. Fold your paper down the middle.

1. Date

   _____   _____

2. Full name

   _____   _____

3. Favorite dinner

   _____   _____

4. My favorite color

   _____   _____

5. My best friend

   _____   _____

6. My favorite singer

   _____   _____

7. My favorite sport

   _____   _____

8. I like to

   _____   _____

9. My favorite game

   _____   _____

10. My favorite TV show

    _____   _____

11. When I grow up, I'll

    _____   _____

12. I like to spend time

    _____   _____

Start-of-Year Activities: People Hunt

....

People Hunt

Hunt for someone who can say "yes" to one of these questions. Have this person sign his or her name. Can you find a different person for each line?

1. can whistle _____
2. has freckles _____
3. has red hair _____
4. is wearing yellow _____
5. loves math _____
6. is new to our school this year _____
7. enjoys reading _____
8. worked on a computer this summer _____
9. lost a tooth this summer _____
10. watched or played baseball this summer _____
11. made a sand castle this summer _____
12. has ridden a horse _____
13. had a birthday in July _____
14. has a birthday in October _____
15. wants to be a business owner _____
16. got sunburned this summer _____
17. can swim _____
18. has a pet cat _____
19. has an aquarium _____
20. loves yogurt _____
21. is left-handed _____
22. has brown eyes _____
23. likes pizza _____
24. wants to be a writer _____
25. has a cheese sandwich packed for lunch _____
26. has flown in an airplane _____
27. likes dancing better than school _____
28. has a great-grandfather _____
29. plays the piano _____
30. likes to rap _____

Start-of-Year Activities: Interest Inventory

Interest Inventory

Name _____ Grade _____ Date _____

1. If you could not watch television at home, what would you most like to do?

2. If your parents told you that you could do anything you wanted to do this weekend, what would you choose?

3. What is your favorite subject in school?

4. What subject is most difficult for you in school?

5. If you could learn about anything you wanted to learn about, what would you choose?

6. What is your favorite television show?

7. What book or story have you read recently that was really exciting for you?

8. Other than watching television, what is the most fun thing to do indoors?

9. Do you like to do your work best in groups or alone?

10. Do you do your best work in groups or when you work alone?

11. If you had to learn something, would you rather read a book or watch a movie?

12. Who are your two best friends in this class?

CHAPTER

Preparing Lesson Plans and Units That Engage Students

Planning Is Important!

Lesson planning is a critical part of effective teaching. Studies have shown that it has important consequences for both student learning and classroom behavior. The old adage "Failing to plan means planning to fail" is all too true in busy elementary classrooms. It is essential that you carefully and thoughtfully prepare for every minute with your students.

Planning always seems to take more time than expected. It requires you to synthesize everything you have learned about teaching, such as models of instruction, cognitive and affective taxonomies, learning objectives, and lesson and unit design, and translate it into useful, significant, practical lessons that meet the needs of your particular students. It is a complex decision-making process. Talk to experienced colleagues about the thought that goes into lesson planning. Ask to look at your mentor's lesson plans. Be aware, however, that it is difficult to learn how to plan effectively from experienced teachers. Most of their planning activities are hidden mental processes that are reflective, intuitive, and nonlinear, taking a large number of factors into consideration. Your own planning must be more specific, careful, and detailed. Experience will gradually give you a better sense of how much to cover and how quickly, how to sequence material, how to start and end an activity, how to modify plans for individual children, and how to make changes if plans are not going as you expected. In the beginning, there are no shortcuts. Plan to spend a lot of time planning.

In college teacher-preparation courses and during student teaching, most new teachers were instructed to start their lesson planning by writing objectives. Don't feel guilty if this is not the best approach for you. Trust your innate sense about where you want to jump into the planning process. Many experienced teachers plan their content and instructional activities first and then cycle back to specify objectives. Of course, you do need to think about outcomes. What do you want your students to understand, appreciate, value, and enjoy? What is the overall result you want to achieve? Then clarify specifically what you will teach and what you expect your students to learn. At the heart of good planning is good decision making. The judgments and choices in teaching are complicated. Use the approach that results in the best instructional planning for *you*.

Steps to Effective Lesson Planning

Successful lessons in the elementary classroom are varied; no one lesson design is functional in all situations. Nevertheless, the design of effective lessons follows general principles. Below is a checklist of important questions to ask yourself when planning:

_____ 1. How will this lesson or unit be relevant to my students' lives?

_____ 2. Are the goals of this lesson or unit consistent with grade-level goals in my school district and/or state curriculum guides?

_____ 3. How will I make provisions for individual differences? Have I provided hands-on learning experiences to support all learning modalities and all types of learners?

_____ 4. Does this lesson or unit require my children to have prior knowledge and skills to complete it successfully?

_____ 5. Did I include enough vocabulary building for limited-English-speaking students? For my students with low reading levels? For my students with special needs?

_____ 6. Did I build from the concrete to the abstract? Does the lesson or unit follow a logical sequence?

_____ 7. How will my daily plan tie into my weekly, monthly, and yearly plans?

_____ 8. Is the content inclusive and at an appropriate depth?

_____ 9. What specific instructional strategies or activities do I intend to use?

_____ 10. In my lesson planning, have I considered not only the cognitive but also the affective domains? Are my lessons building morale and cohesion in my classroom?

_____ 11. Do I have all the resources I need, such as supplementary books, audiovisual materials, speakers, and field trip locales?

_____ 12. What procedure(s) will I use to evaluate student learning?

Lesson Plan Basics

Reserve your least busy time of day for planning. Finding the time to sit down and write plans is a personal matter. Decide when and where it is best for you to do your lesson planning: at school, during lunch or prep time, after school, or on weekends. Check the policy on using the building after work hours and on weekends.

Know what you wish to accomplish. Specify the intended student outcomes toward which you will be working. Two or three goals are plenty for one instructional sequence.

If the grade level you teach now is the same level you student-taught, review notes and lesson plans you already developed. Often, you will find good ideas at your fingertips. Be sure to save any lesson plans that will fit later in the year.

Check existing state and school district documents listing the learning criteria for your grade level or subject. Your state department of education has published official curriculum materials that provide valuable guidelines for content and process selection. Most school districts also produce curriculum guides, frameworks, or courses of study. These important resources, developed by teachers in your local area, outline what is to be taught and provide a clear sense of your district's expectations. Curriculum goals typical for various grade levels are listed in Resource 6.1.

Create a master plan template for the week. Write in routine things—attendance, recess, and breaks. Duplicate this form, and each week fill in the varying lesson activities. Schools sometimes provide blank lesson plan books. Plan books are also available at teacher supply stores. Some teachers enjoy personally selecting a colorful plan book with cartoons or clever quotations.

Relate your lesson plans to student experiences at the onset of the lesson. The opening, or anticipatory set, is especially important because it sets the lesson's focus, hooks into students' past knowledge, triggers memories, and motivates children.

Select specific instructional strategies to achieve your lesson goals. Determine if they need to be completed in a certain format or sequence. Decide how you will group students for instruction.

Think about how one lesson interrelates with others in a unit. Children become more effective learners when you plan continuous, cohesive blocks of instruction that enable them to make connections among ideas. Individual lessons should flow into one another.

Many excellent commercially prepared lesson and unit plans are available. Check educational catalogs and/or your local teacher supply store. Also check magazines such as *Instructor, Teaching K-8,* and *Learning* for special ideas to incorporate in your lesson plans. Monthly teacher magazines contain many quick and easy tips, suggestions from teachers across the country, and current holiday activities.

It's not necessary to reinvent the wheel each time you plan a lesson or unit. A vast number of attractive, user-friendly commercial resources are available with thematic collections of lesson plans. In addition to print materials, be sure to check publishers' Web sites. For instance, Teacher Created Materials (www.teachercreated.com) offers a wide variety of free, ready-to-use lesson plans and activities on their Web site. The plans are referenced to complete thematic units and complementary materials available for purchase if you wish. The Teacher Created Materials Web site also offers a Teachers' Forum, with a Discussion Board to ask questions and share ideas and a section called "1001+ Teacher Links," an extensive Internet database organized into categories, great for locating supplementary materials. Scholastic.com offers similar resources, as do most of the major publishers. Another personal favorite is the Discovery School Web site, which provides sections for teachers, students, and parents (you might want to mention it at your open house). The "Teachers" section offers a teacher-approved library of creative curriculum resources, including lesson plans, quizzes, puzzles, clip art, and Internet links to other resources. Additional Internet sites are discussed later in this chapter in the section on "Computer Technology and Instruction."

Whatever the source of your lesson plans—the teacher's edition, another commercial source, the Web, or your own creativity—you are likely to revise your initial plan after you've taught it. Use colored pens or markers to make comments about the lesson, absent students, what to do differently next time, and what worked especially well. Rarely in teaching can lesson plans be implemented exactly.

Especially at the start of the year, a mentor or colleague can save you time by suggesting tried-and-true lesson ideas. He or she often knows your students and their unique learning interests and needs. Using these suggestions may increase your lesson's effectiveness.

Look for ways to extend students' thinking and to involve multiple learning modalities. For example, students might build models from clay or papier-mâché of animals visited at the zoo or dinosaurs studied in science. Plan a field trip to a museum, farm, or other interesting place. Students can then make booklets, dioramas, puppets, posters, or bulletin boards to illustrate and describe their learnings.

Many instructional models are available. Use one model or part of a model that you feel comfortable with, then branch out and try others. Small-group instruction can flow from periods of whole-class oral involvement; personalized study can be based on small-group or whole-group work. More information on instructional approaches can be found later in this chapter.

Ask if your plan book needs to be turned in at the end of the year. If so, you may want to make copies of your plans each week and make notes to yourself on your copy.

In general, it is better to overplan, or be ready with more than you think can be completed in the period allowed, than to underplan. Spend extra time (above and beyond the workday) for preparing lessons, especially during your first year. Careful planning will give you confidence, knowing that you are fully prepared to work with students in the days and weeks ahead.

Using Materials in the Teaching Manuals as a Guide

An important part of your planning is making decisions about what content to teach. Most new teachers find that their major content decisions are guided by textbooks and the teacher manuals that accompany the students' books. School districts have regular adoptions of textbooks, usually in five- to seven-year cycles. You are often expected to use the officially adopted books to cover the curriculum in each subject area. Your main job becomes making sure you understand the scope and sequence of the content for each subject and then choosing the most appropriate material for your particular group of students, adding supplementary material as needed, and deciding how best to teach it.

The elementary curriculum is crowded. Teacher manuals can be an excellent tool to help you grasp the basic content of each subject at your grade level and how this content is organized in a scope and sequence through time. Teacher guides also include proven activities, suggestions for learning experiences, and information about additional resources and readings to enhance your lessons.

In recent years, it has become fashionable to criticize commercial textbooks and basal series. Nevertheless, teacher manuals to these basic texts can be an invaluable tool for a stressed and busy beginning teacher.

Textbooks will not, of course, be the *only* instructional experience you give your students. Do not overrely on them. Use them as a planning tool. Think of them (especially in certain subjects) as the *base* on which to build higher-order thinking activities.

Consider your students' individual learning styles, needs, and interests, as well as the reading level of the adopted textbook. Then incorporate into your lessons a wide variety of other print and nonprint instructional materials. Below are some ideas to get you started.

Working From a Teacher Guide

1. First, read through an entire section or unit of the material to get a feel for the span and sequence. What are the main ideas?
2. What is your objective, or purpose, for presenting this particular lesson or unit? In some cases, you may not be able to use all the materials in the teacher manual. Do not expect to do everything suggested.
3. Make a list of teaching suggestions and materials related to your objectives. For instance, you might want all lessons to connect to a unit theme, such as the importance of sharing and helping family members. Generate ideas for lessons or activities that fit into this theme from a variety of additional sources: other teachers, community members, fiction and nonfiction books, poetry,

real-life experiences, music, art, television, and even billboards and advertisements.

4. Before using any of this material in a lesson plan, think about how it will enhance the learning and growth of your students. To ensure student learning and growth, take into account different learning aptitudes and styles; varied stages of readiness to learn; and the social, emotional, linguistic, cultural, cognitive, and intellectual needs of students.

5. Have available a short activity, story, graph, chart, picture, or film clip to help focus student attention and develop a readiness for the planned instruction. Once you have decided how to capture your students' attention, consider how you will develop your lesson. Refer to your teacher manual for ideas. Then ask yourself, "What else can I include?" To spark your creativity, here is a listing of various instructional strategies, resources, and activities:

   • Individual packets, graphs, bulletin boards, interest centers, games, problem solving, films, drama/puppets, role playing, field trips, flash cards, puzzles, computers, reference books, magazines, newspapers, book making, manipulatives, maps, questioning strategies, cooperative learning activities, visualization, inventions, skits, video presentations, cartooning, student-created board games, posters, mind mapping, characterizations, rap sessions, debate, mock court, interviews, independent projects, murals, mobiles, team teaching, journal writing

6. After considering various strategies and activities and choosing one or more for your lesson, visualize the instructional sequence step by step:

   • Try to "see" what you and the students will be doing during the lesson. Imagine the lesson from different students' points of view.

   • Visualize the worst possible scenarios, too. Better yet, learn to anticipate. Do you really have enough paste and paint for each group of students? Suppose the students spill paint? What if unscheduled events or behavior problems interrupt plans? Activities that appear ideal in preplanning sometimes misfire. Given the multitude of variables in an elementary classroom, expect to modify and adapt your plans.

   • How will children share what they have learned and produced? Oral sharing, for instance, flows naturally from individual or group writing. If children finish early, how will you turn extra time at the end of a period into a productive learning experience?

Extending and Enriching
the Basic Curriculum

Effective teachers encourage students to go beyond the basic content or skills lessons of the official adopted curriculum. Enrichment activities extend content to related personal interests, pertinent topics, or relevant skills.

Student textbooks, basal readers, and adopted instructional materials are not intended to displace the teacher's instructional decision making or to supplant opportunities for students to experience a wide range of learning activities. Think of your teacher manual as an instructional resource to help you provide basic, sequenced instruction for a wide variety of student abilities. Then, after sampling its contents, take control of your teacher manual so that it becomes only one resource among many for you as an informed and discriminating teacher.

Here are a few examples of curriculum enrichment:

- Regardless of the grade you teach, read to your students every day. If you are unsure where to begin, a list of outstanding "read-aloud" books is provided in Resource 4.1. Read-alouds expand children's understanding of the world around them. Set aside one specific time each day for a story. Read-alouds can enhance your unit themes, but you do not have to tie every book to class work. Allow time for discussion after reading. Your students will look forward to the story if you read one or two chapters at a time and then invite them to predict what will happen next. Read with plenty of expression, slowly enough for each child to build mental pictures.

- Invite your students to choose two favorite stories. Ask the children to imagine what would happen if the character in one story found him- or herself in the second story's setting and had to solve a different problem.

- Small groups of students can choose a favorite author, artist, or musician and then obtain information about that person's life and works. If students choose persons who lived a long time ago, ask them to find world events that their persons might have seen, heard about, or even helped to influence.

- Introduce a new word each day, and challenge your students to include it in one of their stories, use it in conversation at least once, and explore its origins and other definitions. For example, do origins of this word include another language or incorporate a slang term?

- Add an oral language component to your lessons, such as brainstorming, discussing, or dramatization. Build in time for natural oral interaction, collaborative small-group talking, writing, editing, and sharing.

- Take advantage of opportunities for students to participate in hands-on activities. In science, for example, students may be able to test their own hypotheses in an activity or experiment. Scientific concepts are not simply passed down by the teacher and absorbed ready-made by the children. Allow students to demonstrate ideas they have learned, do experiments based on content read, and solve problems embedded in information uncovered.

- Collect and recycle throwaway items, such as empty containers, into useful classroom teaching aids, musical instruments, arts and crafts materials, and toys. Encourage students and parents to help you collect needed items.

- Challenge your students to solve nonroutine math problems, such as soma cubes (seven puzzle pieces that can be assembled into a three-inch-by-three-inch cube) and Rubik's Cube, and then explain how each puzzle was solved.

- Encourage children to keep a learning log as part of content-area study and/or a literature response journal as they read short stories, novels, and poems. They can write in their logs or journals on topics of their own choosing or in response to such questions as these:

    What is the main idea or theme?
    How does this idea develop in the selection?
    What does this idea mean to you personally?
    When have you ever experienced something similar?

- Children enjoy painting or drawing pictures based on their readings and learnings. They can make an illustration to accompany the reading selection. Illustrations may be maps, charts, graphs, or tables, as well as artistic renderings. Invite them to orally share their illustrations. Share a piece of classical music that relates to the mood or theme of a story. Discuss the relationships.

- Students can construct something based on their readings or content-area study—a diorama, a model, a bulletin board, or a time line. They can also respond with a form of drama, such as monologue, dialogue, role playing, choral reading or speaking, and a Reader's Theater rendition that relates to the content read or learned.

Be brave about trying new strategies and materials. Continue to search for ways to improve your lessons. Planning and implementing great lessons takes time, but your extra effort will prove worthwhile.

A Word About District, State, and National Standards

Learning standards are becoming an increasingly prevalent component of teachers' lesson planning. National, state, and local standards can be an important resource for you because they represent an explicit collection of the knowledge and skills students are expected to have at different stages of their education.

Unfortunately, many districts and states have developed standards independently from one another, thereby creating overlapping layers of standards that can easily become overwhelming. For example, has your local school district adopted the state standards, adapted standards from national professional organizations (such as the National Council of Teachers of Mathematics), or created new, locally specific standards using other documents as resources? Important questions for you to ask include the following:

- Which standards are the focus for learning at our school?

- Is every one of my students expected to achieve the complete set of standards?

- How exactly should I use the standards when planning lessons for my classroom?

In most states and local districts, standards are written for each subject area by committees of experts who focus on one area of the curriculum. This process ensures content accuracy and breadth but often leads to fragmented instructional expectations if no one has evaluated the cumulative effect of the standards. In many cases, the various sets of standards don't encompass a realistic scope. For instance, all the science a child ought to know added to all the important social studies, reading, language arts, mathematics, history, physical education, and arts that same child should know might add up to an overwhelming mass of curriculum.

Many teachers don't take these conglomerations of standards seriously. The logistical difficulties alone can deter teachers who must refer to multiple sets of standards documents and search for their grade-level expectations. At your school, you may find that individual teachers make different decisions about which standards to teach and which to ignore. You will find your job less confusing if your district and school have formally identified their curriculum standards. Ask questions to get a clear vision of what your students are expected to learn.

The current standards movement in education is aimed at alleviating situations in which curriculum content and teacher expectations for students in the same grade levels and same subjects vary greatly within and across buildings, districts, and states. Although there is no question that teachers need the freedom to teach in different ways to best meet the needs of students, it is difficult to justify a situation in which a teacher in one first-grade classroom has children memorize five words per week as reading objectives, while the first-grade teacher across the hall has students read books of all genres throughout the week. The logic behind using standards as the foundation for curriculum, instruction, and assessment is therefore compelling. Keep in mind that these standards typically reinforce the best practice of the best teachers.

Basic Instructional Approaches

As you plan lessons, you will decide which teaching models and methods are most efficient and comfortable. In many elementary classrooms, especially in the upper grades, teachers choose the direct presentation model—presenting, explaining, and lecturing. Formal presentations by teachers compose up to one fourth of all classroom time in many schools. Other teachers prefer to break their classes into smaller groups for one or more subjects. During your student teaching, you and your cooperating teacher probably used a combination of these and other approaches. In general, elementary students should experience a succession of group settings for instruction—whole group and small group—on any given day. The specific learning activity often guides the teacher's grouping decisions.

To help you decide on an instructional approach for a lesson you are planning, three basic instructional delivery methods—whole group, individualized, and small group—are outlined below. Two variations, cooperative learning and learning centers, are also described.

Whole-Group Presentations

Description

In the whole-group approach, a teacher or instructor tells, presents, explains, or lectures to a whole class. Wherever applicable, audiovisual materials such as transparencies, slides, video clips, computer-generated images, and other items are used to augment the presentation. Advance organizers are helpful to serve as intellectual scaffolding on which new knowledge is built.

Advantages

- Presentations can be quickly developed because the teacher is likely to be familiar with concepts and related materials.

- Presentations can serve a whole class of students, at one time, in one location, as they proceed together through the lesson.

- Direct class control is easier, because the whole group or class hears the presentation at one time from an instructor in a visible authority position.

Disadvantages

- Students are required to listen and remain passive learners only.
- It is assumed that students are learning the same amount of content at the same time.
- The teacher has to be enthusiastic, knowledgeable, and interesting; a lecture is a performance.
- Not all students learn at the pace set by the teacher.
- Not all students learn by listening.

How to Use Whole-Group Presentations Effectively

- Consider your purpose and rationale for presenting material in this manner—have a specific goal.
- Outline the beginning, middle, and end of the presentation.
- Decide how you will make the presentation interesting and motivating, such as including realia, clever or colorful overhead transparencies, handouts, and humor.
- Encourage students to take notes or, better yet, present notes as a graphic organizer on the chalkboard as you speak. Use key words and simple diagrams. Say before writing.
- Remember that effective elementary teachers do not deliver long lectures with little teacher-student interaction.

Quick Teaching Tips That Foster Student Involvement in Whole-Group Instruction

Ensure participation by all students in whole-group instruction by using the following strategies:

1. Call on students in a random or unpredictable pattern. Ask questions of the class in a fashion that implies that any one of them could be asked to respond. Ask the question *first,* then name the student who will answer the question.
2. Signal the class that someone else may be called on to add to, clarify, or summarize another student's response. Do not routinely repeat students' answers. Expect students to hear, build on, and elaborate each other's answers.

3. Make use of wait time after asking the question and after the student's initial response. Allow your low-achieving students as much time to respond to a question as is given to other students. If the student hesitates, waiting for him or her to think through an answer indicates that you feel confident that a worthwhile response is being formulated. Studies have shown that teachers tend to allow high achievers more time to answer a question than low achievers.

4. Get the students moving and doing—ask several at a time to demonstrate a task at the chalkboard or on the overhead projector; require seated students to perform the same task on paper. Rotate volunteers.

5. Increase teacher-student academic interactions. Ask students more questions that are open-ended and that require critical and creative thinking. When you ask students to give an opinion or make a judgment about a person, situation, or idea, have them cite evidence that supports their judgment so that it is not merely a haphazard guess or recall of something you said.

6. To keep students motivated, vary your routines and materials and keep it short. Provide frequent shifts of activities as opposed to long periods of just listening. Think of minilessons of ten minutes for elementary students.

7. Make certain that high yet reasonable expectations for all students are clearly stated and modeled. Provide equitable response opportunities by calling on *all* the children, not just those with their hands up or those you think will have a correct or thoughtful response.

8. Realize that using "busywork" duplicated worksheets as a follow-up activity may keep students occupied but may not be a worthy on-task activity.

Individualized Learning

Description

Individualized learning is also known as self-paced learning. Unlike whole-group presentations, its structure requires active, individualized participation by each student. The teacher provides objectives and direction for the student, along with a carefully designed set of learning activities to be completed in small, sequential steps.

Advantages

- Students work according to their personal abilities. At-risk learners, as well as gifted students, complete the instruction on their own time schedule.

- The teacher can work more easily with an individual student and tailor instruction to meet individual needs.
- Students' effective study habits are reinforced and rewarded.

Disadvantages

- Additional time may be needed to teach and reinforce students' self-discipline to keep going at their own pace.
- Additional work is required of the teacher to prepare and grade personalized student learning materials and activities.
- Lack of variety in self-paced materials can be monotonous.
- Teacher and student may not interact much in a self-paced program.

How to Use Self-Paced Learning Effectively

- To provide enrichment to students who wish to learn more about a given subject
- To give individual students needed additional practice in a given subject
- To allow students to practice rote facts or skills at their own pace

Sample Types of Self-Paced Learning Materials

- Self-instructional packages (SIPs): Designed to teach a relatively small amount of materials to the mastery level, an SIP is a learning packet developed for an individual student using small, sequential steps and giving frequent, immediate feedback to the learner.
- Tutorial audiotapes and worksheets: The instructor's voice on the tape tells the student what to read or what problem to solve. The recording gives directions and explanations of answers.
- Computer-based instruction: Often used as a drill-and-practice activity, computer-based instruction gives an individual student immediate knowledge of results. Some programs adapt instruction on the basis of the learner's performance.
- Individualized inquiry investigations: The student presents to the teacher an issue, topic, or problem in which the student has personal interest. A contract is drawn up to specify the conditions of the investigation, for example, how much time should be devoted to it, will the student be excused from class to pursue the investigation, how will the student report results, and how will the investigation be evaluated?

Small Groups

Description

Students are given opportunities to complete academic tasks and to improve social and communication skills by interacting with each other, usually in groups of two to six students. Most elementary teachers group students for instructional purposes. Although grouping is prevalent, there is no single best approach to grouping students, nor is grouping in and of itself a panacea for education. Effective teachers put students into groups on the basis of function. They keep groups flexible and move students when the need arises. Students can be placed in

- Interest groups (students choose to study a particular book or concept)
- Teaching groups (when the teacher needs to instruct in a particular skill)
- Cooperative groups (students work as a team, sharing a set of norms)
- Pairs (to work together to complete an assignment)

Advantages

- Students' social and communication skills are enhanced as they work with each other.
- Teachers can obtain feedback, learning more about the effectiveness of a lesson by listening to students' discussions of it.
- Active learning and higher-level thinking are promoted.
- Individual students can share ideas, solve problems, and discuss materials with their peers.

Disadvantages

- The teacher must carefully plan group activities and implement them effectively. Care must be given to group formation and composition.
- Students must prepare for group work by doing assignments, such as readings, before they will be ready to participate.
- The teacher must provide feedback to students on their progress in the group activity.

When to Use Small Groups

- Group work is an excellent supplement to other methods of instruction.

- Small groups are able to discuss topics and exchange facts, ideas, and opinions. Students may offer different viewpoints or special experiences.

- Groups may enjoy open-ended problems, case studies, role playing, and simulation. Educational games may be used in group formats as well.

Cooperative Learning

Cooperative learning is a specific small-group approach that incorporates democratic processes, individual accountability, equal opportunity, and group rewards. A number of types of cooperative learning activities and models are frequently used in today's classrooms, such as student teams achievement divisions, jigsaw, and group investigation. All cooperative learning lessons, however, have three key features: Students work in groups, groups are heterogeneously formed, and reward systems are group oriented. A strong research base supports the use of cooperative learning. Studies have shown that it has positive effects on academic achievement, collaborative behavior, cross-cultural understandings and relationships, and attitudes toward disabled students.

Guidelines for Using Cooperative Learning

- Limit group size to three to five students.

- Compose groups heterogeneously by mixing students as to academic achievement, sex, and race.

- Give each student in the group a specific role, responsibility, or task that contributes to the success of the total group. Sample roles include facilitator, checker, summarizer-recorder, setup, cleanup, and reporter.

- Use cooperative learning as a supplemental activity for review, enrichment, or practice, allowing students in the group to help one another master material. Groups can also complete projects such as reports, presentations, experiments, and artwork.

- Consider room arrangement, task materials, and time frame as you plan cooperative activities.

- Grade individual students' contributions.

- Consider providing a group reward to motivate students in the group.

- Vary group composition so that no student feels labeled by being in a "slow" group and all students have an opportunity during the school year to work with every other student in the class.

- For cooperative learning groups to function effectively, collaborative social skills must be taught, modeled, and reinforced regularly.

Learning Centers

Learning centers or stations are another way to individualize and personalize learning. A learning center is a place to which children can go to do an instructional task on their own (or with a partner), completing the activity outlined there.

- Make sure written directions and all the materials needed to complete the task are available at the station.
- Consider leaving an answer key or correcting guide in the center to enable students who finish the task to self-check.
- Centers are usually set up in classroom corners or along walls so that children face a bulletin board. Sometimes, you can place bookshelves or file cabinets perpendicular to the wall to create a center area.

Computer Technology and Instruction

Until recently, computers were not considered tools for delivering instruction effectively. In reading instruction, for instance, computers could not comprehend oral reading and judge its accuracy. Nor could they accept free-form responses to comprehension questions; their use relied on multiple-choice formats. Those who looked carefully at how computers were first used in classrooms often found them employed primarily as patient drillmasters that sometimes supplied didactic explanations. This type of drilling can help a small group of children with specific types of learning—such as rote memorization of math computations—but it does not enhance thoughtful learning in general and cannot replace the instruction of a human teacher. In short, this type of use is far from the best computers have to offer for instruction.

Drilling programs are still available, but fortunately the situation is much improved in many schools today. New computers have speech recognition capabilities as well as many multimedia presentation functions. The addition of speech to computer-presented text is a promising use of technology in reading instruction, for example. Developments in the Internet, with possibilities of linking schools and instruction, have further increased interest in technology as a teaching device. The possibilities for using technology effectively represent some of the most interesting developments in how new teachers are changing the traditional design of classroom activities.

Using CD-ROMs to Support Instruction

Several newer trends show promise. The use of hypertext (highlighted text that links to underlying definitions or supporting or related text, almost like an electronic footnote) offers an instructional advantage to many students. Following are descriptions of only a few of the many electronic books and hypermedia systems that exemplify how technology today is changing the ways lessons are taught and applied in many elementary classrooms.

Schools across the country are beginning to use simple hypertext systems such as the CD-ROM based on *Compton's Illustrated Encyclopedia* or the *Grolier Electronic Encyclopedia.* In the case of the *Grolier Electronic Encyclopedia,* twenty-one volumes, thirty-three thousand articles, and nine million words of text are available. By typing in a single search word (e.g., *whales*), the student can make the system search every reference to the subject in the encyclopedia. An electronic cutting and editing system allows the student to take notes and compile a personalized data bank.

Another example of hypertext or *hypermedia* (hypertext and visual and auditory sources) is the "Smart Books" program by Scholastic. In this program, electronic books based on existing traditional print books are rendered electronically to take advantage of CD-ROM and hypermedia technologies. The Smart Book version of *If Your Name Was Changed at Ellis Island,* by Ellen Levine, lets children hear stories of immigrants' trips through Ellis Island, meet famous Ellis Island immigrants, meet contemporary immigrant children, use maps and graphs, explore the Ellis Island complex, and visit a Japanese-American internment camp, for example.

M-ss-ng L-nks is an old favorite of reading teachers that is now available in a new format. Students of all ability levels can engage in language play with this award-winning material from Sunburst Communications. In *M-ss-ng L-nks,* passages from well-known children's books, as well as from science and encyclopedic materials, appear as engaging word puzzles. Each passage is presented in cloze format. Students fill in the blanks based on their knowledge of language structure, spelling patterns, context clues, and literary style. Students can work individually, in pairs, or in a collaborative group to solve each puzzle. As they make correct choices, a picture related to the passage can be revealed. Reports can be printed to summarize student responses.

Using the Internet to Support Instruction

Electronic books and hypermedia systems are not the only important innovations in educational computing. Many computer-savvy teachers have found creative ways to use the Internet to engage children in the learning process and to help them broaden their thinking. One teacher, for instance, arranged for her first and second graders to correspond regularly with a fellow teacher who had taken a year off to bicycle around the world. Through their online discussions with the world traveler, the young scholars learned about world languages, cultures, geography, art, time zones, and architecture—and at the same time improved their skills in reading, writing, and communicating. Other teachers have set up "pen pal" relationships with children in different regions of the country, again helping the children to learn from each other in real time while simultaneously improving their communication skills.

Still others have developed buddy projects between classes studying similar subjects. A class doing a field study of pond life at a local site, for example, might compare notes with children doing a similar study at a pond in another region. In another innovative program, a first-grade class created a "butterfly garden," using the Internet to research habitat and to identify species. A sixth-grade class in the same district partnered with the younger group and developed a Web site to document the project.

Using the Internet as a Resource

The Internet also makes many wonderful resources available to teachers who want supplementary information on a topic. A common question heard about this issue in faculty rooms is, "How do I find the time to keep up?" With careful searching, you can find a wealth of useful sites to expand and diversify your lessons. For "savvy surfing," Boolean searches are most efficient. Tell your search engine to look for something specific, thus avoiding sites that contain a word similar to your search word but that have nothing to do with your topic. The search engine can work best for you if you use the following procedures:

- Use quotation marks and a plus sign to provide specific information. For instance, "cat + dog" means you want the searched sites to contain both animals.

- Use quotation marks and the word *OR* to widen the search to include one or both of your key words. For example, "cat OR dog" will bring up sites that have one or both animals.

- Provide enough specific information to narrow the search. The more precise the search, the more specific the sites, such as "Gettysburg + soldiers + journal."

Many lesson plans are available on the Internet. Most are teacher created. These can provide you with the kernel of an idea, or you can download an entire plan. Start with the following:

http://www.csun.edu/~vceed009/lesson.html

http://ericir.syr.edu/Virtual/Lessons/

http://teacher.scholastic.com/index.htm

http://teams.lacoe.edu

http://teams.lacoe.edu/documentation/places/language.html

http://discoveryschool.com/schrockguide/index.html

If you need ideas about literature for the classroom, several sites provide book reviews and suggest related activities:

- Carol Hurst Children's Literature Site: http://www.carolhurst.com
- Children's Literature Web Guide: http://www.acs.ucalgary.ca/ ~dkbrown
- Multicultural Book Reviews: http://www.isomedia.com/homes/ jmele/joe.html
- American Library Association: http://www.ala.org/alsc

Other sites that support classroom instruction are out there waiting to be discovered. For additional lesson-planning ideas, as well as for your own professional development, try these:

- NASA Spacelink: http://www.spacelink.nasa.gov/Spacelink. Hot.Topics/.index.html
- Holidays Around the World: http://falcon.jmu.edu/%7Eramseyil/ holidays.htm
- Multicultural Calendar: http://www.kidlink.org/KIDPROJ/MCC
- Reading On-line, International Reading Association journal: http://www.readingonline.org

For a general resource, try

- TeacherNet: http://www.teachnet.com/

Remember, a good site should lead you to other good sites through "related links." Share your finds with colleagues; such sharing is one of the best ways to discover new resources!

Time on Task

In addition to careful researching and planning of instructional activities, you must also give close attention to how you will use classroom *time.* What is the connection between learning time and student learning and growth? Two major findings have emerged from a number of studies:

1. Students' achievement is higher when they spend more time engaged in learning activities (e.g., practicing skills, discussing, problem solving, and reading).
2. The amount of time students spend learning differs dramatically from classroom to classroom.

The Northwest Regional Educational Laboratory reported that in one fifth-grade reading class, for example, students were observed to engage in reading activities 120 hours during the year. Students in a comparable classroom spent 298 hours on reading—two and one half times more than the other students! Achievement test scores reflected this difference.

In fifth-grade classes, time spent on reading varied from an average of 27 minutes a day to an average of 53 minutes a day. Which children do you think showed greater reading achievement and aptitude?

In one state, second graders are supposed to learn fractions. But a study found that second-grade classrooms actually spent from 0 to 399 minutes during the year on fractions, depending on their teacher.

What Is Engaged Time?

Is engaged time the time the school has scheduled for instruction? The time the teacher devotes? Or is it the time students actually spend engaged in learning tasks?

Just looking at a schedule will not tell you how much work a class really does—or how any one student has spent the time. A schedule gives the broad, official version of how much time every student spends learning a subject.

By scheduling or devoting more time for a subject, you can increase your students' opportunity to learn. But scheduling and teaching do not guarantee that students are actually *attending* to the learning activity.

Engaged time is the essence of classroom learning. It is the amount of time your students actually work on any assigned activity that builds the desired skill—for example, working on written assignments, actively discussing a problem in a cooperative learning group, reading silently, and listening carefully as you explain a subject. It can include reading aloud or rapid-fire drill and practice of math facts. Engaged time will vary from student to student, as well as from class to class (see Figure 4.1).

In a school year of the same number of days, students with an efficient and effective teacher receive the equivalent of many more days of instruction than do those unfortunate children in classrooms in which many minutes in each school day become wasted time. If you eliminate wasted time during transitions, during instruction, and after instruction, not only will discipline problems lessen, but substantial gains in academic learning time will be realized.

Not all your classroom time can be spent in dynamic learning, of course. Some nonacademic time is needed—taking roll, for example, or moving from one task to the next. Some off-task behavior by students is inevitable. Good teaching does not imply that students should be engaged in academic learning every moment they are in school. Research has shown, however, that too much nonengaged time interferes with learning in many classes.

Think about your own classroom during reading or math time. How much time will your students spend getting ready or straightening up? Do they need to wait for your attention? Do some of them daydream? Do

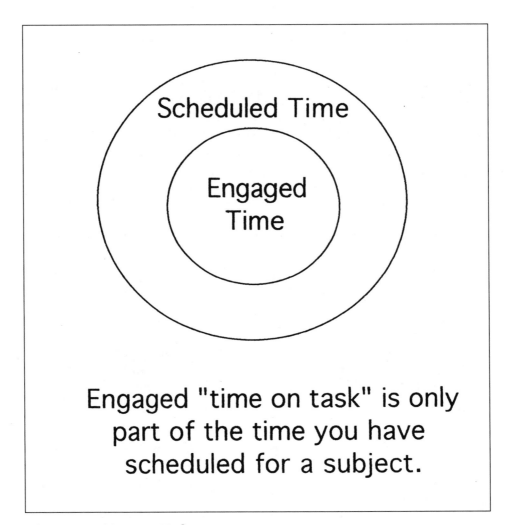

Figure 4.1. Time on Task

they socialize or watch what others are doing? Do they get restless before the end of the scheduled period? How much time is expended waiting for class to start, waiting for the reading group to gather, waiting for papers to be passed out or collected, waiting to be dismissed? All this waiting leaves students with nothing to do but entertain themselves. Usually they fill this time by talking, playing with friends, or getting into trouble. Additional valuable time is lost as you endeavor to regain students' attention and refocus students for the next learning. Pay close attention to how your students use time in your classroom. In Resources 4.2, 4.3, and 4.4 are observation forms and a survey to help you assess your classroom time on task.

The importance of time on task has been well documented for the past twenty years. One of the first studies of beginning teachers in California (Fisher et al., 1978), for instance, showed the importance of maintaining high engagement rates. When teachers allocated and spent more classroom time on a specific topic, their students learned more in that area. Engagement rate (the percentage of allocated time that students were engaged) was shown to be directly related to student learning. Differences in time on task are important. Students who receive less instruction are still expected to do well on the standardized tests given at the end of the year and are compared with students whose teachers maintained high engagement time. In fairness to your students, you must maximize allocated time on academic subjects and manage your classroom so that students are engaged, on task, and achieving success.

At-Risk Students: Effective Classroom Instruction

How should you, as a regular classroom teacher, adapt your instruction to meet the needs of at-risk students in your classroom? The overall picture from the research is one of providing structure and support, yet retaining the best of effective teaching strategies that work with other students. A review of the research in this area turned up little evidence suggesting the need for qualitatively different forms of instruction for students who differ in aptitude, achievement level, socioeconomic status, ethnicity, or learning style. In short, teachers of at-risk students need to do what they do better, not fundamentally differently. Effective instructional practices for at-risk students are outlined in the box on page 98.

Each of these strategies is characteristic of good instruction in general. For your at-risk students, however, teaching in this manner is crucial. Collectively, these instructional practices provide a safety net, helping you create a successful learning environment in which *all* students believe they can and will succeed.

A note of caution: One study of at-risk students found that many of the characteristics of effective practice were being implemented (Northwest Regional Educational Laboratory, 1986). The schools in the study were adapting at every level, from school policies to classroom instruction, and this adaptation was keeping students in school. The researchers also found, however, (a) lowered expectations for students; (b) lack of emphasis on higher-level thinking and problem solving, with a concomitant increase in low-level worksheets; and (c) student apathy and boredom.

Too much teacher-imposed structure and instruction in too-small steps with too much redundancy can result in students' concluding that school is boring, tedious, and trivial. School should be a place in which the excitement of learning something important prevails. At-risk students need both structure *and* challenge.

The dilemma is how to be structured and responsive while still presenting an interesting and challenging intellectual menu. It isn't an easy

---

Effective Instruction for At-Risk Students

Characteristic	Description
Greater structure and support	Class expectations need to be laid out clearly, and assignments and assessments need to be designed to encourage achievement.
Active teaching	Teacher needs to carry the content to students personally through interactive teaching rather than depending on curricular materials, such as the text or workbooks.
Instruction emphasizing student engagement	Interactive teaching with high questioning levels invites all students to participate in lessons. Activity-based teaching/learning, small-group instruction, and/or individualized instruction are used.
More frequent feedback	Student progress should be monitored frequently through classroom questions and assignments. Teacher regularly discusses progress and growth with students.
Smaller steps with more redundancy	Content should be broken down into smaller steps, and student mastery should be ensured before moving on to the next step. Constant review of earlier materials provides for over-learning.
Higher success rates	Classroom questions, assignments, and assessments should be designed to maximize opportunities for success.

---

task, but many teachers do it. A classic example was Jaime Escalante, a math teacher in a low socioeconomic section of Los Angeles. He combined an extremely challenging curriculum with enormous personal support to produce a stunning success rate with at-risk students in advanced placement calculus. The late-1980s movie *Stand and Deliver* was based on this experience. Although he undoubtedly paid an overwhelming personal price in energy and emotion, the accomplishments of his students demonstrate what can be achieved.

Suggestions for Helping Students With Special Needs

Many times, elementary students with special learning needs are reluctant to be risk takers fully participating in classroom activities. Risking participation carries with it the possibility of more failure. You must find ways to break the ice for students and create a classroom safety net. Supported or "buddy" reading is one way. Allow students to read aloud together from the basal reader, chapter book, or subject area textbook. They may take turns or read in unison. Encourage rereadings to improve students' comprehension and fluency. In a similar strategy, the teacher, aide, or adult volunteer and the student can read aloud in unison at a comfortable pace. For younger children, a story with rhyme or a regular pattern can be sung or chanted. Provide peer or adult tutoring whenever possible for your children with special needs.

In addition, you should adapt and modify materials, lessons, and procedures to the needs of special students. Break complex learning into simpler components, moving from the most concrete to the most abstract. Make provisions for your learners who learn best in tactile and kinesthetic modes. Become familiar with your students' learning styles or preferences and vary your lessons, using different individual tasks and capitalizing on students' abilities. Build on strengths. What special abilities do your lower-achieving students possess? How can you incorporate these abilities throughout the curriculum? Draw the class's attention to the special competencies of your at-risk children. Give students frequent and significant success experiences. See "Effective Instruction for At-Risk Students" on page 98 for additional suggestions.

In general, whatever strategies you use to increase the effectiveness of your overall classroom instruction will have disproportionately high positive effects on your underachieving students. Also, in many cases, the teaching methods recommended for at-risk students closely resemble strategies that help second-language learners succeed.

Children With Diverse Language and Cultural Backgrounds

The growing diversity in U.S. schools is undebatable. With large numbers of elementary school students of a racial minority, impoverished, or from nontraditional homes, teachers need to recognize this diversity and organize their classroom activities accordingly.

Ethnicity

According to the Federal Interagency Forum on Child and Family Statistics (1998), one in every three students currently enrolled in elementary school is of a racial or ethnic minority. Students of color will make up about 46 percent of the U.S. school-age population by 2020. Demographers predict that about 65 percent of America's population growth in the next two decades will be "minority," particularly from Hispanic and Asian immigrants. A million immigrants each year are settling, mainly in California, Texas, and Florida. In 1998, 15 percent of the public elementary and secondary school students were Hispanic (National Center for Education Statistics, 2001).

Currently, children of immigrants make up approximately 20 percent of the children in the United States, bringing a host of cultural and language differences to many classrooms. As you review school records at the start of the year, if a student is described as "Hispanic," for example, make sure you know what country that student's family is from, what language the family uses at home, and whether the parents also speak English and how well. If the parents speak only Spanish and you speak it poorly, get a colleague who is bilingual to be on the line with you during your first phone call home. It's a good idea to phone parents during the first week of school, just to say hello and to assure the families that you look forward to working together.

Many immigrants come to America from more rigidly structured societies where social hierarchy is important. If a student won't look you in the eye during the first week of school, don't make a big deal of it in front of the class. Some teachers see this behavior as evasive and prefer students to look at them directly, indicating honesty, trust, and interest in the class. Many children, however, enter school having been told by parents that teachers are authority figures. To show respect, these children may look at the floor when the teacher addresses them. Later, when you have earned the child's trust, you might want to take a minute to talk privately to your newcomer about this cultural difference.

Occasionally, students may be genuinely confused about their ethnic ancestry. Several state courts have indicated that it is illegal to force a child to choose between the mother's and the father's backgrounds. Although it's a sensitive issue, you can communicate clearly to your class that you value all children and that you expect them to do their best. The important thing is the understanding that we are all Americans, regardless of our backgrounds.

Transiency

As you work with the variety of students in your classroom, be aware of the diversity that comes from mobility. Up to forty million Americans move each year, making transiency as important as births (with about three million newborns per year) in explaining population changes. Most migration occurs within the same state, but about six to eight million people move to another state each year. According to the 2000 census, people in the New England, Middle Atlantic, and Midwestern states are moving to the Southeast and Southwest. These growing numbers of migrant families whose children attend school intermittently often present challenges to teachers struggling to help the child fit in and catch up. Find out as soon as possible which of your children are new to the area and may need help getting settled. If half of your students (or fellow teachers!)

are new in town, be prepared to spend extra time, effort, and care. Some teachers have twenty-two students in the fall and twenty-two the following spring—but twenty of the twenty-two are different students.

Family Status

Children live in a variety of settings and with many different types of families. Fewer than half of the children in the United States today live with both biological parents, and 59 percent of all children will live in a single-parent household before they reach the age of eighteen. The number of parents living with a child is generally linked to the amount and quality of human and economic resources available to that child. It's also important to realize that more than one million public school students are the responsibility of their grandparents. Find out which of your students are in this category. Make sure that grandparents get the same level of attention as biological parents do. They may need even more help.

Poverty

One in five children under the age of eighteen currently lives in poverty. In your review of school records, pay particular attention to students who are eligible for free or reduced-price lunches—they may need extra help and may not get enough to eat on weekends. In addition, watch for poverty among children from single-parent homes. Children who live in a household with one parent are substantially more likely to have family incomes below the poverty line than are children who live in a household with two parents (Federal Interagency Forum on Child and Family Statistics, 2000).

Teaching to Diversity

To teach this wide variety of students in one classroom, you will need to organize your classroom activities so that all students can participate meaningfully. The use of integrated curriculum, collaborative projects, and learning centers; the creation of multilevel curriculum units; and the recognition of multiple intelligences are all necessary responses to student diversity in the classroom. You also need to consider the climate of your whole school. How is diversity represented and celebrated throughout the school? What is on the walls? What is the content and format of school assemblies? Do African Americans help students learn about the civil rights movement? Whose customs or holidays are represented on the bulletin boards in the hallways? If there are non-English speakers in your school, are there signs or posters in their languages? Are other languages represented even in monolingual schools? Does the school promote multiculturalism during school assemblies and throughout the year?

You might want to check out the classic resource on student diversity, the Teaching Tolerance project created by the Southern Poverty Law Center in 1991. This project provides teachers with low-cost or free resources to develop students' understanding of and respect for others. Resources described on the project's Web site (www.splcenter.org/teachingtolerance/tt-index.html) include posters, videos, and books, plus the free semiannual magazine *Teaching Tolerance.* Also at the site are suggestions for tolerance-related activities submitted by educators nationwide.

More Information on How Student Populations Are Changing

For a complete, updated picture of the demographics of modern society and schools, the site of the National Center for Education Statistics (http://nces.ed.gov) provides extensive data, including the *Encyclopedia of Educational Statistics.* For other authoritative demographic information, visit the Federal Interagency Forum on Child and Family Statistics (www.childstats.gov), which provides easy access to all U.S. government Web sites with statistics about children and families. Full-text reports on this site include *America's Children: Key National Indicators of Well-Being.*

Second-Language Learners

At least 2.4 million school-age children (ages five to seventeen) speak a language other than English at home and have difficulty speaking English (National Center for Education Statistics, 2001). The percentage of children who speak English with difficulty varies by region of the country, from 2 percent of children in the Midwest to 12 percent of children in the West.

These children are usually referred to as "English-as-a-second-language" (ESL) or "limited-English-proficient" (LEP) students. Many schools offer transitional bilingual classes taught by bilingual teachers. Sometimes ESL instruction is provided in a pullout program, in which ESL children are placed in regular classrooms for most of the day but attend separate classes for part of the day for English language instruction. You will likely find children in your classroom with limited English proficiency.

Specific guidelines for working with LEP students are the subject of numerous current books and articles. In general, the LEP recommendations are good for *all* children in your classroom, providing an activity-based, hands-on, minds-on, caring class environment. For instance, the following teaching methods promote English language development:

- Using the most concrete, most context-rich (least abstract) forms of instruction

- Supplementing the basal reader as much as possible with language experience stories

- Creating a literacy-rich environment in the classroom

- Using small-group, mixed-ability, cooperative learning and collaborative projects

- Encouraging extensive reading—scheduling SSR daily

- Concentrating on the use of multisensory approaches, using various learning modalities—visual, verbal, tactile, and kinesthetic

- Incorporating technology and audiovisual materials, such as videos, photographs, and pictures

- Modeling clear and understandable spoken English

Cultural Diversity in the Classroom

Effective beginning teachers celebrate the great diversity of cultures, races, and ethnic heritage in their classrooms. Understanding and being sensitive to the cultural identities of students allow teachers to serve them better. Effective teachers strive to improve the quality of human relations in the classroom, to promote students' appreciation for the multicultural composition of our society, and to help students appreciate who they are as individuals.

Take time in your classroom to develop awareness and appreciation for cultural diversity. You will help foster respect for the differences in *all* children and create a more empathic, accepting climate in your classroom. As professional educators, it is imperative that we all work to build positive multilingual, multiethnic, and multicultural human relations and foster equity and collaboration in our schools.

The following general suggestions may be helpful in your classroom.

- Acknowledge the importance of having pride in one's background.

- Encourage students to be supportive of friendships that cross cultural and racial boundaries.

- Help students understand that associating with members of one's own group is not a put-down of other groups.

- Examine the verbal and nonverbal styles common to students of different ethnic backgrounds. Be aware of body language.

- Build on the strengths of different ethnic and cultural groups.

- Be flexible in your demands for performance (e.g., students from other cultures may not be accustomed to speaking loudly in front of others).

- Present a curriculum that reflects the cultural diversity of the student population.

- Communicate a sincere appreciation for the culture of speakers of other languages.

In addition, be alert to certain negative behaviors that occasionally occur between culturally diverse groups. For example, students sometimes

- Ridicule other students' use of the English language or their primary language

- Mimic other students because of cultural differences

- Assume that all students celebrate the same holidays

- Ridicule customs, dress, foods, and behaviors of different ethnic groups

You need to adopt a zero-tolerance policy for any such negative behaviors in your classroom.

Obviously, there are many challenges in creating an excellent learning environment for every child in today's diverse classroom. Where do you start? You may need to personally make time to learn about people in different cultures. Read books, articles, and magazines. You will gain a better understanding, along with new teaching ideas. Also, get to know your students. Talk with them. Talk with their families and with people in the community.

You may find the following suggestions helpful.

- If you feel a bit of anxiety about working with students whose culture is unfamiliar to you, realize such feelings are normal and will soon fade.

- Be aware that cultures may differ in attitudes toward educational methods (i.e., cooperation vs. competition), schoolwork, respect of elders, learning styles, and so forth. By being aware of these potential differences, you will reduce the possibility of misunderstanding and miscommunication.

- Consider the issue of respect. For example, in some elementary schools today, teachers are addressed by their first names. In many cultures, however, this is disrespectful. Issues of respect also include etiquette for answering questions and for volunteering—is it seen as boasting, showing off, or acceptable behavior?

- Give all students an opportunity to contribute their perspectives and experiences in class. Value everyone's contributions. Your expectations for individual students affect your relationships with them in and out of class. Expect that each child will succeed.

- Be fair in giving out privileges and prizes. Do not limit yourself to a few able students. Monitor yourself when you evaluate such student work as writing assignments and homework.

- Think carefully about how you assign students to various learning groups in your classroom.

Curriculum Planning for Multicultural Classrooms

Depending on the grade level you teach, you can infuse multicultural education into the basic curriculum by using one or more of the following approaches. In the *single-group approach,* you teach a unit that provides a great deal of information on a certain culture, for example, Mexicans, Native Americans, or Chinese. In the *topical approach,* you present or allow students to present information about one aspect of a given culture, such as its holidays, legends, music, heroes, tall tales, art, houses, and so on.

Both these approaches, although interesting to students and commonly used by teachers, have potential problems. For elementary children, focus instead on similarities between groups, as well as differences. Strive for balance. Be careful of superficial, fragmented lessons and activities. The following approach is considered the most comprehensive.

The *conceptual approach* incorporates such concepts as communications, language, and cultural patterns (beliefs, customs, and rituals) into your lessons in various subject areas, such as language arts and social studies. For example, what legends are similar in many countries (e.g., Cinderella and Little Red Riding Hood)? How do different countries all use the same food (e.g., rice)? Your objective is to incorporate cultural studies as part of the daily life in your classroom. In this approach, you are careful not to represent culture as just "food and fun" (holidays and celebrations). Make sure pictures in instructional materials show people's daily life rather than just special celebrations. Focus on how people are all the same in many ways, rather than just looking at differences.

Planning Integrated Units

Effective elementary teachers integrate curriculum as much as possible. They realize that integrated units help students synthesize information and transfer knowledge across discipline areas. Children become more effective learners when their teachers have planned continuous, cohesive blocks of instruction. This approach differs from the traditional approach of teaching separate subjects at different times in the school day. In an integrated curriculum, subjects are intermeshed, and instructional strategies are used that actively involve students. Cooperative learning, project-based learning, peer tutoring, inquiry, schema theory, and recent models of the brain and learning all find a natural home in curriculum integration. Children communicate actively with one another, make connections among ideas, and think critically and creatively. Recent research indicates that this type of teaching can lead to high levels of thinking and significant learning. It can also lead to enthusiasm and high engagement rates.

Units are integrated, cohesive blocks of experiences in which individual lessons flow into one another. Many natural opportunities are provided for children to listen, speak, read, write, and think. Instructional variety is central to an integrated curriculum. Although you plan integrated units carefully, you generally allow choices and open-ended projects in this type of teaching. Unit teaching enables you to individualize the curriculum to meet diverse learning needs.

The simplest way to plan integrated units is to focus on a topic. "Pets," "Holidays," "Seasons," "Whales," "Bears," "Monsters," "Chocolate," and "Dragons" are common topics in primary classrooms. It is relatively easy to find children's literature (fiction, poems, and nonfiction) that relates to these topics and then to extend the learning experiences into science, social studies, art, music, and perhaps even math activities. (See the unit planning web in Resource 4.5.) The topical approach can be superficial, however, unless students are taught how the facts and topics fit into an understanding of the world and how to transfer information from one topic to another.

Another common type of integrated unit is thematic: Learning experiences grow from a series of activities related to a common theme, message, or idea that underlies the study. The theme explains the significance of the study—it tells the students what the experience means. Examples of elementary unit themes include "Recognizing and Overcoming Our Fears," "Making Things Happen," "I Am Somebody," and "Differences Are Good." Abstract concepts, such as change, patterns, survival, justice, and family, are sometimes used as the key word of the unit theme statement.

Often, a thematic unit is built around literature that demonstrates the theme at its core. Children read the same selections together or alone, as well as additional books, articles, and poems. Experiences in music and art, as well as science and social studies, are part of the exploration of the theme. In some schools, all the teachers at a grade level collaborate on a common theme and its content.

Once you have decided on a topic or theme, you design a unit much as you plan a lesson—identifying objectives; choosing literature that will focus the theme; deciding on the listening, speaking, reading, writing, science, art, music, and physical activities that will be part of the unit; looking for cross-curricular connections; deciding on your means of assessing students' progress toward your unit's objectives; and planning an opening celebration to begin the class's journey. Then you are ready to plan the specific lessons within the unit, including how you will group students and for which activities. See Resources 4.6 and 4.7 for helpful unit planning forms.

In planning an integrated unit, you may likely find that your basal reading series contains literacy selections grouped as units. In this case, you may decide to adapt the ideas and selections in the series. Maybe you would rather begin the unit with a poem or story of your own choosing or have upper elementary students read the original, full-length version of a novel rather than the excerpted one. Keep in mind the lesson planning ideas discussed earlier in this chapter. It is unnecessary to require children to read every piece in the basal unit. Choose what meets the needs of your students. Add and delete. Skip selections and rearrange the order. You may even decide to skip an entire unit in the basal reader and substitute an alternate unit you build yourself.

Planning Instruction and Designing Learning Experiences for *All* Children

Making good decisions about instruction is a complex and demanding process. As an effective teacher, you will plan lessons and units with your students in mind. You will design instruction to respond to individual learners and individual learning modalities. The richness of student diversities will be reflected in your planning. As an effective teacher, you will ensure high levels of student engagement and set high expectations for the success of each child in your class. You know that good instructional planning starts with the goals established by the school district or state, then meets and surpasses them!

RESOURCE

Outstanding Read-Aloud Books for Kindergarten Through Sixth Grade

Title	Author
Kindergarten	
Alfie Gives a Hand	Hughes
Best Friends for Frances	Hoban
Bigmama's	Crews
Born in the Gravy	Cazet
Bread and Jam for Frances	Hoban
The Mother's Day Mice	Bunting
No Good in Art	Cohen
Owen	Henkes
Peter's Chair	Keats
Ruby the Copycat	Rathmann
Sam	Scott
When Will I Read?	Cohen
Zinnia and Dot	Ernst
First Grade	
Amy's Goose	Holmes
The Crying Christmas Tree	Crow
The Day of Ahmed's Secret	Heide/Gilliland
First Grade Takes a Test	Cohen
The Half-Birthday Party	Pomerantz
Jamaica's Find	Havill
Luka's Quilt	Guback
Maebelle's Suitcase	Tusa
Mike Mulligan and His Steam Shovel	Burton
Mrs. Tibbles and the Special Someone	Wine
Niki's Little Donkey	Hol
Petunia	Duvoisin
Rosalie	Hewett
The Signmaker's Assistant	Arnold
Will Gets a Haircut	Landström
Second Grade	
Amos and Boris	Steig
Brave Irene	Steig

By the Dawn's Early Light	Ackerman
Chicken Sunday	Polacco
Evan's Corner	Hill
Farmer Schulz's Ducks	Thiele
Fruit and Vegetable Man	Schotter
The Goat in the Rug	Blood/Link
The Gold Coin	Ada
How My Parents Learned to Eat	Friedman
Mufaro's Beautiful Daughters	Steptoe
Nadia the Willful	Alexander
The Patchwork Quilt	Flournoy
Very Last First Time	Andrews

Third Grade

The Carp in the Bathtub	Cohen
Charlotte's Web	White
Gregory Cool	Binch
I Want a Dog	Khalsa
The Little Painter of Sabana Grande	Markun
Miss Maggie	Rylant
Nathaniel Talking	Greenfield
A Place for Grace	Okimoto
Sam, Bangs and Moonshine	Ness
Song and Dance Man	Ackerman
Storm in the Night	Stolz
Theodore and Mr. Balbini	Mathers
Uncle Jed's Barbershop	Mitchell
Yange the Youngest and His Terrible Ear	Namioka

Fourth Grade

The Bridge Dancers	Saller
Child of the Silent Night	Hunter
The First Strawberries	Bruchac
The Flunking of Josua T. Bates	Shreve
Freedom Train: Harriet Tubman	Sterling
The Great Brain	Fitzgerald
The Green Book	Walsh
The Hundred Dresses	Estes
The Lion, the Witch and the Wardrobe	Lewis
Sadako and the 1,000 Paper Cranes	Coerr
When the Monkeys Came Back	Franklin

Fifth Grade

The Book of Three	Alexander
Bridge to Terabithia	Paterson
Cat Running	Snyder
Children of the Dust Bowl	Stanley
C.O.L.A.R.	Slote
In the Year of the Boar and Jackie Robinson	Lord
The Real Thief	Steig
Sami and the Time of the Troubles	Heide/Gilliland
Sarah, Plain and Tall	MacLachlan
Talk About a Family	Greenfield
The Whipping Boy	Fleischman
The Winter Camp	Hill

Sixth Grade

All Joseph Wanted	Radin
And Now Miguel	Krumgold
Baseball in April	Soto
"La Bamba" (short story)	Soto
"Seventh Grade" (short story)	Soto
Come Sing, Jimmy Jo	Paterson
Cousins	Hamilton
Crow Boy	Yashima
Homecoming	Voigt
Morning Girl	Dorris
Number the Stars	Lowry
Tuck Everlasting	Babbitt
Uncle James	Harshman

Note

This list of outstanding read-aloud books is provided by the Developmental Studies Center (DSC) through the courtesy of the *Reading, Thinking, and Caring* and *Reading for Real* Language Arts Programs. For more information, contact the DSC at 2000 Embarcadero, Suite 305, Oakland, CA 94606-5300 (phone 510-533-0213).

Assessment of Classroom Time on Task

Introduction

Because time on task is one of the most important variables in student learning, it is vital to analyze off-task time in your classroom. The observation form in this Resource will help sensitize you to time spent on organizing and on classroom interruptions that could perhaps be better spent on engaged learning time for students. Ask your aide, mentor, parent volunteer, or an administrator or student teacher to complete the time record for you during the first hour of a typical day. Analyze and discuss your data with your mentor.

A second observation form, shown in Resource 4.3, helps determine on-task behavior. Using a seating chart, you (or someone else) can observe students while they are doing seat work or group work. It is most useful to review actual observational data on your use of time. If an observer is unavailable, however, you may wish to rate yourself using the Effectiveness Survey in Resource 4.4.

Observation Form #1: Time Spent on Organizing and on Classroom Interruptions

Teacher Name _____ Date _____

School _____ Observer _____

	Time Started	Time Stopped
Observation of Classroom Time Spent on Organizing		
Taking attendance		
Collecting lunch money		
Collecting homework or seat work		
Making assignments for seat work		
Making assignments for homework		
Distributing books and materials		
Explaining activities and procedures		
Organizing groups		
Shifting from one activity to another		
Disciplining students		
Observation of Classroom Interruptions		
Students enter late		
Students leave early		
Parents enter		
Administrator enters		
Other visitors enter		
Loudspeaker announcements		
Special sales		
School events		
Outside noise		

Observation Form #2: On-Task Behavior

....

Directions: Observe the class at three- or five-minute intervals. Using the suggested (or agreed-on) behavior categories, note what each student is doing at the specified times, and mark the appropriate symbols in the student's box. In the example, two students were talking with others (and were off task) at 9:00, and all students were on task at 9:03.

Sample of Observation Notes

Teacher

1. 9:00	1-O 6-	1-O 6-	1-T 6-
2. 9:03	2-O 7-	2-O 7-	2-O 7-
3. 9:06	3-O 8-	3-O 8-	3-T 8-
4. 9:09	4-T 9-	4-O 9-	4-O 9-
5. 9:12	5-D 10-	5- 10-	5- 10-

6. 9:15	1-O 6-	1-T 6-	1-O 6-
7. 9:18	2-O 7-	2-O 7-	2-D 7-
8. 9:21	3-O 8-	3-T 8-	3-O 8-
9. 9:24	4-O 9-	4-T 9-	4-O 9-
10. 9:27	5- 10-	5- 10-	5- 10-

Suggested symbols: O = On task
T = Talking with other students
D = Daydreaming or not paying attention

Tip: A seating chart is useful for providing data on whether students are engaged in appropriate behavior at specified times during a lesson.

RESOURCE
Effectiveness Survey: Managing Use of Classroom Time

....

For each practice below, circle the number of the response that most accurately describes the situation in your classroom. (5 indicates strong use; 1 indicates weak use.)

Classroom routines and procedures

- Class starts quickly and purposefully.   1   2   3   4   5

- Materials and activities are ready when students arrive.   1   2   3   4   5

- Seating is arranged to facilitate instruction.   1   2   3   4   5

- Students bring needed materials to class each day.   1   2   3   4   5

- Students have and use assigned storage space.   1   2   3   4   5

- Administrative matters are handled routinely and efficiently.   1   2   3   4   5

- Interruptions are kept to a minimum.   1   2   3   4   5

In controlling use of time in my classroom, I

- Allocate sufficient time for each subject to be taught.   1   2   3   4   5

- Keep students engaged in learning for most (80 percent) of the available classroom time each day.   1   2   3   4   5

- Minimize use of time for nonlearning activities.   1   2   3   4   5

- Use clear start and stop cues to direct student activity.   1   2   3   4   5

- Encourage students to use the clock for self-pacing.   1   2   3   4   5

- Introduce new objectives and activities as quickly as possible.   1   2   3   4   5

- Maintain a brisk instructional pace.   1   2   3   4   5

- Require students to complete unfinished class work after school, during recess or lunch, or in other available time.   1   2   3   4   5

Use of time in our school building is controlled so that

- The school calendar maximizes the time available for instruction.   1 2 3 4 5

- New programs are evaluated relative to their impact on learning time.   1 2 3 4 5

- School, classes, and other activities start and end on time.   1 2 3 4 5

- The school day is organized to minimize time spent on noninstructional time.   1 2 3 4 5

- Class instruction is not interrupted for routine announcements or messages.   1 2 3 4 5

- Students do not have unassigned "free" time during the academic day.   1 2 3 4 5

- Student pullouts during academic class time are minimized.   1 2 3 4 5

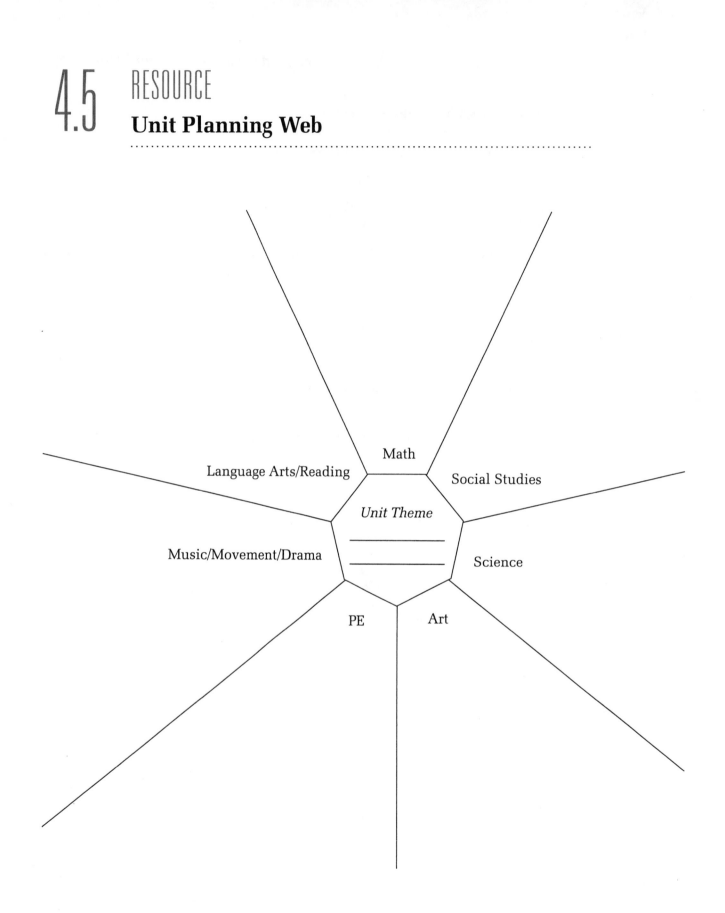

Math

Language Arts/Reading

Social Studies

Unit Theme

_____

_____

Music/Movement/Drama

Science

PE

Art

Unit Construction Checklist

A curriculum unit is normally at least six or more integrated lessons. Each lesson should include two or more learning activities.

The following steps are essential to planning any unit of instruction. Indicate that you have taken each step by placing the date of satisfactory accomplishment in the blank to the left.

_____ 1. Talk with your students as you determine what type of unit you want to teach, when you want to begin, and how much total time will be available for your unit.

_____ 2. Examine your course of study to determine if/how this unit would fit into the total learning sequence.

_____ 3. Draft your instructional objectives for the teaching unit. (Three to five objectives are suggested.)

_____ 4. Clarify your expectations of pupil progress, and plan assessment activities to use with this unit.

_____ 5. In your lesson plan book, lay out a "days and topics" schedule for the unit to ensure that no principal part of the proposed coverage will be omitted from the unit.

_____ 6. Find ideas for your unit in professional books and magazines, textbooks, or related commercial units.

_____ 7. Locate books and materials that may be used in the teaching of your unit.

_____ 8. Locate lists of audiovisual material available for use in your school. Select and schedule titles of movies, records, tapes, and so on that seem appropriate.

_____ 9. Collect and organize materials such as pictures, displays, and models.

_____ 10. Using your "days and topics" schedule, develop at least six lesson plans to be used in this unit. (Suggestion: one lesson plan per day).

_____ 11. Make a check mark in the blank to the left of each of the following activities that you have included in your plans:

_____ Field trip   _____ Making bulletin boards

_____ Visit by resource person   _____ Making displays

_____ Whole-class direct instruction   _____ Viewing educational TV

_____ Class discussion

_____ Small-group activities

_____ Listening to tapes

_____ Making models

_____ Making charts, diagrams, posters, maps, and graphs

_____ Making oral reports or telling stories

_____ Dramatizations/ simulations

_____ Playing instructional games

_____ Viewing films, filmstrips, or videos

_____ Viewing slides

_____ Library research

_____ Panel discussion

_____ Demonstrations

_____ Songs and/or finger plays

_____ Other: _____

_____ Other: _____

Unit Planning Form

....

   I. Duration:
      (Dates and times) _____

  II. Students:
      Grade level: _____
      Student characteristics that need to be considered in teaching this unit:_____

      _____

      _____

 III. Unit Topic or Theme: _____

 IV. Subjects: _____

  V. Unit Objectives: _____

      _____

      _____

      _____

 VI. Materials and Media:
      List curriculum books, materials, and resources to be used. Include at least one
      children's literature book.

      _____

      _____

      _____

      _____

      _____

      _____

VII. Procedures/Instructional Activities:

      A. Introduction:
          Procedure for introducing the unit

          _____

          _____

_____

_____

_____

B. Content and activities within the unit:
    List at least six lesson topics, with preliminary notes on content, teaching
    strategies, activities, and assignments for each.

_____

_____

_____

_____

_____

_____

_____

_____

_____

C. Culminating activity:

_____

_____

_____

_____

VIII. Evaluation:
     Procedure(s) for assessment of learner understanding:

_____

_____

_____

_____

CHAPTER 5

Preventing Discipline Problems

Managing and Monitoring Student Behavior

Discipline is an integral part of teaching. It is also the most often reported concern of beginning teachers. It typically has an ominous connotation. You know intuitively that, without the will and skill to discipline students, you will not be able to teach successfully. Effective discipline and effective instruction are inseparable. Discipline does not have to be distasteful, however. It can be a potentially positive and productive aspect of teaching. Establishing classroom conditions to which students respond with respect and cooperation is as much a part of discipline as authoritarian monitoring, controlling, and intervening.

You have undoubtedly started your teaching career with vows to be good-humored, fair-minded, and enthusiastic. You plan learning activities that will energize students' positive behavior and intrinsic motivation. You will accommodate variety and individual differences and make your lessons relevant to students' lives. You will use time effectively, choosing academic tasks conducive to high student engagement. You will implement grouping strategies for high levels of involvement and low levels of misbehavior. You will communicate rules of participation clearly. Your classroom climate, planning, and instruction will have a major effect in preventing discipline problems. Discipline is much more than spotting and punishing misbehavior. Your primary behavior management task is to establish and maintain positive classroom processes. Rules, procedures, routines, and reprimands all have a role to play, but they can only supplement what you do to orchestrate your overall instructional program.

How you manage and monitor student behavior is closely linked to your teaching philosophy. Reflect on the behaviors and attributes you want to promote among your students (e.g., respect, responsibility, and collaboration), and develop a discipline plan that supports your ideals.

Become familiar with different approaches to discipline to make decisions that work for you and your students.

More than a dozen discipline models of varying degrees of structure have been developed. They range along a continuum from those that are predominantly student centered and use psychotherapeutic and communication principles to those that are decidedly teacher centered and are based on behavioral psychology. Read recommended books and articles on discipline techniques and programs. Discuss "what works" to promote desirable behavior, and share concerns and problems with colleagues. Effective behavior management begins with an attitude that you can and will do something about inappropriate behavior. Being proactive and not reactive puts you in charge—insisting on but also assisting in creating order in a calm, professional manner.

School Discipline Policies

Know what you can and cannot do. Consider district and building policies on student discipline when establishing your class rules. For instance, lunch hour detention or keeping students after school may not be allowed in your district. Get a copy of the teacher handbook, parent handbook, and/or student handbook for your district's approved model, such as "assertive discipline." You will be expected to follow the district system to some degree.

Observe the informal norms of the building, and discuss these with your mentor or principal. Some schools operate as structured, controlled, rather authoritarian systems; others are more relaxed, enfranchised, and even permissive. Ask about the schoolwide discipline plan. How consistent is it? Do teachers enforce the established school rules? Does the principal want to get involved in discipline referrals? Is a time-out or detention room used? Is it effective? Get to know your school's and community's prevailing culture concerning discipline expectations.

As a new teacher, you will have to learn not to take the discipline of students personally. A student's choice to break a rule is not usually an expression of dislike or a reflection of the teacher's ability or personality. Once you realize this, behavior management becomes easier.

Establishing Rules

Rules must make sense to you and to your students. Think deeply about the standards of behavior you want to establish in your classroom and should be able to expect from students. You create the classroom environment you feel best meets students' learning needs. In doing so, you integrate your beliefs about conditions that help students learn (academic, behavioral, social, and emotional) with the practical limitations of the setting.

Typical standards include such behaviors as "using a quiet voice," "responding to a signal," "how to line up," and "what to do when the teacher is busy." Start by brainstorming a list of behaviors you want to see in your classroom. Then select the most appropriate for your group of children. These become the rules for how you want the class to function. You will probably need to establish priorities, however. Cut the list down to the five or six most important behaviors. A list of ten to fifteen is just too cumbersome and too hard to remember. You may have ten to fifteen standards you will eventually want to teach, but save some for later. What do you want first? Clearly define those behaviors in observable terms (respond, line up, and so forth).

Many teachers find it desirable to have their students participate in the brainstorming of classroom rules—this gives children a sense of ownership. Students who have some control over their direction tend to follow the rules more often. In most cases, students arrive at the same set of expectations you originally planned. Many times, you must keep them from being too stringent. Encourage students to state the rules in *positive* terms—what students *will* do in their class. For instance, say "Resolve disagreements by talking" rather than "No fighting." Limit children to about five rules. Avoid the impression that you are more interested in defining restrictions than in promoting learning.

Once you (and your class) decide what the rules and responsibilities will be, spend time during the first weeks of school setting specific expectations. Teach the rules, consequences, and procedures; practice and model correct behaviors; and distinctly point out unacceptable behaviors. Remember that telling is not teaching; students often do not remember by simply being told what to do. Students need to understand clearly what behavior is expected. They need to discuss the behavior and see it demonstrated. Some examples of common rules (with discussion points) are shown below.

- *Speak to fellow classmates with respect.* (Discussion points: People's feelings are not for hurting. Put-downs in this room are forbidden. Teasing others is not OK.)

- *Keep your hands and feet to yourself.* (Discussion points: It is inappropriate to touch classmates, including pushing, shoving, wrestling, and tripping. No throwing of objects—pencils, erasers, rubber bands—at another person, either! Resolve any disagreements by *talking*.)

- *Take care of your desk, classroom, and learning materials.* (Discussion points: Keep your desk clean and organized. Put materials where they belong. Know where your books, paper, and pencils are. Respect the property of others.)

- *Raise your hand for permission to speak.* (Discussion points: Raise your hand and wait to speak. This rule will not be in effect, however, during small-group discussions, class meetings, etc.)

- *Stay in your seat unless you have permission to leave it.* (Discussion points: When does the teacher say it is OK to move around the classroom? Report directly to the assigned area or center. Change from one area to the next quickly and quietly.)

- *Listen the first time instructions are given.* (Discussion points: Wait for directions with no talking. Be quiet whenever someone else is speaking. Eyes on the teacher whenever the teacher is giving directions.)

Effective teachers discuss with their students why rules are needed, provide reasonable explanations for each rule, and explain how the rules will help everyone succeed by making the class run smoothly. Post (in large print) the basic classroom rules. Let everyone sign the rules poster. Give each student a copy. Send a letter to parents explaining your classroom rules. Then ensure that the rules are followed firmly, fairly, and consistently.

Regular reinforcement of the rules is definitely needed. As often as possible, try to "catch the students being good," a phrase commonly used for the reinforcement of appropriate behaviors. If students are already raising hands in a discussion, you might say, "You're all doing a great job of raising hands. That allows me to call on individuals, and everybody gets a chance to think." Positive reinforcement increases the probability of that behavior recurring. When students "forget" the rules, they probably have not been reinforced for following them. One veteran teacher keeps a reinforcement sheet on her desk and records the number of times she has "caught each student being good." It also reminds her how many times she has reviewed the rules. Rule review is often necessary at high-excitement times, such as right before or after holidays and before school ends.

Teaching desirable behavior, just as you teach any lesson, is an excellent way to promote it. For example, a standard that most teachers have in their classrooms is "responding to a signal." As you do with content, you need to first define this learning. What exactly does *respond to the signal* mean? Usually, it means, "Given a signal by the teacher, the students will immediately stop what they are doing and look at the teacher." The process for teaching it looks like this:

1. Make sure students know the signal ("May I have your attention please?" or bell, lights, or arm held high, etc.). Explain the signal. Model it. Have students describe and model it.
2. Make sure students know what to do (pause, stop whatever they are doing, quiet down, and look at teacher). Discuss. Choose a student to model it. Have all the students demonstrate. Have

them write down what the class will look like after the signal is given.

3. Make sure students know when to respond. List sample class activities. Get students into an activity and then give the signal. Have the whole group practice responding to the signal.

The key to teaching a behavior is specifying the subskills needed to complete it properly. Occasionally, an exasperated teacher will declare, "You know how you're supposed to behave!" Unfortunately, this is not always true. You must clearly define the behavior and what is expected of students. Nobody should have to guess.

In addition to carefully thinking through your classroom rules, discussing them with your students, and teaching and modeling them, you also need to consider *consequences*. What will happen if students break a rule? Consequences for unacceptable behavior should be logical and appropriate. They should fit the behavior in a sensible way. For instance, children who are running in the classroom or hallway must turn around and retrace their steps by *walking* the same route. Children who continue to "thump" their neighbors with a pencil are removed to seats away from the table group (and thus are unable to contribute "table points" and participate in today's group reward they earn). Students who write on the desk must stay in at recess and clean *all* the desks. Children who leave their lunch area littered are required to pick up the trash on the entire floor. For consequences to be effective, students must see them as logically and naturally related to their misbehavior.

Much has been written about time-outs, in which students are allowed to sit and think about their choice not to behave. A place out of sight (but not out of sight of the teacher) reduces the emotional impact of the situation, does not lead to escalation, and allows the student a chance to calm down. A time-out is often a logical consequence.

Some school districts use a Saturday study hall for misbehavior. Students who get a "pink slip" for being late or skipping class attend a Saturday session monitored by a (paid) teacher and work quietly on schoolwork they missed while tardy or absent.

When logical consequences are invoked, your voice is friendly and implies good will. Rather than communicating typical negative messages of punishment ("You're bad." "You'll never learn." "You're not acceptable." "You deserve what you're getting." "You'd better shape up." "I'll show you!"), treat the student with dignity, separate the deed from the doer, and communicate respect ("I don't like what you're doing right now, but I still trust you." "You are a worthwhile person." "I'm sure you will learn to respect the rights of others." "I trust you to make responsible choices."). The purpose of using natural and logical consequences is to motivate children to make responsible decisions, not to force their submission. Consequences will be effective if you avoid having hidden motives of winning and controlling.

Tips for Establishing Consequences

- Explain consequences ahead of time.
- Be clear and specific.
- Have a range of proportional alternatives to make the penalty fit the infraction.
- Consequences should not be arbitrary or viewed as punishment.
- Consequences should not be related to lowering of academic grades.
- Consequences should be related directly and immediately to a rule.
- Consequences should follow naturally and logically from the misbehavior.

Some teachers post consequences as well as rules. Lee and Marlene Canter (1992, 1993), well-known authors and workshop leaders of assertive discipline techniques, recommend a specific plan for consequences. Once rules are communicated to students, the students learn that for inappropriate behavior, they will be warned once by putting their names on the board. A second offense—one check by their names—means missing a recess or owing time after school. A third offense—two checks—means two recess or two times after school. The fourth offense—three checks—means two recesses and call parents. The fifth offense—four checks—leads to removal to the office. This plan is communicated to parents and, of course, the principal. Like all consequence plans, it must be modified whenever it does not work.

Students must believe that you will enforce rules consistently and administer the appropriate consequence. Your goal is to be fair, but that might mean not applying *identical* consequences. If students frequently fail to return homework, you may apply a different consequence than you would to students who forget their homework for the first time. It is possible to be fair but not rigidly *equal.* Students can understand that *fair* and *equal* are not always the same. To be consistently fair, however, be certain that the consequences you apply are reasonable and appropriate.

Using Preventive Discipline

Behavior management is more than reacting to problems. It is the total organization of the classroom and the way you communicate that organization to students to promote desirable behavior. Research indicates that what you do to *prevent* punishable behavior, rather than *how* you punish, makes you an effective teacher.

Students' behavior during the first week or two of school is usually good. Use this time to your advantage. Begin the year by establishing positive routines and activities. You will keep students motivated and head off problems.

- Start fresh every day. What happened yesterday is finished. Act accordingly.

- Reward appropriate behavior—praise students when they are doing things right. Tie positive consequences to the desired behavior. Send a positive note home to parents. Have a popcorn party on Friday if the class has earned it with their good behavior.

- Create a warm, friendly atmosphere. Firmness does not negate a warm, personalized atmosphere.

- Observe your class and make notes of the activities that seem to calm students. You can always switch to one of these quieter activities if necessary.

- If a planned activity is out of the normal range of expectations (such as a field trip or lab experiment), take plenty of time before the activity begins to establish behavior responsibilities.

- Establish the signal that calls the whole class to immediate attention. Practice using this signal until you get the expected "freeze and listen" behavior. Some teachers allow the students to choose the word or signal. It may be changed to reflect seasons, holidays, or units of study.

- Communicate to students that you know what is going on. This is called "with-it-ness." It is like having "eyes in the back of your head."

- Develop your ability to deal with more than one thing at a time. For example, if you are working with an individual or small group and you spot inappropriate behavior somewhere else in the class, keep the individuals focused on the task while at the same time dealing with the disruption.

- Maintain a consistent flow in lessons. Effective teachers tend to ignore minor distractions, stay on target, complete tasks rather than letting them "dangle" while imposing discipline, and avoid disturbing on-task students. They keep the lesson activities going in a smooth, consistent manner. Momentum is lost, for instance, when a lesson is stopped to send an offender to the hall to deliver a three-minute lecture while the rest of the students become restless.

- Avoid putting yourself in a power struggle with students. A quiet, private conference later is always preferable to confronting students in front of their peers. In any confrontation, the student always wins. Similarly, avoid making threats that you cannot carry out or imposing arbitrary penalties.

- Modify your instruction to match students' abilities. Many students react negatively to work that appears too difficult, too easy, or pointless.

- Maintain student interest in lesson activities. Interest increases focus on the task. When lessons vary, when they are interesting, when the environment is changed, when you use different techniques for overt responses, when you group and regroup students, and when you do things differently in the mode of presentation, students are less likely to be bored or cause discipline problems. I'll have more on this point later in the chapter.

- By all means, listen to what students are saying. Students misbehave not only when they are bored but also when they feel angry or fearful. Discuss problems to help students understand and solve them. For example, students may feel constantly "picked on" by classmates. You need to find out what the problem is so you can deal with it more effectively.

- Develop contingency plans for individuals for whom your classwide system does not work (e.g., parent conferences and learning or behavior contracts).

Dealing With Misbehavior

No matter how meticulously you have planned and taught the rules, you will likely have to deal with inappropriate student behavior eventually. As an effective classroom manager, you must handle misbehavior immediately and smoothly to prevent a snowballing effect—instead of one or two students being involved, soon there may be several. Students will test the rules to find out whether you will enforce them. Follow through and mean what you say. Children will quickly violate a rule they see classmates violating unless you step in.

To provide maximum time for learning and reduce minor behavior problems, here are some strategies to employ that deal with misbehavior in the least amount of time, with the least disruption, and with the least negative feelings.

- Look at the offending student directly with prolonged eye contact while you continue your lesson.

- Shake your head to stress your message to the student.

- Stop talking for a few seconds.

- Use proximity. Continue your lesson as you move about the room, pausing near "trouble spots."

- Try not to make a big deal out of it. "Soft reprimands," not causing a major commotion while you deliver your feelings of displeasure to a student, will often successfully suppress the misbehavior and also save the student's self-concept.

- Be aware of your options, such as the following:

  Are time-outs in the hall allowed in your school?
  Can you send students to the office for detention or keep students during recess or after school? In what cases should the principal be involved in your discipline procedures?

- Consider changing students' seats or schedule if problems persist.

- Take away privileges, not educational experience. It might take only these words: "You may choose a free-time activity when you finish your work."

In general, when dealing with serious misbehavior, you should talk *less* and act *more*. Many beginning teachers hinder their effectiveness in discipline by talking too much. Students easily become "teacher-deaf" from the continuous sound of the teacher's voice. Do most of your talking with students when you are on friendly terms and they are therefore more willing to listen. When dealing with misbehavior and using logical consequences, keep talk to a minimum as you follow through with action.

Be both firm and kind. Your tone of voice indicates your desire to be kind while your follow-through with appropriate action indicates your firmness. Remain matter-of-fact. If you can view misbehavior objectively, rather than regarding it as a personal affront, you will be more effective.

Motivating Your Students

Effective teachers stimulate children's interest and engagement in the instructional program. Interested, involved students are motivated, successful learners. Also important is the feeling tone of the classroom—how pleasant the learning environment and the particular learning situations feel to the students. A safe, accepting environment enables all children to feel free to learn, grow, and change.

- Begin with your classroom's physical environment. Have you arranged interest centers, bulletin boards, students' desks, tables, and furniture attractively? Do you regularly introduce different books and new materials in your learning centers? Do the walls show interesting displays, pictures, and charts? Have you included plants and an animal or two? In short, is your classroom a place to which students want to come and learn?

- Do you involve students in decisions that affect their lives at school? Do you invite their participation in planning their day, for instance, or in picking or suggesting themes and topics of study? Do you give students choices?

- Do you encourage your students to participate in a range of classroom activities and projects? Do you teach for all the multiple intelligences and learning modalities?

- Have you displayed student work throughout your room? Do you (and/or the students) change it regularly? Are students pleased with what they accomplish in your room? Do they feel successful? Do you emphasize what each child knows and contributes?

- If some of your students complete work earlier than their classmates, do you resist the temptation to hand them a busywork ditto to keep them occupied? Are you conscientious about providing meaningful learning alternatives, such as opportunities to work on a class project, practice on the computer, work quietly at a learning center or the art center, sit in the class library corner for free reading, and so on?

- Do you occasionally reward positive behavior with surprises, such as a walk to the park, a special guest, or a visit or certificate from the principal?

- Do you help students develop pride in self, class, and room? Do you praise their efforts in completing difficult tasks, send a note or a "warm fuzzy," and invite parents and/or another class to see your students' new play or art exhibit?

- Do you remember to smile, give a high five, a pat, a handshake, a word of encouragement? Reaffirm a child's existence? Listen reflectively and genuinely? Give compliments and ask questions relating to children's personal interests and experiences? Let them know you care?

How you attempt to motivate your students depends on your educational philosophy and relates to that mental image of how you want your classroom to feel. Student motivation stems from an enjoyable, interesting class with a positive, personable teacher.

Praise

Children react to praise in different ways. Your objective in using praise is to help children develop an internal locus of control to improve behavior and academic achievement. In general, praise *significant* behaviors or learnings, not just everybody and everything. Also, be *specific*. Suggested uses of praise include the following:

- Give praise for desired behavior and define the behavior: "Thank you for picking up the papers. You really helped the class save time."

- Specify what is praiseworthy about the student's schoolwork. Always give a reason when praising a student's learning performance: "You blended the blues and greens in the sky beautifully—it really shows your knowledge of color groups," or "Kevin read that paragraph so expressively that I could almost feel the pain myself."

- Vary your praise and be creative. Avoid trite, general words such as *great, fine,* and *wonderful.* Praise can become habitual, with a constant stream of *goods, okays,* and *all rights.* Also ineffective are the too lavish, too strong, and gushy tones.

- At times, give praise privately to avoid competition, embarrassment, or singling someone out as "teacher's pet." Many teachers of intermediate students have more success delivering quiet individual praise rather than praising individuals before the whole class.

- Praise needs to be genuine and matched by your body language. Be consistent with your verbal and nonverbal praise. The teacher who says a student is doing a terrific job but reflects insincere body language has "erased" the verbal praise.

- Draw the student's attention to his or her effort and ability. "You sure learned those ten addition facts quickly. You must have spent a lot of time practicing," or "This is great! I would like to display it for the others to see because you have worked so hard on it."

- Avoid comparing children with each other. Such statements as "Gee, you have almost caught up to Karen" are inappropriate in a collaborative learning environment.

- Avoid teacher-pleasing phrases, such as "I really like the way you used descriptive words in your poem." A more powerful message is, "You did an excellent job of using descriptive words in your story. The reader can really hear and see what you meant." Many teachers use too many "I" statements when praising, such as "I like the way you're listening (working, raising hands, lining up, writing, etc.)." Instead, say, "You're listening so well, you'll do it just right!"

- Do not use sarcastic and insincere "praise," such as "Nice going, Blabbermouth!" or "Great shot, Butterfingers!" or "Oh, that's clever, Thomas. Now try putting your brain in gear, too."

- Do not minimize a child's success. Watch out for statements such as "Your math assignment must have been easy. You finished so quickly."

- Delegate extended praise to another student. For example, you might ask Jennifer what she likes about Juan's report. A powerful way to build respect and rapport in the classroom is to facilitate children's sincere praise and appreciation of one another.

Instructional Variety Is Important

A variety of learning activities keeps students interested in school and their schoolwork. Student interest is a powerful motivator. Students who are interested in what they are doing will enjoy it more, do it longer, and learn more from it. When students are interested and engaged in learning activities, they feel more successful, and you have less worry about behavior management and discipline.

A good way to increase student motivation is to vary your instructional methods. As a new teacher, you are probably aware of some teachers' overuse of one instructional method, often a sequence of lectures, convergent questions, and individual seat work. Such teachers seem to forget that students have different learning styles, attitudes, interests, and backgrounds. You know better. Do not slip into the habit of relying on only one or two tried-and-true favorite methods. As you plan a lesson or a unit, look for ways to add variety.

You might begin by reviewing the list of sample strategies and resources below. Is it possible to incorporate one or more into a unit, for example? This list may spark your creative thinking.

Advertisement	Demonstration	Meditation
Album	Diagram	Modeling
Artifact	Dialogue	Montage
Autobiography	Experiment	Myth
Bingo	Fantasy	Panel
Book review	Field research	Pantomime
Case study	Flip book	Pets
Choral reading	Flow chart	Play
Comedy	Holograph	Printing press
Competition	Invention	Puppets
Computers	Jigsaw	Quiz
Correspondence	Letter to expert	Replica
Crafts	Lyric	Sand table
Debate	Machine	Simulation

Questions to Consider for Improving Motivation

- Are students intrinsically motivated or extrinsically motivated? (If you believe, e.g., that students are sometimes extrinsically motivated, then you may be comfortable with some forms of behavior modification.)

- How do you feel about using token systems (giving stickers, badges, certificates, coupons, candies, etc.) for group or individual rewards?

- Do you feel that only "good" student work, or any and all work, should be posted? What about graded work, test scores, skill charts, and grades?

- Is competition a good way to motivate individuals or groups?

- Is teamwork a good way to motivate individuals or groups?

- How does self-esteem relate to student motivation?

- How does the relevancy of the lesson for students relate to student motivation?

- How does the execution of the lesson relate to student motivation?

Homework as a Learning Tool

Management of students' homework is a growing issue of concern for teachers and parents. Many schools now have homework policies and guidelines. Consider these purposes for homework. Homework can provide the following:

- Different ways to monitor student learning
- Opportunity for practice of a skill or concept that has been taught
- Opportunity to tie in school learning with real-world experiences
- Open-ended activities that allow for success
- Ways to actively involve the family in the student's education
- Preparation for in-school activities

Homework Tips

What to Do

- *Do* have a homework policy and be prepared to communicate it to students and parents. The subject of homework comes up surprisingly often during conferences with parents. (See Resource 7.6 for a sample letter to parents regarding homework.)

- *Do* make sure students know objectives of assignments.

- *Do* give feedback and acknowledgment on completion of homework.

- *Do* hold students responsible for completion of homework, but be sensitive to outside obligations.

- *Do* think of alternative ways children can complete their homework at school, such as in the library after school or at recess. Be aware that the resources necessary to complete assignments (encyclopedias, reference books, dictionaries, thesaurus, atlases, and computers) may not be available in some students' homes.

- *Do* help students and parents keep on top of homework requirements with a weekly log or homework assignment sheet. For elementary students who are just learning the homework habit, it is helpful to have parents sign the homework log so you know it went home. A sample is included in Resource 5.1.

What to Avoid

- *Don't* give twenty-five problems if five will accomplish the objective.

- *Don't* give homework as punishment.

- *Don't* use homework as busywork. You will only give yourself unnecessary papers to mark, which will take away time you (and your students!) could have otherwise used more productively.

- *Don't* assume that homework should be assigned every night. Check your school policy. At the same time, realize that some parents expect their children (especially at the intermediate level) to have homework every day and will even complain about you and your teaching methods if they do not.

- *Don't* assign homework simply because a parent requests it. Check with your principal and/or mentor regarding possible exceptions.

- *Don't* make unrealistic demands on students' time. Consider the age level and abilities of your students. For example, it is unrealistic to assign a nine-year-old an at-home project that could take three hours.

Contracts Can Help You Manage Student Behavior

Contracts can be an effective way to help children take more responsibility for their learning (in-class assignments and homework) and for their behavior. The teacher and the student discuss the problem and then draw up a contract that spells out the acceptable behavior and time for completion. Contracts work best if parents are involved as well. Some school districts supply a preprinted contract that you just fill in with name, date, behavior changes, and a place for the student to sign. See Resources 5.2, 5.3, and 5.4 for sample contracts used with elementary students.

Changing Inappropriate Behavior of Individual Students

To deal with individual disruptive behavior—the student who consistently insists on making the wrong choices—you need to implement a strategy. Here is a specific plan you can use to change student behavior:

Identify the Problem and Collect Objective Data. Suppose your class has the rule "Keep hands and feet to yourself," but Shawn keeps tripping classmates whenever they walk by, pushing kids in line, shoving neighbors during circle time, and so on. Start by collecting data to make the problem clear to the student and, sometimes, the parent. Using an index card to make tally marks is a quick method.

Select an Appropriate Consequence and Positive Reinforcer. The question to ask yourself is, "What doesn't Shawn want?" Simply charting the behavior can sometimes be an appropriate consequence. The student sees the result of your watchful eye immediately. Staying in at recess may be an appropriate consequence. A positive reinforcement may be a coveted task such as line leader or calendar person. A note or call home may also be necessary.

Conduct a Conference With the Student (and/or Principal, Other Teachers, and Parents). This is the most important part of the process. The student must hear the problem, see the data, know the consequences, and explain or demonstrate the appropriate behavior ("What does keeping your hands and feet to yourself mean, Shawn? Tell me what you'll do in line," etc.).

Set Up Successful Situations to "Catch the Student Being Good." Be consistent with reinforcement strategies. When Shawn comes in the next day, remind him quietly: "What are you going to do, Shawn? I'm going to keep track of how well you remember." Sometimes the student can keep a personal chart on successfully making or not making the appropriate choice.

Reinforce Regularly. Reinforce positively with social rewards (praise, smiles, an approving nod) every time a student remembers at first. Later, move to intermittent reinforcement. When will Shawn forget? Probably near holidays and especially at the end of the year. You can use this strategy to plug in your own "Shawn's" disruptive behavior and devise your own specific plan to change that behavior.

Increase Positive Interactions

Although students with discipline problems need more positive feedback, they are likely to receive mostly negative feedback because of their misbehavior. Teachers of such students can easily fall into the trap of having mainly negative interactions with them. Negative interactions are emotionally draining for everyone involved. Constant criticism is damaging and drives a wedge between teachers and students. Teachers may even reach the point at which they have difficulty seeing the students' good qualities.

Try to increase positive interactions with your "behavior problems." The world in which we live can be such a negative place. Human nature is such that people complain when something is wrong but say little when things are done right. It is often difficult to change to a more positive way of interacting. Ideally, you should try to get the rate of positive comments and interactions to between 50 percent and 75 percent. Even if this feels a little phony at first, it will get easier and more sincere with practice.

You may wish to "listen and observe" your own behavior toward your students for a day. Count how often you make positive statements. Can you find good reasons to smile at those exasperating children, make positive comments, or give them a quick hug? "You did a great job cleaning up your desk." "Gee, you must be proud of the eighty-seven you earned on your spelling test. You really studied. That's great. Keep up the good work." "The library corner looks so neat and organized. Thanks for picking it up!"

In contrast, how many negative statements do you make? "Your handwriting is so messy." "You aren't even trying." "You've failed the spelling test again." "Don't leave your materials all over the floor around your desk. You're such a slob." "You did a terrible job on this homework assignment. You'll have to stay in at recess again to fix it." "You act as if you don't even care—look at this sloppy paper!"

Are your interactions mostly positive or negative? Teachers especially need to catch their "problem" students being good and compliment the things they do well. If seat work has been a major problem and your students start working on the assignment without being reminded, give them a pat on the shoulder, a smile, or a thanks immediately. Give kudos sincerely and in moderation. Find at least some part of the job to commend. If compliments are too flowery, children may reject them. If you enthuse about schoolwork as if it were perfect and the students recognize that it is not, they may not respond at all positively to your interaction.

Plenty of people in the world are willing to tear down your "problem" students by telling them they are bad, lazy, or wrong. Few people are willing to spend the extra time and energy required to be positive and build the children's self-esteem. It might take a strong conscious effort on your part to be as positive as possible. Make it your personal goal to fill these children's time in your classroom with positive interactions.

Be Consistent

A basic principle of behavior management is to be as consistent as possible with both rewards and consequences. Your students should always know what to expect if they behave in a certain way. To put it simply, they must understand that "good things happen when we behave and unpleasant things happen when we don't."

One of the most difficult aspects of behavior management for new teachers (and many seasoned veterans) is to be consistent with the student discipline program every day—yes, even when you are tired and would love to pretend you didn't see that particular misbehavior. You must step in and promptly deal with it. You must constantly monitor what your students are doing. Use an "active eye." See what is going on. Avoid becoming preoccupied with someone or something and ignoring the rest of the class. It is said that one teacher on his or her feet is worth two in the seat. Staying on your feet benefits your discipline program and is also a potent teaching tactic.

Effective teachers feel confident and in charge of the situation in their classrooms. This chapter has shared a summary of key behavior management techniques that work, as suggested by educational research and by successful classroom teachers. Perhaps most important, remember that in behavior management, your attitudes and expectations will act as self-fulfilling prophecies. Preventing discipline problems begins with the proactive attitude that you can and will promote respect and rapport in your classroom.

5.1 RESOURCE
Sample Homework Log

··

I am aware of this week's homework. _____

Student Name

_____   _____

Date   Parent Signature

- -

Cut off and return to teacher. Keep homework list for reference.

HOMEWORK ASSIGNMENTS

NAME _____   WEEK OF _____

TEACHER'S NAME _____   SCHOOL PHONE _____

SUBJECT	MONDAY	TUESDAY	WEDNESDAY	THURSDAY	FRIDAY
MATH					
SOCIAL STUDIES					
SCIENCE					
LANGUAGE					
SPELLING					
READING					
OTHER					

Sample Behavior Contract
for a Primary Student

Daily Goals for _____

My Daily Goals are:

1. To try hard to complete all my work correctly

2. To stay focused on my work and on class activities

Each day I accomplish these goals, I will get a sticker from my teacher to put on my special chart. On Friday, I will take my chart home and show it to my family.

My teacher and I will check my goals here:

	Goals	9-10:30	11-12:00	1-3:00
Monday				
	I tried			
	I focused			
Tuesday				
	I tried			
	I focused			
Wednesday				
	I tried			
	I focused			
Thursday				
	I tried			
	I focused			
Friday				
	I tried			
	I focused			

Sample Behavior Contract
for an Intermediate Student

....

Student-Teacher Contract

Student Name _____ Date _____

1. The behavior I will work on: _____

_____

2. What I am willing to do: _____

_____

3. Where and when I will do this: _____

_____

4. The amount of time I think I need to work on this behavior: _____

_____

Signed: _____

(Student)

For the successful completion of the above, you may: _____

_____

_____

Signed: _____

(Teacher)

Cut off. Tape to student desk.

Weekly Progress Chart

Student Name _____ Week of _____ to _____

Behavior to work on: _____

_____

Put a mark every time you: _____

_____

Monday	Tuesday	Wednesday	Thursday	Friday	Weekly Total
Teacher Initials	Teacher Initials	Teacher Initials	Teacher Initials	Teacher Initials	Teacher Initials

Sample Homework Contract

HOMEWORK CONTRACT

✓Each day that I complete all my homework assignments, I will put a sticker on one square of my chart.

✓When I have filled in _____ squares, I will earn a reward. My reward will be _____

_____

_____

Student Signature _____

Parent Signature _____

Date Started _____ Expiration Date _____

6 CHAPTER

Assessing Student Learning and Performance

As an elementary classroom teacher, you will use many types of assessment on a daily basis. Sometimes, you will jot down anecdotal notes about how well your students are performing classroom learning activities. You may use observational checklists and scales. Your students' own records, such as reading logs, science notebooks, and journals, will provide additional information on their learning progress. In addition to informal measures, you will also evaluate class work and homework and develop and administer a variety of formal tests.

Like the behavior management models discussed in the previous chapter, assessment practices range on a continuum from informal, continuing classroom assessments to formal or "objective" measures. Teachers vary in their need for formality. As with other aspects of classroom life, some educators regard controlled conditions and rigorous standards as imperatives. Others, whose classrooms are more flexible and naturalistic, tend to see assessment as significant only if it is an integral part of the continuing learning situation.

In Chapter 3, you reflected on your own philosophy of education and the type of classroom in which you feel most comfortable. Assessment is another dimension to consider as you develop your personal educational credo and inquire about the philosophy and expectations of your school and district.

Schoolwide and Districtwide Testing Programs

Most public and private schools rely extensively on commercial standardized tests. Formal, norm-referenced group tests that compare students with other children who have taken the same test provide district administrators with feedback on the overall success of the educational program. Standardized tests, which are available in different forms, also allow school systems to assess students at the beginning of a school year or program and then to assess again at the conclusion to determine growth. A major problem with formal, norm-referenced tests, however, is that they do not inform classroom instructional practices. These tests tell you in only a general way about your students' achievements. They let you know how your students did on the test compared with other students nationally who have taken the same test. Pending federal legislation will surely exacerbate the issue. Unfortunately, standardized tests provide you, the teacher, with little or no usable information for modifying your classroom curriculum.

Many educators are worried that schools seem to be drowning in a sea of standardized tests. The trend seems likely to continue. Congress's recent decision to expand the National Assessment of Educational Progress (the "Nation's Report Card") and the movement toward new national education goals foreshadow an even greater emphasis on standardized tests. Proponents argue that a number of constituencies have a legitimate interest in the achievement levels of students and that they are entitled to accurate, adequate, and timely assessment data. Parents often request this information. In larger school districts, whole departments of specially trained evaluation experts coordinate and manage schoolwide assessment programs. As a beginning teacher, you will not have any say in the selection of tests to be administered on a schoolwide basis, nor in their scoring or initial interpretation. Your main job will be to communicate test results clearly to parents and, perhaps, to upper elementary students themselves.

To communicate results effectively, you need to be aware of the limitations, criticisms, and objections to standardized tests. The criticism you are likely to hear most often is that multiple-choice tests focus on lower-level cognitive skills—that standardized tests are skewing the curriculum toward what is easily measured by machines: basic skills and isolated facts. School districts may require teachers to cover material because it is "on the test," and too much instruction is reduced to rote memorization and skill drills.

Another major criticism is that standardized tests measure students' knowledge of standard English and test-taking skills as much as they measure content knowledge. Critics contend that the tests are biased in culture, race, and gender. Such criticism is especially significant when these test scores are used for tracking students into remedial or special programs. Standardized test results are sometimes used to make decisions that can affect students' entire lives.

You will probably be asked to review test scores with parents at conferences or explain test results that are published in a local newspaper to parents or students. Be prepared to discuss in nontechnical terms what a norm-referenced test is and its limitations. Generally, you will communicate that standardized, norm-referenced tests only compare children against a norm group and do not provide a good measure of how well a particular child is achieving particular objectives. Focus parent attention on your own classroom assessment program that considers the prior knowledge of students and then tailors instruction for the capabilities of your particular classroom.

High-Stakes Testing

Currently throughout the nation, state-mandated standardized tests have become the centerpiece for standards-based school reform efforts. These tests are "high-stakes" because they are used as the basis for decisions about everything from student placement, promotion, and graduation to teacher and administrator pay raises to school rating and funding. Newspapers around the country now routinely rank local schools on the basis of students' standardized test scores. Despite cautions and caveats from testing experts, high-stakes tests have become the public benchmark of educational quality. The increasing accountability that has accompanied reliance on high-stakes testing has profoundly affected the content of classroom teaching.

Unfortunately, the atmosphere of importance surrounding the exams can promote a success-at-any-cost attitude that brings out the worst in some schools. Whole subject areas are being omitted from the curriculum—art and music, especially, but also science and social studies in some cases—to make more time in the school day for teachers to prepare students for standardized tests. Instead of "teaching toward the test" and using assessment as an opportunity for thoughtful curriculum restructuring, some schools are actually teaching the test *itself* as the curriculum. This emphasis on the test, including repeated practice drills, may boost scores but can lead to rote teaching and disengaged learning. Good teachers in many areas are worried that their schools are focused more on accountability to the state or school district than to their students.

Your Classroom Assessment Program

Most beginning teachers are less interested in systemwide assessment than in the use of assessment in their own classrooms. Systemwide testing does not assist you in helping children succeed. Norm-referenced data (e.g., stanines, grade equivalents, and percentiles) do not tell you which strategies students are or are not using during reading, for instance. It is usually not enough to know simply whether students have reached a certain standard. You also need to know your learners' areas of strength and weakness, so you can build on one and remediate the other.

Effective elementary teachers tend to avoid "snapshot" assessments. These one-shot evaluations, just like commercial standardized tests, have similar limitations. Single tests, such as the ubiquitous unit culmination examinations in math or social studies, often do not do justice to a student's competence. What if a child has high levels of test anxiety or is ill on the test day? It is preferable to build a cumulative, continuous record of student performance. For example, many teachers now have their children keep a writing folder or portfolio containing all the writing assignments, formal and informal, completed during the year.

As a classroom teacher, you will be interested in where each student is on a continuum of learning. You can refer to your school district's scope and sequence documents (see Resource 6.1) for benchmarks that will help you identify and chart each student's progress, as well as help you understand the whole continuum of learnings for children at your grade level. Children's learning tends to go through a series of phases, in spurts and splutters, as children accommodate additional elements of information, build relationships among separate elements, and become able to construct abstract concepts or general principles. Continuous assessment fits the integrative, developing nature of children's learning.

Performance-Based and Authentic Assessments

Alternative assessment tools seek to measure the students' ability to perform in a given subject area directly. These tools demand that students demonstrate real competencies, probing students' minds to reveal what they know and what they can do. By presenting students with more complex tasks, these tools provide additional motivation for students to excel. Many alternative assessments involve students in genuine meaning-constructing activities—ones that are authentic, from students' perspectives. Performance-based or authentic assessments resemble real tasks and can take a wide variety of forms. Common types of authentic assessments include culminating exhibitions or presentations; writing tests (students write on assigned topics, and the results are rated by a team of readers); portfolios (collections of student work that show development in progress); checklists and rating scales; and anecdotal records, which are used for recording atypical and routine behaviors that you observe as you move around the room.

Classroom Observations of Children

Experienced teachers use "kid watching" a great deal as an assessment strategy. Careful, systematic observation is a critical tool for early assessment of students and their abilities. You need to be constantly aware of

---

**Suggestions for Using Classroom
Performance-Based Assessments**

Designing the Assessment
- Have a clear purpose in mind for the assessment; ask yourself how you will use the results.
- Devise tasks directly related to instructional goals that require students to apply what they have learned.
- Use tasks that have more than one correct answer or outcome.
- Use tasks that require more than one step to complete.
- Consider asking students to design their own question, problem, or project.

Administering the Assessment
- Have students complete the assessment task during their regularly scheduled class time. More complex tasks may take a number of class periods and might include out-of-class work also. For such assignments, students should keep a log of their progress. Identify checkpoints at which you record pupil progress. This gives you a more comprehensive picture of student performance and enables you to diagnose weaknesses.
- Specify clearly what the students are to do and under what conditions.

Scoring the Assessment
- Avoid mental record keeping because you may forget important information about students' performance. Relying on memory can also result in your perceptions' being filtered as you observe subsequent students. Decide whether holistic or analytic scoring is appropriate on the basis of your purpose for the evaluation.
- Establish scoring criteria prior to using the assessment activity.
- Decide on a method of recording scores, and prepare the necessary materials such as a checklist or rating scale.
- Refer to a written copy of the scoring criteria when evaluating students' performance.

---

which children are having difficulty or are becoming distracted. Start a logbook in September to maintain a record of your observations of students' work habits, their reading and math progress, and so on. You may find it handy as you move about the classroom to carry a pad of Post-it notes in your pocket to jot down observations, which can later be stuck in the logbook under the appropriate children's names. Be sure to check off names to ensure that you observe every student. Additional suggestions for effective use of observation as an assessment tool follow:

- Make a number of observations through time. Just as one-shot tests are of questionable validity, one-shot observations are unreliable indicators of student stability or growth. By looking at children in many different instances, you can detect patterns, document growth, and spot areas that you will need to address in minilessons to a small group with similar problems.

- Know what you are looking for. To make effective observations, you need to be aware of developmental and academic expectations at your grade level: What learning strategies are appropriate for children of this age doing this task? (Refer to Resource 6.1, "An Overview of Learning Objectives for Elementary Students.")

- Observe children in a variety of learning situations. Many commercial tests are poor evaluative tools because they pose artificial situations, are boring, use stilted language, or are limited to a few multiple-choice items for each topic or skill. As a teacher, you can observe your children in varied class settings—in whole groups, small groups, and individualized situations.

Written notes are only one way to document your observations. In addition, try using a tape recorder to capture children's story retellings and oral readings and a camera or videocamera to capture children's work in groups and active and interactive performances. Such documentation is wonderful to share with parents. Sometimes older children can take turns being the class photographer. Older students can also keep journals to record their daily learnings, reactions, and further questions.

Checklists and Scales

Authentic assessment relies in many ways on your understanding of developmental milestones. It is essential to know these observable behaviors and abilities. Checklists can then be used as a quick reference tool. Often teachers who begin with general observational techniques find the use of various checklists helpful to formalize their expectations and to facilitate the process of collecting data. Some checklists include Likert-type scales (e.g., 1 to 5, or *seldom* to *often* ratings) because many skills, such as reading fluency, increase through time.

Checklists are valuable for students to use, too. They help learners be clear about the exact expectations. Various writing checklists developed through the National Writing Project allow older students to become their own evaluators. Many teachers also have students keep reading logs as a daily record of their reading habits and interests, usually during self-selected reading periods. A sample log form is included in Resource 6.2.

Questionnaires and Surveys

Questionnaires are most useful to assess students' attitudes and to stimulate children's thinking about their learning. Used as one aspect of your total classroom assessment program, questionnaires can generate student reflection on such activities as working in cooperative groups.

Family surveys are another way to generate additional information about your children. For instance, a survey could determine how often children read at home and their favorite books. Keep in mind that checklists, questionnaires, and surveys are intended only as a beginning point in a comprehensive assessment program.

Oral Questions and Interviews

Questioning is perhaps the most basic and effective way to assess children's learning. Classroom questions are also a teaching strategy. Although not technically an assessment instrument, questioning is a form of assessment because it provides feedback to teachers. Research indicates that most classroom questions ask for only low-level knowledge, facts, and details. To truly assess your students' learning, make your questions more thought provoking. Also, remember that pausing between the question and the naming of a student increases the quality of children's thought and response. Distribute your questions evenly among all the learners in your classroom. Unfortunately, research shows teachers have a natural tendency to ask more questions and higher-level questions of students they perceive as their more able learners. Be equitable in your questioning if you expect it to yield valuable assessment information.

Individual interviews with children can give you valuable data. An individual reading inventory (IRI) is a similar tool found to be useful by many elementary teachers. Consisting of graded word lists and story passages, an IRI provides an individualized, holistic assessment of a child's reading ability. Many large text publishers (e.g., Houghton Mifflin) provide a supplementary teacher's resource guide on how to conduct IRIs. If such a guide is unavailable in your district, an excellent resource is *Alternative Assessment Techniques for Reading and Writing* by Wilma H. Miller (1996).

Portfolios and Records of Student Work

Portfolios, or samples of students' work collected through time, can be used for classroom instruction and assessment activities. Students examine and analyze their work and then decide with the teacher what items to include in their portfolios.

Some schools require students and teachers to work together developing portfolios to both assess and report student achievements. The use of portfolios no doubt adds an additional dimension in assessing student performance. Be aware, however, that the implementation of an authentic assessment program using portfolios can be challenging for new teachers as well as for seasoned veterans. Most teachers are accustomed to more traditional assessment schemes that require less time and are more structured. In comparison with the neater forms of data collection and achievement tests, portfolio assessment can be messy, bulky, "unreliable," and time-consuming. Everyone involved needs to plan carefully for an efficient and successful experience with portfolios.

Portfolio assessment, like other forms of assessment, must be an integral part of the instructional program. The purpose for keeping the portfolios must be clearly established at the outset for the stakeholders (teacher, students, parents, and administrators). Useful portfolios evolve from and are based on curriculum outcomes and student outcomes. Portfolios are unique and especially worthwhile because they provide a look at texture, layers, and diversity of student work—at depth and breadth, at the "big picture," not just a snapshot. Portfolios give teachers insights into student growth not possible through traditional assessment measures.

Portfolio Structures

Portfolios include a physical structure, such as chronological order, subject area(s), and style of work. Portfolios also must include a conceptual structure, or goals for student learning. On the one hand, classroom portfolios are simply collections of students' papers, tapes, drawings, and other materials. The varied collection is put into the portfolio by the student and the teacher. The container or holder can be an expandable folder, a box, or even a special decorated shopping bag. On the other hand, the portfolio is far more than just a holder or a set of papers. It becomes a growing repository of the student's thoughts, ideas, and accomplishments.

Guidelines for Portfolio Development

Use the following guidelines to set up a portfolio system:

1. Determine which student work is to go in, as well as which work stays out (see next sections). Most important, if you are doing "best shot" portfolios, determine what constitutes excellent work. Develop standards to measure the excellence of work in various subjects. Ask your students to rate their own work according to rubrics or scoring systems that you provide or that students have developed as a class project.
2. Select student work samples at the end of a unit or quarter. Select a variety of daily and weekly student assignments. Have students

write personal reflections or self-evaluations of their work samples to place in their portfolios.

3. Establish a rule that your students may not take their portfolios out of the classroom.

4. Develop a cover letter that summarizes the types of information readers will find in the student portfolios. This enables you to use the portfolio to report to parents and others. Monitor the frequency with which you examine portfolios by including a sheet that you initial and date at each viewing.

5. Remember that your students may need some time to become accustomed to the idea of keeping portfolios, as well as evaluating their own work.

What to Put in Portfolios

Examples of work that other teachers and students have chosen to include in portfolios are listed below:

- Documentation of the writing process, including brainstorming notes made by the student, drafts, notes on additional ideas, and a final copy of the written work

- Other writing samples—prose and poetry

- Peer comments/review of student work, teacher reflective comments, and parent reflective comments

- Lists of books read, lists of words learned, and other proficiency lists

- Audio- or videotapes of the child reading aloud, oral presentations, skits, and debates

- Cooperative group projects

- Graphs, charts, maps, diagrams, pictures, and favorite artifacts

- Journals

- Autobiographies

- Attitude inventories

- Interest inventories

- Diagnostic tests

- Anecdotal records

- Parent conference notes

- Photographs of science models

- Solutions (with written explanations of how the answers were obtained) to math problems

Types of Portfolios

Consider which portfolios would be most useful to you. One type of portfolio documents *processes* in learning and includes such items as

- Entry/exit skills checklists and pre- and posttests
- Anecdotal observations
- Multiple examples of classroom work selected by students and teacher
- Records of individual conferences
- Oral reading on tape—early, middle, and end of year
- Process examples (at least three) reflecting the writing process for the first and fourth quarters
- Math problem solving
- Science lab sheets from experiments

Another type of portfolio contains *best shot* examples such as

- Final copies of "published" stories or poems
- Math project
- Congratulatory note from teacher with a "big smile" or happy face
- Selected journal entries
- Audiotape of a polished book report presentation
- "Star" homework assignments
- Research paper
- Visual arts (drawings, paintings)

Most teachers choose to begin with best shot portfolios.

In summary, portfolios provide a cumulative record that shows pupil progress through time and that is much richer in detail and substance than a mere list of scores. Papers and other items are placed in your students' portfolios at regular intervals. Portfolios not only can hold students' best work but also can represent evidence of student performance on a given range of categories or genres of work.

Portfolios can do the following:

- Assess outcomes as well as processes of learning
- Provide information that facilitates effective instruction and learning
- Involve students in their own assessment by enabling self-selection of work samples to submit for evaluation
- Result in more reliable evaluation by using more than one sample

Portfolios provide a number of benefits for students, including the following:

- Allowing students to see how much progress they are making
- Increasing students' knowledge about the scope of what they have learned
- Promoting teacher-student interactions and collaborative learning
- Supporting student ownership and responsibility for learning

At the end of the year, get together with other teachers who want to know what your students have accomplished, particularly teachers who will have your students in their classes next year. Share your students' portfolios. In the meantime, discuss and review portfolios with individual students. Ask students to decide what work they wish to keep—perhaps the best or favorite or most unusual work. During portfolio conferences, students can decide what pieces of work will help next year's teacher understand them better.

Guidelines for Preparing Written Tests

One of the most traditional assessment activities, especially in the upper grades, is preparing written tests. A number of guidelines exist for teachers to follow as they construct their own classroom tests to measure student learning and as they make judgments and assign grades for student work. The principles of test construction include making sure that test items match instructional objectives, cover all instructional tasks, and are appropriate for the students.

Teacher-Made Tests and Quizzes

Custom-made tests prepared by teachers have a number of advantages when compared with commercially prepared tests. They can address learning goals unique to particular classes and grades, provide immediate detailed feedback, and are scored by teachers, which allows teachers to accept more than one answer as correct. Most important, such tests are more significant to students than are commercial ones.

As a student teacher, you probably developed quizzes and tests in subjects such as spelling, math, and social studies. To be sure, you will now be able to apply much of what you have learned about test construction. Feel free to use those techniques that have worked for you as you write a rough draft of the test. After you have completed it, review the questions below as you check your work. Then you will be ready to type and administer your test.

- Are you including only those skills and concepts you have taught in class?

- Do you provide a variety of questions instead of presenting a single type, such as only true-or-false statements?

- Have you included the right number of questions for students to answer? For example, include at least five examples focusing on the same concept, such as subtraction, in an arithmetic test. Establish how much time your students will need to take this test and include an appropriate number of questions.

- Is this test only one of the many samples of work completed by individual students? Or are students' entire grades in a subject determined mainly by quizzes and tests?

- How will you plan for any absent students to make up tests? If students do poorly on the test, how will you reteach and assess again? Will you encourage students to rework specific test items on which they did poorly?

- Do some of your test questions encourage your students to apply concepts?

What Do You Think About Testing?

- What do you consider to be a fair test?
- What sorts of assessments are developmentally appropriate for students at your grade level?

Discuss with a mentor or colleague what makes tests fair and/or developmentally appropriate.

Using and Assigning Letter Grades

General Guidelines

Consider *why* you are assessing students, then find the proper tool. Sometimes, it may be portfolios. Sometimes, it may be a multiple-choice test provided by the textbook publisher.

- Carefully explain to students how they will be graded and the quality of the work you expect. Use rubrics and models whenever possible.

- In general, students should be assessed on their daily class work and homework, as well as on special projects.

- Decide lesson by lesson the following:

    Will it be graded?
    How will it be graded?

Who will grade the lesson?
When will it be graded?
Where will it be graded?

- Discuss with your mentor or school principal any building policies on late work, grade breakdowns, homework policies, and grading systems (A-F or S-U). If your school uses letter grades at the intermediate levels, here is a traditional grading scale:

	Traditional Grading Scale	
	97-100	A+
(95 percent = 4.0)	93-96	A
	90-92	A-
	87-89	B+
(85 percent = 3.0)	83-86	B
	80-82	B-
	77-79	C+
(75 percent = 2.0)	73-76	C
	70-72	C-
	67-69	D+
(65 percent = 1.0)	63-66	D
	60-62	D-
	59 and lower	F

- Progress reports (weekly or monthly) are an excellent way of letting the students and parents know the current status of the students' grades. They are also a good way for you to keep on top of grading.
- Informal, continuous assessment of children's performance on a variety of measures is essential to good teaching.

Reporting Evaluations

There are many ways to let students and their parents know about progress made in school. Some of these ways include the following:

- Sending notes
- Checking and returning work
- Calling home
- Sending progress reports

- Holding teacher-parent conferences
- Sending report cards

See Chapter 7 for more specific information about working with parents.

Suggestions for Using Any Assessment Tools

Never lose sight of the main goals of schooling. For example, you undoubtedly want students to learn strategies for solving problems and reading independently, rather than simply rote knowledge and facts. To challenge your students to apply, analyze, synthesize, and evaluate what they have learned, use a variety of methods for evaluating them, such as observations, checklists, reports, projects, and portfolios.

Performance-based assessment puts newer theory into practice. Recent research on learning endorses the old adage that the best way to learn something is to do it. Many teachers now believe that the best way to determine whether a student can effectively construct meaning is to assess the meaning the child has constructed.

Tips for Assessing Student Learning

- Have a procedure for evaluating and grading in place at the beginning of the year because
    1. It will help you determine the assessment methods you will use.
    2. You will need to explain this carefully to students and parents.

- Talk with your mentor or other teachers at your grade level to learn about assessment techniques commonly used at your school and school policies about assessment.

- Develop good observation skills, focusing on the whole child (social, emotional, physical, and academic).

- Keep an anecdotal record of specific student behaviors. (For example, "Jillian stared out the window for ten minutes today during instruction." "Arturo spoke out for the first time during reading group today.")

- Keep a folder for each student to file samples of daily work, all correspondence to and from home, copies of student self-evaluation, and student anecdotal records.

- Refer to student cumulative records ("cum file") to gather information such as age, family unit, previous teachers' comments, health, and referrals for special services.

- Talk with other professionals who come in contact with the student. Be careful not to be unduly influenced by comments. Keep an open mind.
- Try to give tests midweek, because students tend to perform better.
- Determine a specific objective for each assignment, and check the assignment for that objective.
- Develop methods for students to check papers occasionally. It is not necessary for the teacher to grade all assignments.
- Keep students and parents informed about school progress with a report at the midpoint of a marking period.
- Make sure students and parents understand your evaluation criteria. Go over expectations outlined in grading rubrics and/or what is needed to earn each specific grade on a general grading scale such as the traditional grading scale shown earlier.

In summary, assessment serves many purposes, including

1. Gathering information on student progress to report to parents
2. Gathering information on student progress to better meet students' instructional needs
3. Gathering information to make students aware of their strengths

Student assessment is a continuing, cooperative process among teachers, students, and parents. It begins when the children walk into class the first day and you begin observing daily skills and behaviors.

Assessment may not be your favorite activity as a teacher, but it is of utmost importance to parents and students. If done well, assessment will make a major contribution to your effectiveness as a teacher.

An Overview of Learning Objectives for Elementary Students

··

Introduction

These objectives are representative of basic learning expectations in language arts, reading, and mathematics at grades 1, 3, and 5. This composite set of objectives was derived from several sets developed in school districts in the state of Washington, but the expected learnings are typical of what is required throughout the United States.

Use this overview as a reference to focus your instruction. If your school or district has provided a similar list, refer to it instead. For more information when you want to explore, understand, and use the standards and benchmarks that have been developed in all the major content areas, an excellent reference is *Content Knowledge: A Compendium of Standards and Benchmarks for K-12 Education* by John Kendall and Robert Marzano (1996). This reference was developed by the Mid-Continent Regional Educational Laboratory and is available from the Association for Supervision and Curriculum Development (toll free 1-800-933-ASCD; also available on CD-ROM). This 610-page resource has more than 250 standards and 4,800 benchmarks organized into three broad categories of knowledge (procedural, declarative, and contextual knowledge), making it possible to identify targets for learning at every grade level.

It is often worthwhile to carefully review the objectives for the grade level just below and above yours. Know where your students have been academically and where they are expected to go when they leave your classroom.

First Grade

Language Arts, First-Grade Learning Objectives

In a language arts program, all students should receive instruction and practice in writing, speaking, and listening. The curriculum enables students to communicate skillfully, to listen critically, to write and speak effectively, and to think logically and creatively. Language arts skills spiral through the grades, with each level expanding on previous skills and experiences. Major instructional topics and student objectives include the following:

A. Composition Skills

The student understands that writing is a process that involves several steps: prewriting, writing, revision, and presenting.

1. Writes for a specific purpose and audience
2. Writes complete sentences
3. Uses editing skills

B. Handwriting Skills

1. Forms manuscript letters correctly
2. Demonstrates proper size, spacing, and appropriate speed
3. Demonstrates neatness in printing

C. Language Study Skills

1. Recognizes a sentence as expressing a complete thought
2. Develops skill in using nouns, adjectives, and verbs
3. Uses capital letters for first word in a sentence, *I* used as a pronoun, and proper nouns
4. Uses correct punctuation at the end of a statement or question
5. Recognizes correct verb tense
6. Recognizes correct subject and verb agreement

D. Listening Skills

1. Listens attentively at appropriate times
2. Follows oral one- and two-step directions in sequence
3. Practices common directional clue words (e.g., *first, last, next, left,* and *right*)
4. Listens to paragraphs and stories and identifies
   a. Important details
   b. Topics
   c. Main ideas
   d. Predicted outcomes
5. Identifies correct sequence of events

E. Reference and Study Skills

1. Reads for information
2. Begins to use alphabetical order
3. Categorizes words and ideas into similar groups

F. Speaking Skills

1. Speaks with clarity and appropriate voice control
2. Focuses on a topic
3. Answers questions in complete sentences
4. Participates in show-and-tell/group discussion

G. Spelling Skills

1. Spells words at first-grade level
2. Learns weekly lists of words
3. Uses assigned spelling words correctly in sentences
4. Applies spelling generalizations (rules)

Reading, First-Grade Learning Objectives

An elementary reading program is designed to develop competent readers who read for information and pleasure. Decoding, comprehension, and literary skills are developed through a variety of instructional approaches. Major instructional topics and student objectives include the following:

A. Decoding Skills
  1. Distinguishes alphabetic letter forms
    a. Recognizes similarities and differences between upper- and lowercase letters
    b. Identifies upper- and lowercase letters by name
    c. Recognizes vowels and consonants
  2. Distinguishes letter-sound associations
  3. Distinguishes beginning sounds and letters
  4. Distinguishes ending sounds and letters
  5. Substitutes initial and final consonants
  6. Discriminates short and long vowel sounds
  7. Uses picture clues to decode unfamiliar words
  8. Uses sentence context to decode unfamiliar words
  9. Recognizes letter blends (clusters) in initial and final position
  10. Distinguishes digraphs in initial and final position (*sh, ch, th, ck, kn,* and *wh*)
  11. Recognizes the addition of *-s, -ing, -ed, -or,* and *-er* to base (root) words
  12. Recognizes the addition of *-s* or *-es* to indicate plural
  13. Recognizes the addition of *-'s* to nouns to indicate possession
  14. Understands spelling generalizations:
    a. When action words end in a single consonant following a short vowel, the final consonant is usually doubled before adding *-ed* or *-ing.*
    b. When action words end with a final *e,* that *e* is usually dropped before adding a suffix that begins with a vowel.
    c. When action words end in *y,* that *y* is usually changed to *i* before adding a suffix that begins with a vowel.
  15. Identifies base words
  16. Understands contractions as two words combined with an apostrophe representing one or more omitted letters
  17. Identifies vowel combinations and their sounds
  18. Differentiates between hard and soft sounds of *c* and *g*
  19. Recognizes compound words as two combined words
  20. Identifies a suffix as a common syllable added to the end of a word
  21. Identifies a prefix as a common syllable added to the beginning of a word

B. Comprehension Skills
    1. Derives word meaning from picture context clues
    2. Distinguishes among multiple word meanings
    3. Identifies word referents (pronouns)
    4. Recognizes and interprets punctuation (. ? ! " " ,)
C. Literary Skills
    1. Reads for enjoyment
    2. Demonstrates beginning library use skills

Mathematics, First-Grade Learning Objectives

A mathematics program should strive to give all students instruction in skills, applications, and concepts. The process of developing thoughtful behavior in mathematics requires that throughout the grades and within each strand, instruction should progress from the concrete level, through pictorial representation, to abstract symbolization.

Problem solving, rather than exercises, should be the mainstay of instruction and learning. Students should apply their mathematical skills and understanding, inquiry skills, and thinking skills to formulate and solve problems.

Major instructional topics and student objectives include the following:

A. Place Value and Counting
    1. Recognizes zero to twenty objects
    2. Recognizes number words *zero* to *ten*
    3. Reads and writes numerals 0 to 100
    4. Counts by ones, fives, and tens to one hundred
    5. Identifies ordinal numbers 1st through 10th
    6. Understands place values of 10s and 1s to 100
    7. Counts on and back
    8. Determines which numeral comes before, after, or between to compare numbers one to twenty
B. Adding Whole Numbers
    1. Adds two- and three-digit numbers
    2. Estimates sums
    3. Understands addition as a joining process
    4. Understands sums through eighteen
    5. Adds quantities of money using pennies, nickels, dimes, and quarters
    6. Solves addition problems using horizontal and vertical forms
C. Subtracting Whole Numbers
    1. Understands subtraction as a separating process
    2. Demonstrates knowledge of the mental math techniques of counting back one, two, or three to find differences
    3. Uses mental math technique of subtracting with zero

4. Memorizes facts to twelve
5. Solves subtraction problems using horizontal and vertical forms
6. Uses mental math technique of subtracting nine and subtracting doubles to find differences
7. Understands add-to-check fact to subtract

D. Fractions
1. Identifies equal parts of a whole unit
2. Recognizes $\frac{1}{2}$, $\frac{1}{3}$, and $\frac{1}{4}$

E. Problem Solving and Applications
1. Collects and organizes data
2. Reads a bar graph and pictograph
3. Uses a variety of data sources to solve a problem (data sources may include information from a story, chart, table, or graph)
4. Understands how to choose the operation that fits a given problem
5. Determines reasonable estimates
6. Uses pictures of coins (penny, nickel, dime, and quarter) to solve problems
7. Determines whether answers to problems are reasonable

F. Critical Thinking and Logic
1. Identifies number, color, and position patterns
2. Understands sorting and classification by attributes
3. Compares and contrasts attributes
4. Demonstrates use of critical thinking to identify differences

G. Measurement
1. Estimates and measures length using a ruler to measure inches and feet
2. Estimates and measures using a centimeter ruler
3. Estimates, measures, and compares weight

Third Grade

Language Arts, Third-Grade Learning Objectives

A. Composition Skills
The student understands that writing is a process that involves several steps: prewriting, writing, revision, and presenting.
1. Writes for a specific purpose and audience
2. Writes a paragraph using at least three related sentences
3. Uses correct form to write a personal letter
4. Uses editing skills

B. Handwriting Skills
1. Writes using correct manuscript form, spacing, and size
2. Reviews lowercase cursive letters and joining strokes taught in second grade
3. Writes uppercase cursive letters

    4. Uses margins, titles, headings, and indentations correctly
    5. Practices good penmanship habits and skills

C. Language Study Skills
    1. Writes complete declarative, interrogative, and exclamatory sentences and uses correct ending punctuation
    2. Uses capital letters for first word in a sentence, *I* used as a pronoun, and proper nouns
    3. Identifies nouns, pronouns, verbs, and adjectives
    4. Uses correct verb tense
    5. Practices correct subject and verb agreement
    6. Identifies subject and predicate
    7. Writes abbreviations and initials correctly
    8. Uses comma for date, city, state, and series of items
    9. Uses colon for writing time of day
   10. Identifies apostrophe for writing contractions and possessives
   11. Uses *a* and *an* correctly
   12. Uses subjective pronouns correctly (*I, we, you, he, she, it,* and *they*)

D. Listening Skills
    1. Listens at appropriate times
    2. Follows one-, two-, and three-step oral directions
    3. Practices listening carefully and responding to others in a group discussion
    4. Listens to an oral presentation for important details, topic, main idea(s), and predicted outcomes

E. Reference and Study Skills
    1. Alphabetizes to the third letter
    2. Uses guide words to locate entry words in a dictionary
    3. Uses alphabetical order for reference in
       a. Dictionary
       b. Glossary
    4. Understands key information found on title page
    5. Uses table of contents to locate information

F. Speaking Skills
    1. Strives for appropriate expression when reading aloud
    2. Practices speaking with clarity and appropriate voice control
    3. Gives informal talks and oral presentations
    4. Participates in group discussion
    5. Focuses on topic of discussion

G. Spelling Skills
    1. Spells words at third-grade level
    2. Learns weekly lists of words
    3. Applies spelling generalizations (rules) in written work
    4. Spells words correctly from dictated sentences
    5. Proofreads for spelling errors

Reading, Third-Grade Learning Objectives

A. Decoding Skills
   1. Demonstrates ability to use skills taught in first and second grade, including
      a. Distinguishing letter-sound associations
      b. Distinguishing short and long vowel sounds
      c. Recognizing the addition of -*s* or -*es* to indicate plural
      d. Using context and picture clues
      e. Recognizing base words
      f. Recognizing common syllables (prefixes and suffixes)
      g. Recognizing compound words
      h. Recognizing consonant clusters (blends) and digraphs
      i. Recognizing the function of an apostrophe in contractions and possessives
   2. Determines the number of syllables in a word
   3. Applies syllabication rules to divide two-syllable words
   4. Recognizes synonyms, antonyms, and homonyms

B. Comprehension Skills
   1. Demonstrates ability to use skills taught in first and second grade, including
      a. Following oral and printed directions
      b. Understanding sequential order
      c. Remembering important details
      d. Recognizing multiple meanings of words
      e. Categorizing groups of like words
      f. Understanding that a pronoun may refer to a noun in a previous sentence or in the same sentence
      g. Deriving meaning from punctuation marks (. ? ! — , . . . " " :)
      h. Identifying the topic and/or main idea of a paragraph or story
      i. Drawing conclusions and making inferences
      j. Predicting outcomes
      k. Recognizing cause-effect relationships
   2. Derives additional meaning from punctuation:
      a. Commas for added emphasis
      b. Italics for emphasis
   3. Uses dictionary and glossary to locate information
   4. Draws appropriate conclusions
   5. Distinguishes cause-effect relationships
   6. Recognizes supporting detail

C. Literary Skills
   1. Distinguishes between fiction and nonfiction
   2. Distinguishes between fantasy and realistic fiction and between fact and opinion
   3. Recognizes elements of story:
      a. Character

       b. Setting

    4. Recognizes various types of literature: stories, plays, poems, and informational articles

Mathematics, Third-Grade Learning Objectives

A. Place Value and Counting
1. Demonstrates ability to use skills taught in first and second grade, including
   a. Identifying 1s, 10s, 100s, and 1,000s place
   b. Counting by ones to 999 and writing standard numerals
   c. Counting by twos, threes, fours, fives, tens, and twenty-fives
   d. Using ordinal numbers to the tenth place to indicate position in line
   e. Comparing numbers (greater than, less than)
2. Develops understanding of negative numbers
3. Rounds numbers to the nearest 10 and/or 100

B. Adding Whole Numbers
1. Demonstrates ability to use skills taught in second grade, including
   a. Addition facts through eighteen memorized
   b. Finding missing addends in basic addition problems
   c. Adding three or more single-digit numerals without regrouping
   d. Adding two-digit numerals with regrouping from 1s to 10s
   e. Estimating sums
2. Develops understanding of the properties of whole numbers and addition
3. Adds three- and four-digit numerals with regrouping in two places

C. Subtracting Whole Numbers
1. Demonstrates ability to use skills taught in second grade, including
   a. Subtraction facts through eighteen memorized
   b. Subtracting two-digit numerals with regrouping from 10s to 1s
   c. Developing mental math techniques (counting up, fact families)
2. Develops understanding of the properties of subtraction
3. Subtracts three-digit numerals with regrouping in two places
4. Estimates differences

D. Multiplying Whole Numbers
1. Demonstrates ability to use skills taught in second grade, including
   a. Understanding multiplication as repeated addition process
   b. Using objects to find the product of two numerals (5 or less)
2. Develops understanding of the properties of multiplication
3. Completes related multiplication sentences for basic facts through $9 \times 9 = 81$
4. Memorizes basic multiplication facts through $9 \times 9 = 81$

5. Multiplies by a two-digit numeral without regrouping
6. Multiplies by a two-digit numeral with regrouping

E. Dividing Whole Numbers
1. Understands division as sharing or separating to make equal groups
2. Perceives the relationship of multiplication to division
3. Completes related division sentences for basic facts through $81 \div 9 = 9$
4. Uses two-digit quotients and one-digit divisors with remainders

F. Fractions
1. Demonstrates ability to use skills taught in second grade, including
   a. Writing a fraction to identify part of a whole
   b. Writing a fraction to identify part of a set of objects
   c. Finding a fraction of a number
2. Compares and orders fractions
3. Computes with fractions and mixed numbers
4. Adds and subtracts like denominators
5. Converts decimals and fractions

G. Problem Solving and Applications
1. Demonstrates ability to use skills taught in second grade, including
   a. Solving problems using the following strategies:
      Missing data
      Making a list
      Looking for patterns
      Guessing and checking
      Using logical reasoning
      Drawing a picture
      Acting it out
   b. Determining reasonableness of answers by estimation
2. Chooses correct operation to solve word problems

H. Geometry
1. Demonstrates ability to use skills taught in second grade, including
   a. Identifying, sorting, and making solid figures
   b. Drawing and making plane figures
   c. Identifying and making symmetric and congruent figures
2. Identifies plane and space figures
3. Develops understanding of patterns, symmetry, and congruency

I. Measurement, Time, and Money
1. Demonstrates ability to use skills taught in second grade, including
   a. Identifying quarter and half-dollar
   b. Finding the value of a collection of coins, including pennies, nickels, dimes, and quarters (total less than $1.00)
   c. Measuring with nonstandard units
   d. Measuring to the nearest inch and centimeter
   e. Measuring weight with pounds
   f. Measuring mass with kilograms

g. Measuring capacity with cups, pints, quarts, and liters

h. Reading thermometers (Fahrenheit)

i. Beginning to tell time to nearest five-minute interval

2. Develops understanding of perimeter, area, weight, and volume

3. Compares units of temperature

4. Measures to nearest half-inch using inch, foot, and yard

5. Recognizes centimeter and meter as linear measures

6. Tells time from the hour to one-minute interval

7. Finds the value of a collection of coins (less than $2.00) and records the amount using correct symbols

8. Adds, subtracts, multiplies, and divides money

J. Decimals

1. Understands place value

2. Compares and orders decimals

3. Adds and subtracts decimals

4. Converts decimals and fractions

5. Rounds decimals

6. Relates decimals to money

K. Consumer Math

1. Applies mathematical knowledge in shopping and travel situations

L. Critical Thinking and Logic

1. Demonstrates ability to use skills taught in first and second grade, including

a. Predicting and verifying

b. Evaluating evidence and conclusions

c. Classifying and sorting

d. Comparing and contrasting

e. Using spatial visualization

f. Making generalizations

2. Understands patterns

3. Develops spatial visualization and logical reasoning

4. Evaluates and generalizes

M. Algebra

1. Understands and uses variables and equations

2. Develops knowledge of patterns, functions, relations, and algebraic expressions

N. Data Collection and Analysis

1. Collects and records data

2. Makes graphs

3. Makes questionnaires and tally charts

4. Takes surveys and summarizes results

O. Statistics and Problem Solving

1. Collects data

2. Presents data graphically

3. Makes choices based on probability

4. Makes predictions

P. Graphs and Graphing
   1. Demonstrates ability to use skills taught in first and second grade, including
      a. Making and using bar graphs
      b. Reading pictographs
   2. Uses various graphing methods

Fifth Grade

Language Arts, Fifth-Grade Learning Objectives

A. Composition Skills
   The student understands that writing is a process that may involve several steps: prewriting, writing, revising, and presenting.
   1. Writes for a specific purpose and audience
   2. Writes a topic sentence
   3. Constructs paragraphs
   4. Writes concluding statements
   5. Writes on a given topic
   6. Writes specific types of poetry
   7. Writes dialogue
   8. Writes paragraphs from notes
   9. Organizes information
   10. Lists sources of information
   11. Uses editing skills
   12. Writes and uses correct form of personal letter
   13. Begins writing business letter in correct form

B. Handwriting Skills
   1. Continues to demonstrate proper shape of letters
   2. Demonstrates uniform slant
   3. Leaves adequate margins
   4. Begins papers with proper headings

C. Language Study Skills
   1. Identifies the following parts of speech:
      a. Nouns
      b. Verbs
      c. Pronouns
      d. Adjectives, adverbs, and prepositions
      e. Conjunctions
   2. Uses correct verb tense and form
   3. Identifies forms of the verb *to be*
   4. Identifies noun and verb phrases
   5. Practices rules for capitalization
   6. Practices rules for punctuation

       7. Refines proofreading skill

D. Listening Skills
    1. Derives meaning from listening to oral reading of various forms of literature
    2. Understands oral directions
    3. Demonstrates appropriate etiquette as part of an audience
    4. Takes notes from oral information

E. Reference and Study Skills
    1. Uses library card catalog
    2. Demonstrates dictionary skills by locating words and interpreting pronunciation keys
    3. Locates and uses index
    4. Locates and uses table of contents
    5. Uses encyclopedia to locate information
    6. Takes notes from written material
    7. Begins to summarize information

F. Speaking Skills
    1. Reads with appropriate interpretation and expression
    2. Answers specific questions
    3. Speaks on a topic for a specific purpose
    4. Recites poetry

G. Spelling Skills
    1. Spells words at the fifth-grade level
    2. Learns weekly lists of words
    3. Applies spelling generalizations
    4. Writes spelling words from dictation
    5. Proofreads for spelling errors

Reading, Fifth-Grade Learning Objectives

A. Decoding Skills
    1. Uses prefixes, suffixes, and base words
    2. Applies pronunciation rules
    3. Uses accent marks
    4. Uses dictionary pronunciation key

B. Comprehension Skills
    1. Uses context clues
    2. Differentiates between facts and opinions
    3. Follows directions in sequence
    4. Identifies cause-effect relationships
    5. Draws conclusions
    6. Notes details
    7. Uses glossary and dictionary for word meanings
    8. Derives meaning from idioms, metaphors, and similes
    9. Recognizes main idea of paragraphs
   10. Identifies topic sentence

   11. Uses clue words to establish sequence
C. Literary Skills
   1. Recognizes types of literature
      a. Biography
      b. Autobiography
      c. Fiction
      d. Nonfiction
      e. Fantasy
   2. Identifies main and minor characters
   3. Distinguishes between narrative and dialogue
   4. Recognizes plot
   5. Identifies point of view
   6. Describes setting
   7. Identifies story elements

Mathematics, Fifth-Grade Learning Objectives

A. Place Value and Counting
   1. Uses critical thinking to find number patterns
   2. Understands the meaning of place value through millions
   3. Rounds numbers to the nearest 1,000 or 10,000
   4. Recognizes concept of one billion
   5. Explores algebra by evaluating algebra expressions with one variable

B. Multiplying Whole Numbers
   1. Divides three- and four-digit numerals by one- and two-digit divisors with and without zeros in the quotient

C. Fractions
   1. Uses the concept of least common multiple to determine the least common denominator
   2. Changes fractions to simplest forms, or lowest terms
   3. Adds fractions with and without like denominators
   4. Subtracts fractions with and without like denominators
   5. Adds mixed numerals with and without regrouping
   6. Subtracts mixed numerals with and without regrouping
   7. Multiplies a fraction by a fraction

D. Decimals
Most mathematics programs integrate decimals with whole numbers for all operations.
   1. Recognizes decimals to thousandths
   2. Practices adding and subtracting decimals
   3. Begins to multiply by hundredths
   4. Divides a decimal by a whole numeral
   5. Rounds decimals to the nearest whole numeral or thousandth place

E. Problem Solving and Applications
Most math programs integrate critical thinking, problem solving, and math reasoning into every major unit of instruction.
1. Solves story problems using one or more whole number operations
2. Solves problems using measurements drawn to scale
3. Solves computer and calculator problems

F. Geometry
1. Identifies and measures acute, right, and obtuse angles
2. Investigates, identifies, and measures perimeter, area, and volume of common types of triangles, quadrilaterals, polygons, and circles

G. Measurement: Customary and Metric
1. Recognizes millimeter as unit of measurement
2. Adds and subtracts linear measures using fractions to the nearest sixteenth of an inch or to the nearest millimeter
3. Understands, calculates, and uses appropriate units of measurement for linear distance, area, volume, weight, time, and temperature

H. Ratios and Percentages
1. Solves proportions
2. Writes ratios/fractions as percentages and vice versa
3. Finds percentages of a number

I. Probability
1. Finds probability of equally likely outcomes
2. Conducts experiments to compare experimental with mathematical probability
3. Uses critical thinking and simulations to predict possible outcomes

Reading Log

Name _____

Week of _____

Read for 20 minutes a day.

Date	Book		Pages	Tell about the book or chapter you read. Boring? Good? Interesting? Fantastic? Funny? Scary? Why?
Monday	Title			
	Author			
Tuesday	Title			
	Author			
Wednesday	Title			
	Author			
Thursday	Title			
	Author			
Friday	Title			
	Author			
Saturday	Title			
	Author			
Sunday	Title			
	Author			

7 CHAPTER

Developing Partnerships With Parents

....

As a beginning teacher, you have probably received little information on dealing with parents. Yet this is a crucial part of your job. Parents need to be involved in their children's school life. Research confirms that parent involvement in the education of their children is fundamental to effective teaching. Parent involvement improves student achievement, attitudes toward learning, and self-esteem. Teachers who undertake strong comprehensive parent involvement efforts and have strong linkages to the communities they serve are much more apt to have high-performing, well-behaved students. Parent involvement in children's education is more important to student success than family income or educational level.

Although extremely important, developing partnerships with parents is not always easy. Some parents have attitudes toward school that make initial efforts at two-way communication difficult. Time and tact are necessary to enlist them as allies. In some communities, parents feel intimidated by schools and may at first respond with sensitive, negative, or even hostile emotions. Some parents may think the school's values conflict with their own values or religious beliefs. Other parents may have busy work schedules that prevent them from participating in classroom activities when they would sincerely love to be involved. On the other hand, parents in a number of communities will be exceptionally interested and available, ready to respond to your every request. Research shows that children, especially children from low-income, ethnically diverse neighborhoods, experience greater success when their teachers consistently involve their parents and build on the strengths of their families.

Seek to establish positive relationships with all the parents of your students early in the school year. Most parents are willing to help however they can, but it is up to you to contact them first. For example, consider calling home to parents in early September to introduce yourself and begin establishing positive interactions. By doing so, at least you will make dealing with any later problems an easier task.

If you are unfamiliar with the community, get to know as much about it as you can. Drive around, go into stores, read the local newspaper, or even ride the school bus.

Remember that more and more contemporary children live in one-parent homes and that one in four children has stepparents. Others live with adoptive or foster parents or with relatives or guardians. *Parents* is used in this chapter to refer to all primary caregivers.

Getting to Know Parents

Use your mental image of what it means to be a professional to help you decide exactly how you will help parents get involved. Discuss this with your mentor. How do other teachers in your school develop partnerships with parents?

Early in the school year, send a letter home to each parent and/or student, welcoming the student into your classroom and briefly outlining expectations and needed supplies. You can also let parents know your procedures regarding students' absences and homework. Samples of such new school year letters are provided in Resources 7.1, 7.2, and 7.3.

Decide to what extent you want parents to participate on a daily basis in your classroom. As a general rule, you will want only two parent volunteers in the room at one time. Schedule volunteers for certain days in specific time slots. As I discussed in the first chapter, some of the ways parents can assist in the classroom include

- Reading with individual children
- Supervising learning or interest center activities
- Taking dictation writing from children
- Laminating and binding children's stories
- Correcting student papers
- Filing
- Changing bulletin board displays
- Helping children with arts and crafts projects

Resource 7.4 is a sample letter asking for parent help. If you do choose to use parents as volunteers, check school policies and informal norms about parents in the classroom. Also, find out if parents are allowed to drop in to observe your class and, if so, what procedures they are expected to follow.

As a rule, parent participation in schoolwide functions will vary. Discuss with your mentor which events specifically invite parents. Use a district calendar and your mentor's experience to highlight and plan for these regular activities. Examples include open house, back-to-school night, parent-teacher conferences, school music programs, fund-raisers, and sports events.

Before the opening day of school, ask your mentor or a teacher who had some of your students last year to suggest the name of a parent who might be willing to volunteer in your classroom for at least the first few days of school. Call this parent and ask if she or he would help get the year under way. Especially if you do not have an aide, the parent helper can answer questions, answer the door or the class phone, take students in the wrong classroom to the correct one, and generally assist you in getting off to a smooth start.

Plan to contact parents as often as you can during the school year using memos, notices, student work, newsletters, phone calls, visits, progress reports, report cards, meetings, and conferences to provide information to families. A weekly student-produced newsletter or "Friday Flier" is an excellent method of keeping parents informed of what is happening in the classroom. Here are some quick and easy ways to write a newsletter:

Quick Ways to Write a Student Newsletter and Actively Involve Your Students

Grades K-2

At the close of each day, have the children brainstorm things they worked on that day. List suggested topics on chart paper. Decide what should go into the newsletter, and write it by the appropriate day on an enlarged newsletter form. On Fridays, fill in the newsletter (see page 175) just before lunch. Copy it for each child and send it home Friday afternoon.

Grades 2-4

Give each child a copy of the newsletter form (see page 175) on Monday. Brainstorm things worked on each day. Children can decide what will go into the newsletter and record it themselves from ideas listed on chart paper. This could be done individually, in small groups, or as a whole class.

Grades 4-6

Do a newsletter for the week as a summary activity on Friday. Help your class list ideas from the week. Then, as a writing assignment, have them write a weekly newsletter. Model the process several times, but let students compose their own newsletter entries. This is a great way to work on grammar, communicate with parents, and review what has been worked on in class. Remember to proofread!

Student Newsletter Form

Ask an artistic child (or children) to create a fancy heading with name of school, room number, and names of students. Duplicate multiple copies and fill in each week.

Room _____ Newsletter

Week of: _____

Monday:

Tuesday:

Wednesday:

Thursday:

Friday:

Notes and reminders:

Contacting Parents

Letters from the teacher to parents should usually be in formal typewritten form and should certainly be proofread. It is important to appear competent and professional, especially during your beginning years, when parents and community are still getting to know you. State your purpose clearly. Decide whether to request proof of receipt, either in a return note or a signature on the original letter. It helps students remember to give school correspondence to their parents when you require a returned signature. It is imperative that parents with limited English receive information in their primary language. Check with your site administrator for translators.

In addition to welcoming the student and introducing yourself, a first-day letter home can also inform parents about the following:

- Classroom rules and procedures
- Homework policies
- List of ways parents can get involved
- Forms that must be returned to school
- An invitation to call you at school with questions (include phone number)

Check to see if a parent handbook is sent home to parents from the school office. Sometimes your principal will send a school newsletter home on the first day, too. Adapt your letter to harmonize with the amount of information that is provided by the school itself.

Many times, the best way to communicate with a parent is by phone. School phones may be used for such purposes. Before contacting parents, consider the following:

- What you will say (Make notes in advance about what you would like to say, and keep the conversation focused.)
- When you will call (Decide the hour of your call.)
- How you will sound (Immediately put the parent at ease with a friendly tone.)
- What you are saying (Take notes, including the date.)
- What you will do in the event that the telephone number is false or is really the number of an older student's room at home
- How to end the conversation (Make an agreement and a plan to follow up.)

In addition, if the purpose of your call is to set up a conference, consider beforehand exactly how you will ask the parent(s) to come to school and meet with you. State the goals of the meeting. Describe the problem briefly and objectively. Indicate past efforts by you and/or the school to address the problem. Outline the proposed home-school collaboration. Reinforce any past support and willingness to confer. Make notes of what was agreed on, and let the parent(s) know you are looking forward to the meeting.

Dealing With Many Different and Sometimes Difficult Parents

As I mentioned earlier, parents' attitudes may differ toward your school and toward schooling in general. Some parents will naturally be easier to work with than others. Whatever attitude parents bring to school, it is your responsibility to establish and maintain a positive relationship. Usually, poor attitudes reflect poor communication or a lack of communication between you and the parent. The parent, in the meantime, has made certain assumptions and is acting as if these assumptions are true.

Here are a few examples of the many types of parents with whom you will interact:

Belligerent. Many times, belligerent parents wish to address a perceived wrongdoing. Do not let their initial anger intimidate you. After greeting them politely, ask them to tell you what the problem is. Then listen carefully. You may find that you are not really at fault. For instance, a beginning teacher had a first-grade student who typically arrived at school an hour late. The teacher set up a conference with the parents to discuss the tardiness problem. The teacher didn't realize that the parents felt threatened and belligerent at being asked to come to school to discuss it. In the parents' view, the early grades of school consisted primarily of fun and games, and it was therefore unimportant exactly what time the child arrived.

Such a situation takes every bit of your diplomacy and tact. But don't back down. In this case, the teacher felt that chronic tardiness was a serious problem needing to be discussed in a forthright manner. The teacher explained to the parents her belief that the child was learning a bad habit that would hurt the child later on. The parents were able to "hear" the teacher's sincere conviction that school, even first grade, is important and requires a commitment by everyone—the student, the parents, and the teacher. Lack of commitment and effort would result in the student's doing poorly in school. The teacher's sincerity, concern, and care not to blame the parents turned a potentially difficult situation into a healthy one. The teacher asked the parents to help get the child to school before the tardy bell and expressed support for their efforts. The next week, when the student arrived on time several days in a row, the teacher wrote the parents a note appreciating their efforts and describing how their child was enjoying and participating in the morning circle activities in a special role as calendar monitor.

Indifferent. Indifferent parents appear to have little or no interest in their children's schoolwork or activities. They rarely come to school or return necessary forms on time, if at all. When you try to contact them by phone or notes, you wait a long time for a reply, or worse, you hear nothing at all. You may feel tempted to end further efforts to get in touch with these parents. You are busy, and it seems a waste of time. It is important to maintain contact through notes, memos, and calls, however, even if you do not hear back from them. In the meantime, verify information such as telephone numbers and addresses with your school's main office. Let your mentor and principal know about your efforts to contact this child's parent(s) and the results. Keep a record of your attempts, because occasionally you need to refer to this record at a later date.

Reluctant. You may hear sporadically from reluctant parents, but not as often as you would like. You wish you had more opportunity to talk with them about their children's progress or lack thereof. Sometimes, the students may volunteer information about their home situation that sheds light on your difficulty in establishing two-way communication. Nevertheless, do not give up on your attempts to involve these families.

Cooperative. These parents are usually a joy to work with. They return requests for information promptly and assist whenever asked. One or two of these parents can be recruited as "class parents" (formerly called "room mothers"!) who serve as liaisons between you and the other parents—arranging volunteer schedules, planning class celebrations, driving for field trips, organizing fundraising, and so on. Let them know you appreciate their efforts!

Interested. These parents are also cooperative and fairly easy to work with. In some cases, however, they seem to be overly concerned about their children's social or academic progress. Perhaps there is a valid reason. After all, parents know their children best. Sometimes, children are experiencing difficulties of which you are unaware. Make an effort to invite the parents for a conference to answer their questions, discuss their concerns, and share their knowledge of their children. If there is a problem, you will have an opportunity to help solve it.

Unfortunately, many contemporary parents lack the time or opportunity to get involved in their children's school as much as you or they might like. They still care deeply for their children, however, and desire a quality education for them. Let all parents know how much you value and encourage their support and participation in this important part of their children's lives. Anticipate that they will respond in a positive way and in any manner they can. Once you have reached out to them, encouraged an honest exchange of expectations, and invited them to keep you informed of important events in their children's lives, you can look forward to a rewarding partnership and a smooth school year.

Conducting Parent Conferences

The parent-teacher conference is the most commonly used means of sharing information between the home and the school. Many schools schedule two regular conferences per year, fall and spring, to coincide with report card periods. Often, one specific day or a series of minimum days are set aside each year for conferences. Individual conferences last twenty to thirty minutes. Check your school policy regarding these annual conferences. Of course, you can schedule additional conferences with parents as needed.

Inform parents ahead of time about the purposes of the conference. A sample letter to send home prior to your meeting is provided in Resource 7.5.

Be prepared to listen. Parents often come with their own concerns. Asking an open-ended question at the beginning of the conference gives them the opportunity to express their interests and/or worries. Also, many of your parents and students will have different backgrounds, attitudes, beliefs, and socioeconomic status than your own. You need to help them feel welcome and comfortable. Host them graciously.

It is sometimes helpful to ask students to participate in conferences, especially if there are behavior problems to resolve. This can help clear the air and ensure that everyone understands the expectations. On the other hand, students who are doing well enjoy being complimented in front of their parents.

Be prepared with ideas for parents to help their children at home. For example, prepare handouts of curriculum outlines, grading procedures, homework criteria, and so forth. Share a list of upcoming projects that would benefit from parent monitoring and assistance. You will handle this differently depending on the student, the parent, and the material. Have a list of good books your students can read alone or parents can read to them. (See Resource 4.1 for a list of outstanding read-aloud books.) Also, share suggestions of good children's magazines, educational TV shows, and library and museum programs. You may be surprised at the number of parents who are unaware of the variety of enrichment opportunities available. If you choose to have parents work with their children on particular skills, provide them with specific directions and materials.

If you plan to share standardized test scores with parents, be ready to explain what these scores indicate, as well as what they are *not* intended to mean. Your district may have a policy on this. Check it out ahead of time.

Have samples of each student's work ready. Dated samples showing improvement or decline help provide specific information for parents and direction for the discussion. Avoid comparing the student's work with that of other students. Mention something about each student's strengths as well as areas that need improvement.

Suggestions for Getting Through the Conference

Think about the four purposes of a typical conference: information getting, information giving, joint problem solving, and development of mutual trust. The conference is also a good time to get parents to sign necessary forms.

Collect all needed materials for each child in a folder, with folders ready on a table. Side-by-side seating (instead of your sitting behind your desk) is less formal and less intimidating to most parents. Set a positive climate by introducing yourself with a smile and a friendly voice and establishing a feeling of caring and collaboration. Set out a bouquet of flowers, a dish of candy, and toys for younger siblings whom the parent might have to bring to the conference.

Try to get a realistic picture of the home situation before you make any suggestions about the student. Often, your perspective is changed when you understand the student's background. Find out what you can about the child's history *before* the conference. Review cum files, former teachers' notes, social/discipline history, referrals for testing, past standardized test results, and report cards. Changes in family structure such as divorce, death, birth, and so on are also helpful to know.

Ask the parents for their perception of their child's strengths and weaknesses before offering yours. Seek their input. Discussing the child's strengths first helps relax ill-at-ease parents. Encourage them to tell you what they expect of their child, of you, and of your school. Their facial expressions, gestures, and tone of voice can provide clues concerning their feelings for the child. Always give parents the chance to express possible reasons for a child's poor work or misbehavior in the classroom, explore the possibilities together, and discuss strategies that might help the child. Thank them for their helpful insights. Avoid using "educationese." Use language to which parents can relate, but be positive and professional, too.

Conversely, do not let a parent berate you. If a parent becomes verbally abusive, simply say, "I do not think that the purposes of this conference are being met. Perhaps we can schedule another conference date." Never argue with parents. The next conference should be scheduled in the school office with an administrator and/or union representative. If you expect a difficult conference, ask the principal or a more appropriate person, such as the special education director or the vice principal, to sit in.

If you suspect that some parents may not speak English, ask their children if this is the case. Unless you are fluent in their language, arrange for an interpreter to attend. If the school does not have an interpreter, suggest that parents bring a close friend or adult family member along. It is usually best not to ask the child to translate. For any of your students who attend special programs, either get information from their other teachers to relay to parents or ask other teachers to sit in on the conference.

During the conference, avoid negative expressions, such as "troublemaker," "lazy," and "sloppy." Put yourself in the parent's place. How would you feel? Instead, substitute positive suggestions and/or specific descriptions of the behavior. Rather than "sloppy," you might say, "could do neater work"; rather than "lazy," "has a chance to earn a higher grade"; rather than "hyperactive," "often out of seat without permission"; and so forth. Be extremely circumspect about using labels such as ADHD, dyslexic, and learning disabled.

Stick to your schedule during the conference day or evening. Especially if other parents are waiting, and the parent seems reluctant to respond to your lead, ask if you can schedule another time and date to finish up loose ends.

You may need to set up a special conference to focus on a specific problem situation. Your purpose in this type of conference is to define and clarify an issue and make plans to solve it. Here are some tips to make this sort of problem-solving conference go more smoothly:

- Tackle only one problem at a time—don't try to change everything at once!

- Choose what seems to be the most critical problem.

- Refer to records and notes to support any additional type of intervention, if needed.

- Outline the proposed home-school collaboration.

- Plan for follow-up. For example, will you send home a daily report, and will they return the completed form to you?

- Allow an hour for any specially scheduled problem-solving conference.

- Make agreements and responsibilities extremely clear at the end of the conference. Write them down. Give parents a copy.

End the conference on an upbeat, positive note. If you have agreed to find out information for the parent or send information home, add it to your "to do" list and keep your word.

Whether the conference was a regular school event or a special meeting to discuss a problem, spend a few moments afterward to assess its effectiveness. Ask yourself the following questions:

- How well prepared was I?

- How well did I use time?

- Did I start on a positive note?

- Did I listen attentively?

- Did I involve the parents?

- Were follow-up plans made, if needed?

- Did I gain any insights?

- What needs to be changed?

Back-to-School Night
and Open House

In most schools, your first formal introduction to parents will be in the form of some sort of "Meet the Teachers" event, such as "September Open House" or "Back-to-School Night." To prepare, talk with colleagues to find out what parents at your school normally expect from this session.

In some schools, a back-to-school night is held in the fall, and an open house is scheduled in the spring to showcase what your students have been doing all year. If your school does not schedule these events, consider holding a parent orientation meeting in September just for your own class.

Back-to-School Night

Traditionally, back-to-school night has been a schoolwide event at which teachers communicate to parents their discipline policies, schedules, academic programs, homework policies, and so forth. In most cases, the teacher talks almost every minute of the allocated hour.

Consider giving parents a more active role. How can you transform back-to-school night into a process that promotes the concept of parents as partners with teachers in the education of their children? Here are some suggested goals for your back-to-school night:

- To build relationships with and among parents

- To build a strong home-school connection in which parents feel like partners in their children's education

- To inform yourself and your instructional program with the ideas and expectations of parents

- To inform parents about the academic and social program, expectations, and standards in the classroom

Preparing for back-to-school night is demanding and exciting. Just as for the opening day of school, you should be *over*prepared. Because you are a first-year teacher, many parents may be coming to "check you out." Your classroom should be spotlessly clean and organized, with bright bulletin boards and student work on display. Some teachers even decorate the chalkboards with student work to dress up the classroom and give it a finished look. Hang student projects from the ceiling, too. Place additional work in special folders or booklets on each student's desk. Parents enjoy looking through their children's accomplishments, and this gives any early birds something to do. Make sure that you have names on all desks and that students have cleaned their desks inside and out.

Write the daily schedule on the board so parents can actually see what their children do each hour they are at school. Have a sign-in sheet ready for parents and a welcome sign outside your classroom door with the room number and your name. Set out extra chairs for students who participate that night and for grandparents or additional adults who attend.

Agenda

Carefully plan your agenda for the evening. Not only must your classroom look great, but also you must be well organized and your student participants well prepared. Here are some possible agenda items:

1. Welcome (Warmly greet parents and students as they arrive.)
2. Get-acquainted activity (optional, depending on time available)
3. Parents as partners

   - Let parents know that you see them as important partners in their children's education and want to learn what their expectations are for the year.

   - You could combine a get-acquainted activity with this step by asking parents to introduce themselves to another parent and share on this topic: What do you want your child to gain from school this year?

   - Conduct a whole-group brainstorm, and record parent responses to the question on chart paper with colored pens.

4. Teacher's presentation of goals and classroom educational program

   Now you can link your instructional program with what parents want for their children. Refer to the list as you present your goals and program. Here you have the opportunity to communicate your sense of purpose as an educator. Be sure to emphasize that you have high expectations for the academic success of each child. Instead of giving parents a list of policies and schedules, share the heart of your program with them. Focus on curriculum and highlights of the year.

5. Question/answer period

   Allow several minutes to answer specific parent questions. If some parents tend to monopolize the time (often with questions about their own children), say, "Our goal tonight is to overview the instructional program, but I would be happy to meet with you for an appointment at another time." Let parents know your door is always open.

6. Homework and discipline policies

   These policies are fundamental to share with parents. Instead of presenting them in detail, consider preparing a handout of these important items that you will not have time to go into extensively during the presentation. If you do not have time to prepare the handout before back-to-school night, let them know orally and through a posted sign that you will be sending home a letter with these policies soon. A sample letter is provided in Resource 7.6.

7. Continuing communication and volunteers

Let parents know that you will be communicating with them throughout the year and that they are always welcome to send you a note, give you a call, or make an appointment. Let them know how to contact you. Write the school phone number on the board and, if you wish, your home number, too. Use the evening as an opportunity to recruit volunteers. Provide a sign-up sheet.

Other Considerations

You may want to involve students in back-to-school night. If you are far enough into the school year, students could share examples of each concrete element of the curriculum as you explain it (e.g., literature response journals, writing folders, and computer logs). Specific students could also lead different center activities and explain to parents various other aspects of the instructional program. All students should give their parents a tour of the work areas in the classroom.

With these preparations, your back-to-school night will be a success. You will find it was worth the extra effort to start the school year in such a positive manner.

After back-to-school night, the faculty of many schools meet for dinner at a local restaurant. Join them. Allow yourself this celebration time for socializing, comparing experiences, and relaxing.

Open House

Preparations for open house in the spring (usually May) are similar to those for the back-to-school event in the fall. Rather than introducing parents to your curriculum and expectations, however, the major goal in a spring open house is celebrating students' accomplishments. Make your classroom come alive with student projects and displays. Showcase major reports completed by your students several weeks prior to open house night, such as a state, country, or animal project. The spring of the year is an especially good time to have students take an active role in planning and presenting the open house program for their parents. Select a student committee to help you pick out papers for display. Have students write invitations to their parents. Perhaps your class would like to select a student master of ceremonies. At the least, each child should prepare to serve as a tour guide who will explain the year's highlights to his or her parents. Make open house an interactive learning experience for parents and students.

Building Relationships
With Parents

Your goal is to build a trusting relationship with parents. In addition to traditional school events such as back-to-school night, open house, and conferences, develop regular communication with parents via phone calls and newsletters from the start of the school year. Schedule meetings throughout the year for which parents contribute to the agenda. Recognize parents for the positive things they do to help their children succeed. Your perspective can be one of a learner, too. Certainly an attitude that reflects that you have all the answers shuts down two-way communication. Project your belief that you also have much to learn—especially about your students as individual learners. Open up two-way communication, and invite parents to be your partners. It's worth the time and effort. Building positive home-school relationships will make a much smoother school year for you and for your students.

RESOURCE

Sample New School Year Letter
to Parents of K-1 Children

....

Date

Dear Parents:

It's exciting for me to start another school year at _____
[school name] with your children. I did notice a few frightened faces and
a few slow steps into Room 111, but believe me, this is normal.

The following are a few suggestions that you might want to consider:

1. Put names on all materials brought to school.
2. Put names inside any clothing that your child might take off and
   misplace.
3. Have a set bedtime on school nights, so your child is not tired in
   school.

We do provide some basic supplies. If you want to supplement these, the
following is a suggested supply list that may be helpful:

1. Shoe box or cigar box for supplies
2. Pencils, crayons, paste, and blunt scissors
3. Folders with pockets for carrying papers home
4. Old sock to store chalk and erase student chalkboards

I am looking forward to meeting and working with all of you. If you need
to contact me, I am available at school from 7:30 a.m. to 3:30 p.m. daily.
You can reach me through the office by calling _____. If I am
unavailable, I will return your call as soon as possible.

Cordially yours,

Sample New School Year Letter to Parents of Children in Grades 2–3

....

Date

Dear Parents:

I look forward to sharing a successful year with your child. Second grade has many new and exciting experiences in store. Together we can share in the growth and development of your second grader.

It would be helpful if your child could bring the following items:

1. Gym shoes for gym day
2. Art shirt with your child's name
3. Box of tissues to share
4. School box to keep in desk
5. Small spiral notebook

Please make certain that all your child's clothes, supplies, and personal items are clearly marked with your child's name.

If at any time you have questions or concerns, feel free to contact me. I look forward to meeting you at our Back-to-School Night on _____.

Sincerely,

Sample New School Year Letter to Parents of Children in Grades 4–6

Date

Dear Parents:

A new school year is here, and I would like to take this opportunity to tell you that I am excited about it—and I hope your child is, too. Fifth grade is an exciting learning year. Children begin to progress rapidly and pick up new ideas quickly.

The daily schedule for the fifth grade is as follows: I will teach Reading, English, Spelling, Creative Writing, and Social Studies (Science will replace Social Studies in the second semester) to your child every day. From 12:05 to 1:00 each afternoon, the fifth graders will go to Mrs. _____'s room for Math. Mrs. _____ is currently on maternity leave and is being replaced by Mrs. _____ for approximately six weeks. This schedule will help the children get used to having more than one teacher but also provide the benefits of having a homeroom.

Please take a moment to look over the notes and papers your child brings home each day, and remember to look for the Friday folder that will be sent home each week containing the work your child has completed and other important information.

I am looking forward to getting to know you and your child better. Please make every effort to attend the Back-to-School Night on September 22 at 7:30 p.m. If you have questions before then, please feel free to call the school at _____ and leave a message. I will get in touch with you as soon as possible.

Once again, I am looking forward to an exciting year with a lot of learning taking place. I will see you at Back-to-School Night on September 22.

Sincerely,

Date

Dear Parents:

I realize you are busy with your jobs, lives, and families. If time permits, I'd love your help in the classroom. Please take a few minutes to look over the list below to see if you can help.

- Typing/computer work (commitment: twice a week)
- Handling book club orders (commitment: once a month or every six to ten weeks)
- Working with individuals or a small group with math (commitment: once a month to several times a week)
- Listening to children read aloud (commitment: once a month to several times a week)
- Serving as room parent (general support for class parties and field trips)
- Talking to the class or small group about your career (commitment: one time to be arranged after December)
- Cooking with a small group of students
- Reading to the class once a week
- Anything I missed? _____

If you have any questions or need more information before making a commitment, please feel free to call me at school (phone number) or home (phone number).

Sincerely,

RESOURCE

Sample Parent-Teacher Conference Letter

···

Date

Dear Parents:

Next week, you and I have a special opportunity to talk about a very special person. That special person is your child.

I want to be as well prepared as possible, and I know you feel the same way.

When we meet, I'll be talking about the following:

1. What we're doing in class this year and what I expect of all students
2. How well your youngster is doing and what he or she needs to work on
3. How you and I can work together to help your youngster get the most out of this class (school)

You probably have some things that you want to talk about, too, and perhaps some questions on how you can help. Because of the limited time we have scheduled, it would help if I knew what questions and concerns you have ahead of time. There is some space below to jot down any questions or concerns that you might have. Either send them back to school with your child or bring them with you when you come to conferences.

Questions I have:

_____

_____

_____

_____

Thank you for your help.

Cordially,

Sample Letter Informing Parents About Homework

Date

Dear Parents:

This is a note about homework. Your child will have homework every weekday night except Fridays. The intent of the homework is threefold:

1. It helps to build responsibility in the children, because they are responsible for the completion and the transportation of the work.
2. It gives the students an opportunity to practice skills taught in the class.
3. It gives you a chance to become involved with your child's class work.

Children are most successful with homework if the time and place for it are consistent. A quiet area to work and a regular time such as right before or after dinner seem to be the most beneficial.

Below is a copy of your student's regular homework schedule. Please keep it as a reminder.

Thank you,

- -

Homework schedule for (child's name) _____

Monday: _____

Tuesday: _____

Wednesday: _____

Thursday: _____

(Teacher lists all regularly scheduled homework, such as spelling practice lists on Mondays and Wednesdays, math skills on Tuesdays and Thursdays, independent reading every school night.)

8 CHAPTER

Frequently Asked Questions (and Answers!)

··

When experienced teachers talk about their most difficult problems during their first years of teaching, they mention classroom management and discipline most often. It is normal to feel insecure about managing your first classroom. Even when your students are for the most part happy and well behaved, you are still likely to encounter a number of anxious situations and problems.

Many of the problems associated with behavior management are dealt with through preventive, proactive approaches. Through the years, effective teachers develop strategies that work for them consistently, fit their personalities, and are relatively easy for them to implement. You will learn what works best for you to gain students' cooperation and respect and how to tailor various suggestions to meet the needs of specific situations and students. Actively search for ideas. Ask other teachers, "How do you handle the situation when you must deal with _____?" or "What do you do when students do _____?"

Following are some specific questions that beginning teachers ask. Seemingly insurmountable problems may appear less so as you take a few minutes to review these questions and answers.

Entire Class Is Misbehaving

I hate to admit it, but there are times when my whole class is misbehaving! Sometimes, the students are just too rambunctious, or the room gets chaotic during small-group activity time, or someone makes an annoying noise and the whole class begins giggling uncontrollably. What should I do to get them back on track?

Any time the class as a whole gets too noisy or exhibits inappropriate behavior, turn off the lights. Keep the lights off until the class settles down. Explain to students that the lights-out signal means they have misbehaved and that therefore the entire class must stay in from recess sitting quietly at their desks for two minutes plus the time the lights are out. Record the amount of time owed in a corner of the chalkboard. There is no need to scold them. Losing recess time is a sufficient consequence. Repeat this procedure any time student behavior gets out of hand. The time owed is paid back only when students are quiet. Therefore, if students are noisy during payback time, they don't begin to pay back the time until they have been quiet for the allotted number of minutes. Some teachers have children put their heads down on their desks during the quiet time. Use this technique sparingly. Be cautious about imposing consequences for whole-group misbehavior if the problem is really only a few troublemakers.

If two or more students are setting each other off, stop what you're doing and wait for them to be quiet. Sometimes, students are reinforcing each other's misbehavior. If you determine that it is only a few kids causing the problem, have the individuals owe one minute from recess for each misbehavior. Record minutes owed on a daily record sheet. The individual students must pay back this time by sitting quietly at their desks until the time is paid back.

Usually, it is best to continue teaching your lesson and praise students who are cooperating with you. If children are unsuccessful in getting attention from you or the other kids for misbehaving, they will stop. When the students begin to behave, praise them. Show them that you are aware of their efforts and are pleased, but be consistent in requiring that time be paid back for misbehavior.

In administering any consequence, remember to implement it in a calm, neutral, nonemotional manner. You're simply enacting a previously agreed-on consequence of behavior, and there is no need to get angry while you do so. Your nonpunitive attitude will go a long way toward minimizing the bad feelings that tend to result when students must face the consequences of their misbehavior.

Students Are Apathetic About Poor Performance and Grades

When I have to give certain pupils a zero, they shrug, saying, "Zero is just another number. I don't care." How do I deal with such apathy?

Students who are apathetic have probably experienced a lot of failure in the past and have, in essence, given up trying. Because they imagine being unsuccessful this time, why should the students bother? In working with such students, you may feel tempted to give up, too. It seems impossible to convince these kids that they *can* succeed. Instead of lecturing, try to give jobs and activities that the students can handle successfully, perhaps designing a bulletin board or some other creative task. Then praise the students for a job well done. When the students make apathetic remarks, ignore the negative and concentrate on the positive. Point out the students' talents.

Make sure you provide academic assignments in which the children can succeed. Focus on the students' interests. Try taping a story, reading picture books to younger students in the school, shortening the spelling list, or focusing on one type of math problem.

Some students, especially those with learning disabilities, seem to have no idea whether they have passing or failing grades. School grading seems to be a complete mystery. They may make high grades on some tests but forget to turn in homework, not complete class projects, and end up with a failing grade overall. They remember the occasional high grades and are baffled by the overall failing grade. They feel confused and may conclude that regardless of how hard they try, they are going to fail anyway.

If you have students in danger of failing, you, the parents, and the student might jointly develop a plan to monitor school grades or homework completion on a weekly basis. The students could keep a running tally of grades and regularly confer with you about how they are doing. Some teachers of students who are apathetic have found success by helping the students graph their grades. Charting weekly grades on graph paper may give them the visual aid they need to realize what grades actually mean. Encourage them to decrease the distance between the high and low points of their grades on the graph. The children can visually observe improvements in their grades, which provides concrete positive feedback.

Students Are Not Bringing in Materials for Projects

We're short of supplies, and I've asked students to bring in various "junk" items for art projects, such as orange juice cans, egg cartons, hangers, scraps of fabric, and string. Few bother to do so, however. What should I do?

You might get better results by sending home a short note to parents requesting these and other needed items. If you provided a sign-up sheet for parent volunteers during your back-to-school night, check this list for help. Explain that you need their assistance to give their children supplementary learning experiences. Parents whose schedules will not allow them to volunteer in the classroom are often pleased to help by providing arts and crafts materials. Contact them.

Actively enlist the students' help through election or appointment of a materials committee. Suggest they do a phone tree to remind each other to bring designated items. Write a reminder on the board each day. Let students know you will have to postpone the project until you find a way to obtain these materials. Also, discuss the supplies problem with colleagues. Perhaps you can set up an exchange, through which each of you can help the other gather and share materials for a given project.

Students Are Not Cleaning Up After Themselves

I am tired of cleaning up after my students. They just won't stop an art project or center activity when I announce cleanup time. They dawdle, and I end up scolding, nagging, and doing too much of it myself. I'm exhausted. Help!

It is much more fun to continue with an art project or center activity than to stop and clean up. Decide if you are allowing enough cleanup time. You probably need at least ten minutes. Then explain the time allotment to the students. Write it on the chalkboard, and start a countdown. Note every elapsed minute (and announce in a referee's voice) on the chalkboard. Don't nag or scold. If they can get the room cleaned up by the time limit (without running or pushing!), give a group reward such as leaving for recess five minutes early, marbles in the jar (see description later in this chapter), or stickers on the chart. Each time the class cleans up, discuss what their previous cleanup time was. Begin timing to see if they can break the record. Make cleaning up a fun activity, too.

Students Are Not Doing Homework

The same four or five students in my fifth-grade class fail to bring in their homework almost every day. They always have an excuse for missing homework. What should I do?

Students sometimes don't do homework because they believe it is not really important to the teacher. For instance, one teacher had a "time-saving" idea that backfired: Instead of collecting homework every day, the teacher had students keep it in a folder and collected it only once a week for recording. The students gradually did less and less of their homework.

As you collect homework, make sure you verbally acknowledge each student who has it completed, correct it promptly, and discuss the answers in class. If you show you care, students are more likely to care also. Let your students know that incomplete homework will have to be done before participating in a recreation activity planned for later in the day.

Figure out how much homework is appropriate for your students' ability levels. For example, thirty minutes a day is reasonable for fifth graders. It is also important to inform parents about homework in your class. See the sample letter in Resource 7.6.

The threat of a lowered grade for incomplete homework seldom motivates elementary children to do it consistently. The report card seems a long way off and unrelated. Elementary kids perform better when the teacher notices and praises their homework efforts each day. They also do better when some fun might be involved.

Some teachers give students who have turned in homework on time a special privilege, such as five minutes of extra time at morning recess. The privilege could be extended on a different day each week, so students are never quite sure which day their homework might influence the privilege. Other teachers declare a "No Homework Day" after a predetermined number of consecutive days in which everyone completes and returns homework assignments. Others bestow occasional "Homework Certificates" allowing recipients to turn in the certificate rather than completed assignments.

For students who seem incapable of completing independent work, first carefully verify that the work is of an appropriate difficulty level. Then sit down individually with the students and arrange homework contracts (see Resource 5.4) with them.

Some students have non-homework-friendly home environments. You might need to approach students individually to find out how to help them arrange to do homework in the library or classroom after school.

Students Are Slow to Shift From Task to Task

When it is time to move on to a different subject, my kids seem to take a long time to settle down to the next task. How can I get students to move more quickly and work more efficiently?

These children may not know how transitions should take place. In addition, they are probably not held accountable for moving efficiently from one task to another.

Take another look at your transitions. Do you keep your students waiting too long between lessons or activities? Have you reviewed transition problems with your students, along with rules you expect them to follow during the next transition? Be sure to let students know when they are doing a good job. If the students "forget" the rules for moving from one lesson or activity to another, have them return to their original positions and practice how to move correctly. Express your appreciation when transitions go smoothly and quickly.

A concrete transition routine usually helps. It defines the time students will have to make the change. (It also keeps you on task, too. It is easy to get distracted by students and other things. This torpedoes transitions just as often as student behaviors alone do.) Try a "Transition Tune," such as the theme song from a game show or an easily recognized classical piece (e.g., Beethoven's Fifth Symphony) to play during transition time. In addition, a Transition Countdown with a timer or counting backward to "Zero = Blast off into the next lesson" works well to keep students focused during transitions.

Students Are Unruly
or Noisy in Lines

I really dread taking children out of my classroom to gym, assembly programs, recess, and the lunchroom because they are so unruly. They are noisy, they push each other, some rush ahead, and some lag behind. What should I do?

Discuss this problem with the children. Explain what behaviors have been a problem. Determine together exactly how students *should* behave in the halls. For instance, discuss and decide if students should be able to talk in hall lines. Why or why not? Write the hallway rules, have each child sign the poster, and post it near the door.

Especially in the primary grades, have the children practice and role-play how to get in line and walk in an orderly manner. Reinforce the correct way by praising children doing a good job. Be clear about expectations. Use positive statements, reminding them what is expected: "We will walk in a single file with no talking," rather than what not to do: "We will not run in the hallway." Make sure you have discussed with students the consequences for not following the hallway rules, such as "An aide will take you back to the room for a three-minute time-out." Children need to be reminded not only of expectations but also of consequences. Be prepared to carry out the stated consequences. If you do not have an aide to take individuals back to the classroom, take the whole class back when a student or students violate the hallway rules.

You can also implement a group incentive for proper line behavior. One such incentive for primary children is the Secret Star Walker game. Place student names in a jar. Just before leaving the classroom with your line of children, draw out a name, read it silently with a flourish, and then keep it secret in your pocket. As you walk together, observe the line and make comments such as "Oh, our Star Walker is being so quiet in line today!" Use the secret person's behavior as the basis for a whole class reward or points.

Another method is this Quiet Lines game: Choose one student from the class to be in charge of selecting the quietest person in line. That person then gets to move forward five places. In the intermediate grades, the student selected might also be allowed to choose a friend to move forward with him or her. Make sure that the "chooser" is carefully selective. This procedure can quiet down a noisy lunch line within seconds.

Students Call Out Answers

Help! My students are always calling out answers. I have tried to stop this habit, but lately this problem has become worse. What should I do?

First of all, take a close look at your daily schedule. Determine which classroom activities are truly more successful and effective if students raise their hands to volunteer answers. Then determine activities in which students may speak without first obtaining permission. Discuss with your students these two types of activities and the hand-raising expectations for each. Let your students know that you will ignore anyone who calls out during an activity requiring a raised hand. Then be consistent! As soon as *you* forget and start responding to students who blurt out, you reinforce that behavior.

Students Come Late to Class Every Day

A few of my students come late to class every day. I have sent notes to their parents, called their homes—all to no avail. Any ideas?

Start by talking individually with the offenders about their tardiness to find out as much as possible about *why* they are late to school so often. Sometimes, especially with younger students, it is the parents' fault as much as the children's. Parents oversleep, have younger children that need care, have car trouble, and so on. Unfortunately, if parents act as if it is inconsequential that children get to school on time, young children are unlikely to be punctual on their own. Schedule a conference to discuss the problem of tardiness with the parents. (See section on parent conferences in Chapter 7.)

You might consider not starting academic instruction the moment the bell rings in the morning. Allow some transition time for students to settle in. It might be more efficient to spend ten to fifteen minutes on morning routines that can be missed rather than to keep repeating instructions or be interrupted by late students.

If you are dealing with older students who are chronically tardy, discuss the problem with them privately in depth. Emphasize the importance of coming to school on time every day. Sometimes, students are responsible for getting themselves up and off to school after the parents have left for work. Some teachers have actually purchased alarm clocks for students who oversleep. Others arrange "buddies" who phone at wake-up time each morning. Give a lot of encouragement and support.

Do you have specific consequences for tardiness? Especially with older students, develop one or two effective consequences (e.g., lunch detention and making up missed work) and bring them to students' attention at regular intervals during the school year. Speak with your mentor or other colleagues to find out which strategies have worked for them. Check the district policies regarding tardiness and absenteeism.

Students Finish Work Early

Some of my students finish their seat work much more quickly than others. What should I do?

No matter what type or how much seat work you assign, you will always have some students who complete their work sooner than others. Brainstorm a list of "things to do when you are done early," such as finding a book from the library corner to read at their desks, working on a project, working at a learning center, and helping a classmate. After completing the list of brainstormed ideas, select four or five and copy them on a large chart to hang in the classroom. Then, discuss it often with your students, reminding them that they may choose one of these items after they have completed their seat work.

A related problem is the students who often do not finish assignments or cannot work independently without the teacher's constant monitoring and assistance. Make sure the assigned work is appropriate to each student's skill level. Consider giving struggling students less work or work geared specially to their ability and/or work speed. You can quietly go to such students and whisper that today they need only complete the odd- or even-numbered math problems, for instance. Be concerned less with amount and more with competence in completion.

Sometimes, it motivates students to designate a special class activity to be enjoyed when *everyone* has completed the work. Enlist your students' help in suggesting the activities. Student-generated ideas in one fourth-grade class included ten minutes of free time at the end of the day, an extra-long recess, a special art project, a musical session, free reading time, hearing the teacher read aloud an additional chapter in the class novel, ten minutes extra PE, and a video. The teacher placed the written suggestions in a container from which to draw when the entire class earned a reward. Providing occasional positive reinforcement such as this makes necessary seat work less tedious.

Perhaps you are giving too much seat work. Take a few minutes to assess whether more activity-based lessons would involve all students more equally and naturally.

Students Have Messy Desks

Several students in my fourth-grade class have terribly cluttered, messy desks and are unable to find books, materials, and even their completed work when needed. How should I handle this problem?

Share with your students *exactly* what you believe is an organized desk. Select a "volunteer" desk and sit down to model a desk cleaning. After your demonstration (which you can make funny and exaggerated, if you'd like), brainstorm with your students a list of clean desk criteria. For instance, suggest that instead of pushing loose papers in their desks, students place these papers neatly in folders or loose-leaf notebooks. Some teachers have students file all corrected work to be sent home each week in a Friday folder. Others require older students to keep a three-ring binder with sections for each subject and conduct unannounced binder checks to ensure that papers are organized. Organization is a skill that must be *taught* to many children.

Inspect your students' desks every now and then for compliance with the criteria. Compliment students who are making an effort to keep their desks uncluttered. Regularly remind students to take home books, toys, and supplies that are no longer needed. Consider having students vote in a "Clean Team" whose job is to inspect desks each Friday and help disorganized classmates clean up.

Students Hide Candy and Food to Eat in Class

My students frequently hide candy, gum, and sunflower seeds to eat while they are in class. Our class rules forbid this. Should I just go ahead and confiscate the students' food?

First, ask yourself if you specified consequences for eating in the classroom at the beginning of the school year. Even if you suspect that students are hiding food in their desks or book bags, you cannot do anything, including confiscating the food, if you have no rule concerning it. Then you still must catch the offending students in the act. In the meantime, review the no-eating rule with your class. Sometimes, "no eating" is also a schoolwide rule you are expected to enforce. Discuss problems, such as sunflower shells or gum on the floor. Then, when you notice students munching, implement the consequences, including confiscation of the food. Some elementary schools allow a midmorning snack time. If so, encourage your students to wait until regularly scheduled breaks to eat. Recommend fruit rather than sweets.

During a quiet time alone with your snacking students, ask whether they normally eat breakfast and lunch. Find out why they are snacking. You may be dealing with children who are truly hungry.

Do not do something yourself that you forbid students. Too many teachers sip coffee or sodas in class in front of their students when students are not afforded the same privilege.

Students Hit and Push Other Students

A couple of my first graders are always hitting or pushing other children. Reprimands from me and the other kids have not stopped it. I am afraid that parents will soon complain about this. What should I do?

If children are generally happy and outgoing but occasionally hit or push when they get in an argument, it's probably of no great importance. But if certain students are tense and unhappy much of the time and keep hitting other children for no good reason, then something is wrong. Such children may not know of other ways to interact successfully with peers. Perhaps the children have had too few opportunities to become friendly with other children.

Many young children who hit others, whether in a playful or angry spirit, do so to get attention from other kids and from the teacher. Getting a rise out of the other children, making them scream and tattle, is better than being ignored. A lecture from the teacher at least results in some undivided attention. So the hitting behavior will often continue, even escalate.

Implement a consequence for hitting, perhaps taking away a few minutes from a favorite activity. Discuss the problem with the students who are hitting. Be firm about the consequences for hitting another child. But also let these students know that you care. Tell them that you will be watching for *good* behavior. Make some subtle arrangements for the children to interact successfully in a friendly group.

Continued hitting or similar behaviors will make a parent conference necessary. Talking with both children and parents might give you further insight into the misbehavior. Perhaps the students are being bossed and disciplined too much at home and are in a frantic, high-strung state. Perhaps the students are jealous of a baby at home and carry over the fear and resentment to all other children, as if they were competitors, too. Sometimes, if the cause and cure are complex, a school psychologist can provide help.

Students Keep Tattling

Two of my third-grade students cannot stop tattling. This happens every day! I have told them to stop, but the children do not seem to listen. What should I do?

Often, tattling concerns a situation that you will not have to pay attention to immediately. Once you listen to tattlers, you encourage them to continue. Stopping the tattling then becomes harder and harder. Let your students know that you will ignore all tattling. Explain that from now on, you will listen only to *positive* comments about others. As students stop tattling, praise them and let them know how much you appreciate their ability to take care of themselves.

Although most effective teachers ardently forbid tattling, there are times when tattles do point up problems about to blow up. Consider trying a "problems or concerns box" for upper grades to write questions and tattles. With guidelines, these can provide good discussion topics for class meetings about behavior and social interaction. Class meetings, with strict rules to prevent deterioration into name-calling ("You did/I didn't" arguments), work well in lower grades, too.

Students Misbehave
on Playground

I've been asked by the principal to serve on the playground problems task force for our school. Students are exhibiting undesirable behavior on the playground. Teachers have talked to them about it, but they seem to relapse quickly. How can we motivate students to follow proper playground procedures?

Some playground problems can be effectively dealt with by setting up the following classroom group incentive procedure. Each class starts out the week with twenty-five points. When a problem arises on the playground, the supervising teacher gives out a pair of tickets, one to the student causing the disruption and the other to the homeroom teacher of that student (this solves the problem of students' not turning in their tickets). If a student does not immediately turn in the ticket after receiving it, a penalty is enforced. Each time a ticket is received, two points are subtracted from the initial total of twenty-five points. Each day that an entire class goes without receiving a ticket, they may add an extra five points to their total (i.e., Tuesday, thirty points; Wednesday, thirty-five points; Thursday, forty points; Friday, forty-five points). The maximum number of points that any one class may earn per week is forty-five points. On Friday, an awards assembly is held for the entire school, and the class that has earned the most points for the week is awarded an honor banner, which may be hung in their classroom until the following Friday.

Students on Contract Are
Not Improving Behavior

I have two students who are working on individual behavior improvement plans that I've set up with them and their parents. But lately, I'm not seeing the desired behavior in the classroom. Any ideas to refresh their motivation?

Use a copy machine to duplicate "catch me being good" cards. Explain to students who are working on individual behavior improvement contracts that you will be watching for times when they are engaged in appropriate behavior. You are going to try to "catch them being good" and give them a "Good Behavior Coupon." Determine a reinforcer that each student would like to work for and the number of coupons he or she must attain to receive the reward.

For a variation, determine a *class* reward such as a popcorn party, extra recess, or free time. Tell the class that they can help and encourage the individual student to improve his or her behavior. When the individual student obtains the required number of coupons, then the whole class can partake of the reward.

Good Behavior Coupon

I caught _____

being good by _____

_____

Signed _____

Date _____

Students Talk Back to Teacher

I have a couple of students who always argue with me and talk back disrespectfully, saying things such as "You're not being fair!" Should I ignore this?

Children who feel that they can get their own way by arguing with the teacher will not respond to attempts to ignore them. This is especially true if these students want more attention from you in the first place. If what you have done or said was fair, simply tell the students that this is the way things will be done, end of story. State your bottom-line position, and then walk away. Remember that it takes two people to have an argument. If your students continue to talk back, change your own behavior by refusing to argue about it. Rarely is anyone ever argued into submission.

You can, if you wish, remind the students that they can discuss the matter quietly with you during recess or lunch. Allow them to air their feelings, while depriving them of the audience of classmates. Most effective discipline is done on a one-to-one basis.

Students Talk While Teacher Is Presenting Lessons

I have tried to ignore students' whispering and talking when I am presenting a lesson or explaining a concept, but to no avail. I cannot keep reminding them to be quiet! What should I do?

If you teach in the primary grades, is your lesson longer than twenty minutes? Or thirty minutes if you teach at the intermediate level? Are your students sitting passively during these times? If so, consider changing your lesson format, such as including more hands-on activities. Look also at the content of your presentations. Students talk when lessons are boring, too hard, or repetitious.

Unfortunately, many children have learned that talking and misbehaving are good ways to get the teacher's attention—they can make the teacher stop and tell them to be quiet. In addition to ignoring the talkers, make sure you praise students who are listening. Give your attention primarily to students who are behaving appropriately.

Because your students talk even when you ignore them, consider imposing a penalty such as taking a minute from their recess or free activity time for each instance you must stop the lesson because of too much noise (see first question). In addition, review your seating arrangements. Do certain seating groups create pockets of talking, perhaps special friends, perhaps conflicts, that students "can't resist"?

Students Throw Temper Tantrums

How should I handle temper tantrums?

Most elementary-age children have grown out of true temper tantrums. The prime age for these tantrums is two to three years. But some children have learned at home that this is still a good way to get what they want when thwarted.

You certainly do not want to give in and let the children have their way, or you will be dealing with children who persistently throw tantrums. Such children are testing your limits.

Take tantrums casually, with patience and tact. Avoid getting angry yourself. If you get angry, you will find yourself arguing, which is futile, because these children will be in no mood to listen. Assign tantrum throwers to a time-out, a quiet spot to cool off in private. Kids usually cool off rapidly if the teacher "fades away," ignoring any yelling and thrashing. If the noise is disruptive to your class, consider having an aide temporarily remove the tantrum thrower from the room to cool off. In addition, train the other children in your class to ignore other students' tantrums.

Occasionally, older students will throw a tantrum, perhaps crying, screaming, swearing, or pounding on the desk. Such students need help in learning acceptable ways of dealing with unpleasant tasks, frustration, and anger. The tantrum may be serving as an escape mechanism. Students, especially those with attention deficit disorder and/or learning problems, may respond to stress with angry temper outbursts and aggression. Sometimes, when such children do something wrong, they get defensive and become angry at the person correcting them, rather than apologize or accept a punishment. If the angry outbursts are minor, or if you suspect that the students are intentionally trying to get a rise out of you, ignore the behavior. Teach techniques for dealing with anger, or refer the students to a counselor who can help. Keep in mind that low frustration tolerance and impulsivity contribute to emotional blowups even when some youngsters truly wish to remain calm.

Whenever you observe such students behaving well (working hard on a task or being helpful to another student), praise them. Let the students know you see their successes. Compliment the students on their maturity.

Avoid negative interactions with students who are angry and frustrated. Some of these children seem to be constantly butting heads with their teachers. They often do irritating things. If you chose to do so, you could spend your whole day correcting these students' behavior. You will only end up feeling exhausted and hostile, and so will the students. Many effective teachers of angry children who misbehave frequently make a conscious decision to address only the most important misbehavior or emotional outbursts.

Especially if children have learning problems, their chances of becoming frustrated over difficult schoolwork and blowing up are high. When this occurs, stay clam and *lower your voice.* You might say, "I know this is hard, and you are frustrated. Let's take a break." Send the student to the library corner or bathroom to regain his or her cool. Researchers have found that loud emotional responses from adults result in students' becoming more aggressive and producing less schoolwork.

Teacher Has Hall Duty and Still Must Supervise Class

I have hall duty first thing in the morning, but at the same time, I also have to supervise students in my own class. What's the best way of doing this?

By law, you cannot leave your students alone and unsupervised in your classroom. Consider assigning a short warm-up exercise or sponge activity and having an aide supervise your class while you are in the hall. If possible, stand near your doorway and check the classroom frequently. If you do not have an aide to supervise children in the room, you may have to lock your door during your hall duty times. Check with your mentor or principal about school policy regarding this matter.

Teacher Has to Share Classroom With Another Teacher/Class

I just found out that I have to share a classroom with another teacher. What should I do? What do I tell my students?

Try to meet with the other teacher as soon as possible and establish a good rapport. Chances are that she or he is also concerned about sharing a classroom. If possible, arrange to get separate teacher desks. If you share a single desk as well, discuss which drawers and even which side of the desk each of you will use. Talk with your new roommate about dividing classroom shelves, files, and storage space. For primary classrooms, set up separate student cubbies and storage areas with agreed-on rules about student access. Think carefully about how you will share textbooks and instructional materials. Will you each have teacher manuals? Find out who will use which of the bulletin boards. Agreeing on one set of posted classroom rules (and consequences) will make it easier for yourselves and your students. Make sure that the room is always left clean and neat. Remember to discuss your concerns with your students. They might enjoy setting up "desk pals" so they can correspond with and get to know the students who share their desks. Ask them for their ideas and cooperation, and then try to incorporate their suggestions. You and your roommate may be in for a pleasant surprise. Two heads are often better than one.

Teacher Helps Limited-English-Proficient Students

One of my students doesn't seem to understand what is going on in class. He is new to our community and goes to ESL pullout sessions but is in my room most of the day. How can I help this student? (My class is large—32 students.)

Help your LEP students feel at ease when they arrive in your classroom by assigning each of them a personal "buddy" who, if possible, speaks the language of the newcomer. The job of the buddy is to help the new student through the school day, with routines and so on. Arrange your classroom seating so that the LEP children are sitting next to their buddies. It is often best to partner LEP students with fast, confident, independent workers who can help them keep on task, as well as help them adapt to everyday school life. Avoid changes in the classroom schedule by following a regular, predictable routine each day, which creates a sense of security. If your classroom is arranged in table groups, assigning each LEP student to a "home group" for an extended period helps create a sense of belonging.

Many grouping strategies are effective. Students can read aloud with their partners, pausing to ask questions, make predictions, and clear up misunderstandings. In general, cooperative learning and collaborative projects with a lot of opportunities for informal oral language are beneficial to second-language learners. Make sure that your LEP students hear models of clear and understandable language, dramatized with gestures and facial expressions, as necessary.

Teaching methods that promote English language development for your LEP students are good approaches for *all* your students. Examples include the following:

- Previewing and reviewing lessons with visual schematics (semantic mapping, webbing, and advance organizers)

- Technology and audiovisual lesson materials (videos and photographs)

- Simulations and role playing

- Student journals and learning logs

- Direct experiences (math manipulatives, science experiments, and field trips)

Create opportunities for newcomers to share their language and culture during daily events in the classroom. Together you will all learn new things.

Teacher Helps Student Deal With Death in Family

A parent of one of my students died in a sudden accident. My student shows little interest in class work. What should I do?

Every child reacts differently to a severe change or loss in life. Let the student bring up the topic—don't try to get the child to "open up." Quietly welcome the child back, and express that everyone is sorry to hear of the tragedy. Then immediately help the child get involved in a classroom activity with other students. It is best to carry on as usual. Let the student find comfort in a familiar environment and routine.

If possible, before the student comes back to school, send a card and note of sympathy signed by everyone in the class. Discuss with your class how it may be stressful and overwhelming for a grieving student to have thirty classmates all personally offering condolences on the day the student returns.

Most children do not understand that death is an irreversible event until they are about nine years old. Younger children may think that the parent will come back somehow.

It takes children, as well as many adults, at least a year to put their lives back together. Be as supportive as possible. The child's emotions of fear, anger, guilt, and sadness may need to be expressed openly in the classroom. If the student breaks down in class, don't make a fuss. Give quiet comfort when the rest of the class is engaged in an activity. Both the child and the surviving parent may need special help during this time. For further resources and/or suggestions, contact your school or district counselor/psychologist or community resource center.

Teacher Uses "Marble Jar" and Similar Class Reward Systems

When I was student teaching, a teacher down the hall used a "marble jar" class reward. She liked it a lot, and so did her children. Can you tell me how to do it?

The marbles-in-a-jar system is easy to use and is popular with younger students. The brightly colored marbles and the sound they make as they are dropped into the jar are motivating in themselves.

Here's how to use a marble jar:

- Place a jar on your desk. Tell your students that when they follow the class rules, you will drop several marbles into the jar. Explain that when the jar is full (or when the marbles reach a certain level), the entire class will earn a reward.

- Look for opportunities to reinforce the group.

  Are students quiet?
  Are students on task?
  Do all students have their pencils sharp and ready?
  Did they leave the closet neat after recess?

- Be sure to add marbles throughout the day to maintain students' interest. Mark lines on the jar with tape to note daily goals.

- Restate the behavior you are reinforcing as you put marbles into the jar.

- The reinforcing activity can be a surprise or something the class selects, such as

  Class game
  Popcorn party
  Free time
  Extra story
  Extra afternoon recess
  Art
  Music and social time
  Skating party after school

Similar to the marble jar is the popcorn jar. You will need a bag of unpopped popcorn, a small scoop, and a large transparent container. Each time you notice students working well together (or whatever behavior you want to reinforce), place a scoop of popcorn in the jar. When it is full of popcorn, plan a popcorn party.

Still another similar way to increase desirable classroom behavior and work toward a common goal is the "Bubble Gum Machine." Post a copy of the Bubble Gum Machine picture (see Resource 8.1) where all students can see it. (If possible, use a duplicating machine to enlarge the picture.) Establish positive classroom behaviors that you want to reinforce, such as a quiet return after recess and a smooth transition between activities. When one of the established behaviors occurs, use colored markers to color in a ball on the picture. Decide with the students what reward activity they would like when all the balls are colored in. See the previous list of reward ideas, or consider bringing in bubble gum and allowing students to chew gum on the specified reward day.

Teacher Uses Rapport-Building Strategies

All my students are wonderful. I tell them frequently. What else can I do to build positive rapport in my classroom?

Try the "Stars of the Week" activity.

1. Cut out a star for each student in your class. Use construction paper in bright colors.
2. Ask each student to bring a recent photo of him- or herself. (Photo must fit inside middle of star—wallet-size is best.)
3. Put all photos in a large manila envelope.
4. Once a week (every Monday), draw two photos from the envelope.
5. Call each student individually to the front of the class or circle. Tape the star on the board. As that week's star student stands with you, ask for volunteers from the class to tell what they especially *like* about the person. As volunteers offer positive comments, write the adjective on a corner of the star. Encourage students to use specific and descriptive words—for instance, rather than *nice*, they could say *outgoing, generous, courteous,* or *kind;* rather than *funny*, they might say *energetic, hilarious,* or *class clown*. Give each Star of the Week a small gift (such as a pencil with "Star of the Week" embossed on it).
6. Paste the photo in the middle of the star. Put the completed star with others in a row at the top of the chalkboard.

A similar rapport booster is the weekly "Mystery Person" activity. For this, duplicate the certificate in Resource 8.2. Give each student a copy of the certificate or a brief questionnaire of five to six questions about their likes, dislikes, special qualities, and funny incidents. Have students write answers "secretly" without sharing them with others. Collect the filled-in certificates. Roll up and tie each with a ribbon. Place the certificates in a basket. To spotlight a student each week, draw a certificate from the basket (make an elaborate show of the drawing!). Then unroll the certificate with drama and suspense, and without revealing the student's name, read aloud the answers to the questionnaire. Ask the class to guess who it is. Create a special "Mystery Person Revealed" spotlight bulletin board with photographs of each student.

Here's one more self-esteem promoter that is easy to implement: Ask students to write their names on sheets of blank paper. Students can use markers and make their names as fancy and colorful as they wish. Then tell them to clear everything else off their desks, leaving just their name paper out on the desktop. Explain that they will each take a pencil and move from desk to desk, stopping at each one to write a positive comment on each person's paper. (Discuss and give examples of *positive* comments.) For easier traffic management, have students move along a predetermined route. How pleased students will be when they return to their own desks and read the happy messages that are awaiting them! If you'd like "strokes," too, put your name on a paper and join the fun.

Bubble Gum Machine

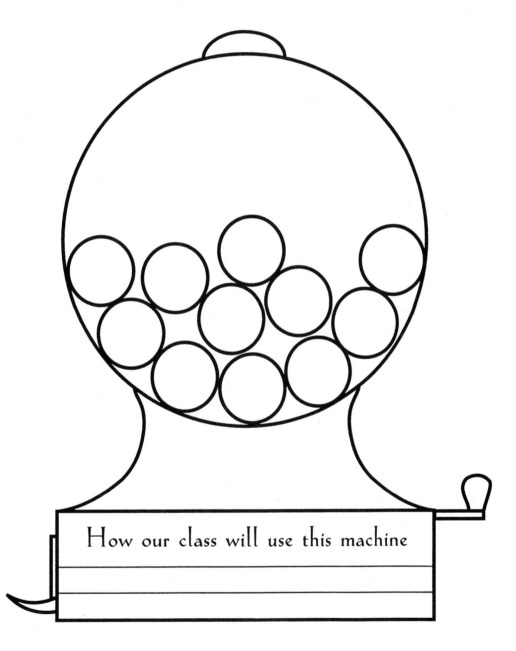

How our class will use this machine

Mystery Person Certificate

Name _____

Born in what state _____

Born in what month _____

Color of hair _____

Color of eyes _____

Favorite food _____

Favorite sport _____

Favorite pet or animal _____

Favorite TV show _____

Favorite color _____

Favorite book _____

Favorite saying/quote _____

Things I like to do with my friends _____

Something I do well _____

❑ Only child   ❑ Youngest   ❑ Middle   ❑ Oldest

❑ Boy   ❑ Girl

Your Own Professional Development

Learning to teach is a lifelong process. Successful teachers grow in effectiveness throughout their professional careers as they gradually hone their style and strategies through trial and error, reflection, and critical inquiry. Beginning teachers may often feel as if daily responsibilities to students totally consume their lives. New teachers typically report thinking about "their kids" every waking hour. They even dream about them!

You undoubtedly care deeply for your students and are working hard to ensure a positive, flourishing year for them. But how about *you*? You have needs as a learner, too. Don't neglect your own professional growth and development.

The educational profession is teeming with changes and trends. Research and practice regularly recommend new techniques to engage children in learning. It is important to stay abreast of these innovations. In time, you may want to throw your energies into school reform issues and help tackle some of the current problems in the profession.

For now, however, concentrate on consolidating what you learn as you become more confident in your ability to teach and to deal with students. One of the best ways to learn from experience is through reflection and problem solving about situations in your own classroom.

Reflecting on Your Practice

When you reflect on experience, you have an opportunity to grow from it. Thinking about what you are learning helps consolidate teaching knowledge and skill. Develop a habit of analyzing what you do and why. Monitor your decisions about what and how you teach and how you interact with children. Don't ignore what your discoveries are trying to tell you. Become a student of your own teaching. Evaluate your successes as well as your errors. Contemplate what "works" to engage students in learning. As you consider alternative courses of action, you'll expand your teaching repertoire and refine your approach for the next time. Look back thoughtfully and accurately to assess your effectiveness. Define what specific strategies were successful, and begin building personal principles and theories that will apply to other instructional issues. Let these insights serve as springboards for discussions and new discoveries. If you merely "survive" your first year of teaching without thinking closely about it, you will miss profound opportunities to examine and savor your experiences.

Perhaps the most productive way to reflect is *out loud,* talking with a mentor or a peer. Mentoring is really just one teacher's facilitating the growth of another. Reflect on specific teaching problems as well as larger professional and career development issues. When teachers are collaborating in an active, honest search for answers, this is reflection at its most powerful. Reflecting with a supportive listener may be your best source of information and emotional succor. From this, you will learn, grow, and gather strength to be a truly professional teacher.

Becoming an accomplished teacher is a complex process. No matter how well you learn to execute specific teaching models and procedures, building a repertoire takes time. Because discussion time with your mentor and colleagues will probably be limited by the press of events, keeping a journal of your personal reflections and self-assessments is also valuable. Despite the constraints of classroom life, a certain degree of reflection is possible. A good idea is to write in your journal whenever you have students write in theirs. You will be modeling good writing habits while giving yourself a lull in the action and a chance to record events and personal reactions. Sometimes, the simple act of writing about an issue will clarify it for you. What happened? Why did it happen? What was my role? What beliefs did my actions reflect? How should I act in the future? Reflection will give you perspective on events. It is one of the best (and cheapest!) professional development activities available.

Thinking About Teachers as "Professionals"

American teachers have an image problem. As teachers, we are members of the largest, most complex, and most important profession in the world. Yet true professional status eludes us. In many cases, teachers simply are not viewed or treated as professionals—by the public, by school and district administrators, or even by themselves. The issue of professionalism is a critical ingredient of this country's efforts to improve education. In reflecting on the public school puzzle, you'll find that professionalism, public confidence, and school improvement are important interlocking pieces.

What is a professional? Different people will give you slightly different definitions, but in a comprehensive literature review on professional development commissioned by the North Central Regional Education Laboratory (NCREL) in Naperville, Illinois, a professional is defined as someone "characterized by the ability to make informed judgements and perform important tasks in complex environments. These judgements and performance are grounded in an identifiable, empirically supported knowledge base" (NCREL, 2001).

Teachers certainly fit this definition. From reams of research reports emerges the image of a teacher as a *decision maker.* Even in the most routine situations, teachers must make multiple and simultaneous judgments. They must continually gather and organize large amounts of information and juggle several sometimes contradictory goals. They apply their special knowledge of students and classrooms in deciding when, what, and how to teach.

As a new teacher, you stand at a special point in time as a teaching professional. This is not only because it is the beginning of a new decade, century, and millennium, but more important to this profession, the "art" of teaching is swiftly transforming into the "science" of teaching. More and more researchers are systematically studying teaching in a scientific manner and reporting the positive effects of instruction on student learning.

In previous decades, the public believed that schools made little difference in the achievement of students. This was, in fact, the conclusion of the now-famous "Coleman report" of 1966 (see Unger, 1996, for a description), based on data from more than six hundred thousand students and sixty thousand teachers in over four thousand schools. Coleman and colleagues rocked the educational world when they reported the results of their research, saying what many had secretly believed all along: that schools make little difference. They concluded that the quality of schooling a student receives accounts for only about 10 percent of the variance in student achievement. The vast majority of differences in achievement were attributed to factors such as the student's natural ability or aptitude or "intelligence," the socioeconomic status of the school, and the student's home environment. These same findings were reported in other studies, especially by Christopher Jencks (1972) in the book *Inequality: A Reassessment of the Effects of Family and Schools in America.*

The conclusion that schools make little difference was widespread. It did not paint a very hopeful picture for educators and education. If most differences in test scores are due to factors that teachers do not control, why even try? This gloomy attitude devalued the teacher's professionalism. Unfortunately, a pessimistic view of what schools and teachers really can do has stuck in the public mind. You may even have graduated from a teacher-credentialing program that subtly or not-so-subtly gave you a similar message.

Recent research paints a much more hopeful picture, however. For instance, after reviewing hundreds of studies examining effective teaching practices, respected researchers Thomas Good and Jere Brophy (2000) concluded, "The myth that teachers do not make a difference in student learning has been refuted." Based on an analysis of achievement scores of more than one hundred thousand students across hundreds of schools, William Sanders (1997) noted that the individual classroom teacher has even more of an effect on student achievement than originally thought:

> The results of this study document that the most important factor affecting student learning is the teacher. In addition, the results show wide variation in effectiveness among teachers. The immediate and clear implication of this finding is that seemingly more can be done to improve education by improving the effectiveness of teachers than by any other single factor.

Teachers *do* make a difference! Keep this in mind as you grow as a professional and master the complexities of schools and classrooms. The desire and commitment of new teachers is perhaps the most powerful resource for change that exists in public education today. (For more information on William Sanders's work, see www.tvaas.com and www.mdk12.org/practices/ensure/tva/.)

Professional Development Through Inservice and Graduate Study

Many school districts sponsor induction workshops and seminars just for beginning teachers. Make sure you attend. Take advantage of the opportunity to establish a professional network with other beginning teachers in the school system. Furthermore, topics are usually selected for the workshops through surveys and input from the beginning teachers. You will find useful and practical ideas about managing student behavior, engaging students in active learning, and using instructional materials and resources.

Other inservice workshops are offered for *all* teachers at your school, district, or perhaps a local agency. These programs are scheduled when teachers are available to attend—usually on minimum days (when students have a short school day) or in late afternoon or evening. Inservice workshops are often led by veteran teachers with expertise in special curriculum areas. At other times, the topics covered in these workshops can be as diverse as time management, investment options, and violence in the schools. Short descriptions of featured workshops are available in flyers or a school district professional development catalog. You have the option to select inservices of special interest to you.

Pursuing a master's degree at the university is another fine way of continuing your professional development. Look into master's degrees in your teaching subject, in curriculum and instruction, in counseling, or in educational administration. School districts provide pay increases for teachers who earn graduate credit units and degrees.

Professional Development Through Regional and National Conferences

To keep abreast of the latest instructional research and to recharge yourself with new inspiration, attend every convention and conference you can. These professional meetings are one important way for beginning teachers to feel less isolated and more empowered. You may not agree with everything you hear or see, but you will expand your awareness. The intellectual stimulation will generate options that enable you to make informed choices. Efficacy, the confident feeling of success, results when you continue to learn.

In your search for professional growth opportunities, subscribe to (and read!) at least one educational journal. Join at least one professional association. Many professional organizations are subject specific, such as the International Reading Association, the National Council of Teachers of Mathematics, and the National Science Teachers Association. A similar state organization is usually affiliated with the national group. See Resource 9.1 for a list of names and addresses of recommended professional associations. These organizations publish regular newsletters and journals for their members, with interpretive articles on educational research and practical teaching tips.

Local, state, and national organizations also have annual meetings with speakers, workshops, exhibits, and socials. Educational publishers are invited to set up displays. You will leave these conferences with bags of sample materials, freebies, teaching packets that workshop leaders distribute at their sessions, and pages of notes and new ideas. Plan that in time you will become a conference presenter yourself! Professional development means sharing and learning together. Teaching other teachers about your special skills is an important component of the professional growth process.

Conference attendance gives you an opportunity for professional networking beyond your school and district. Talking, laughing, and sharing with teachers from other places sometimes includes discussing "war stories" and confirming that you are not alone in your concerns. But most important, you will gain ideas and descriptions of new programs and techniques that work for others and may work back home for you.

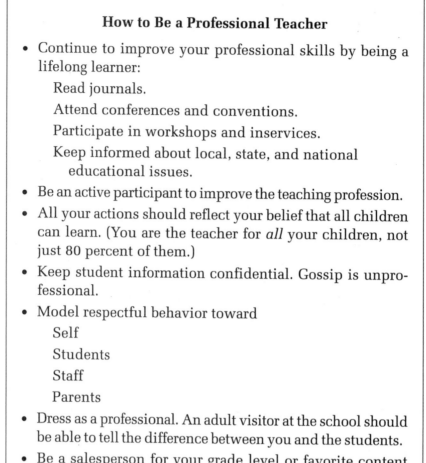

How to Be a Professional Teacher

- Continue to improve your professional skills by being a lifelong learner:

    Read journals.

    Attend conferences and conventions.

    Participate in workshops and inservices.

    Keep informed about local, state, and national educational issues.

- Be an active participant to improve the teaching profession.

- All your actions should reflect your belief that all children can learn. (You are the teacher for *all* your children, not just 80 percent of them.)

- Keep student information confidential. Gossip is unprofessional.

- Model respectful behavior toward

    Self

    Students

    Staff

    Parents

- Dress as a professional. An adult visitor at the school should be able to tell the difference between you and the students.

- Be a salesperson for your grade level or favorite content area as well as for the whole profession.

Your Teaching Portfolio

Many beginning teachers develop professional portfolios. Portfolios serve as tools for reflection, a way to thoughtfully document teaching practices and progress toward goals. Portfolio entries can inform professional growth plans. As actual artifacts of teaching, portfolios are conversation starters for you and your mentor or colleague and provide focus for your discussions. Portfolios also work well as a tool for *self*-reflection—helping you think systematically about your practice, reflect on the issues you face, and learn from experience. They provide direct evidence of what you have accomplished.

Portfolios allow you to "walk your talk." If you are having your students develop portfolios to reflect on their learnings, you can benefit from doing the same. Let students know about your personal portfolio. Perhaps they can suggest entries. Typical classroom artifacts include, but are not limited to, lesson plans, a unit plan, and student work samples.

In addition to using the portfolio as a spur for reflection, you can also use it to showcase your best efforts. Although a personal reflective portfolio can include samples of lessons that flopped and notes on strategies that do not seem to work for you, a showcase portfolio should include your "best shots." A showcase portfolio is typically used in employment interviews and in assessment of teaching competency. A portfolio can strengthen your résumé and supplement the interview or tenure process. It provides multiple sources of evidence that you have collected through time, sorted, and refined to reflect your best work. The final, polished presentation portfolio, similar to the artist's portfolio, is an important marketing tool for promoting your skills and abilities.

Your school district may require beginning teachers to develop teaching portfolios. Such a portfolio is a reflection of your first year, as well as a resource in future years. Typically, it consists of your documentation of at least one entire teaching unit. It could contain a written unit plan, including the unit's goals, rationale, sequence of lessons, and learning activities. Your portfolio could also include a videotaped lesson, instructional materials, assignments given to your students during the unit, and examples of student work with your evaluative feedback.

The portfolio shows your ability to plan and design instruction, create and use instructional materials, and evaluate student learning and, to a lesser degree, your knowledge of content. It will be strengthened if it documents a *series* of lessons. Any inconsistencies and contradictions among such entries will immediately become evident, so choose carefully.

School districts require portfolios for the following reasons:

1. Portfolios are useful for assessing professional growth and documenting the knowledge, skills, and abilities of beginning teachers.
2. Portfolios are useful as a resource for new teachers for ideas in future years.
3. Portfolios are useful as a framework from which to begin discussions of the growth of new teachers and a way to build rapport and communication between beginning teachers and their assessors.

Developing a portfolio requires you to integrate knowledge, skills, and attitudes acquired from a variety of practical experiences with teaching. It requires you to establish your own standards of excellence and decide how to demonstrate these standards through tangible documents. As an organizing center, a portfolio guides you in defining your values and beliefs about teaching and learning. It helps you reflect on your teaching practices and on what you have observed in your classroom and school. In many states and locales, you will be encouraged to extend the development of your portfolio throughout your induction years of teaching.

In most cases, your school district will have established criteria detailing the knowledge and skills to be demonstrated in the portfolio. You should be able to examine available rating rubrics and other assessment forms. You may be able to organize much of the required information into the following categories:

- How I organize and manage my classroom
- How I plan and design instruction
- How I deliver instruction
- How I demonstrate subject matter competence
- How I diagnose and evaluate my students' learning
- How I participate as a member of a learning community

Using these six areas of teaching competence as a framework, you could build a portfolio that exhibits your effectiveness in each area.

Important projects such as portfolios simply cannot be assembled at the last minute. Portfolio materials and necessary documents should be completed and gathered one stage at a time. Components should be arranged in sequence with captions, explanations, and reflective comments. Generally, portfolios include written documentation of lessons you have actually taught. Specify in detail the learning activities in which you engaged students, and provide samples of your instructional materials. Include photographs of students participating in the lesson activities, bulletin boards related to the lesson, models constructed, learning centers, and so forth. Make sure your lesson plans show active learning, a variety of strategies and modalities, and sensitivity to language and culture issues.

It is important in your portfolio to provide concrete examples of your teaching effectiveness in classroom management and discipline/behavior management strategies. Sample portfolio entries might include

- "Our Classroom Rules" poster (photo, with explanatory caption, of poster on your classroom wall)
- Samples of behavior awards or positive recognition certificates, incentives, rapport-building activities, "warm fuzzy" notes, and positive notes to parents
- "Consequences" poster ("What happens if rules are broken?") and parent information letter about rules and consequences
- Your "freeze and listen" signal (a description and a photograph of all students imitating the signal)
- Effective planning for transition time (including sponge activities and group rotation chart)
- Procedures, routines, and classroom organization (photos showing your "supplies tubs" organization, labels, directions, short de-

scriptions, and photos with captions that illustrate how well you have planned for routines and procedures that happen daily or frequently in the classroom)

- Class meetings (photographs, description, and rationale: Why are class meetings important in your classroom management plan?)

What Should the Presentation Portfolio Look Like? There is really no prescribed blueprint for a portfolio. It should reflect your own particular focus and preferences. Four rules of thumb, however, will help you produce a quality document:

1. Use a three-ring presentation binder that allows you to insert materials and move them around.
   - Two-inch thickness is probably fine for now; larger binders become too bulky and cumbersome.
   - Select a dark-colored binder (avoid bright neon, reds, plaid, etc.).
   - You may want to use a binder that displays the school district logo.
2. The appearance of your portfolio should be *impeccable,* because it is a tangible representation of your personal standards of excellence. It should have
   - Laser printing
   - Quality bond paper
   - Plastic page covers
   - Absence of typos and spelling errors
   - Clean, attractive pages (no coffee stains, whiteouts, etc.)
3. Begin your portfolio with a title page and table of contents.
4. Be selective in adding the materials. More is not necessarily better. An assessor or a prospective employer will want to peruse the portfolio and abstract information quickly.

What Materials Should I Include in My Portfolio? Your portfolio will begin small and will become more extensive and refined as you get more involved in the professional life of your school and district. Some of the materials will not be developed until you complete your first year of teaching. Those marked below with an asterisk (*) are optional.

Title page

Table of contents

Statement of your philosophy/educational credo

Résumé

Professional goals

Letters of reference

*Honors and distinctions (e.g., certificates; award letters; list of achievements such as conference presentations, honorary societies, and other recognitions)

Photos of you with your students, engaged in whole-group and small-group instruction and related professional activities (each photo should be captioned)

*Newspaper clippings that cite your achievements

The following are to be added as you complete your first year of teaching:

Samples of classroom management plans/techniques/routines

Sample unit plan(s)

Sample lesson plan(s)

Sample learning/interest center plan

Samples of student work with your written feedback and evaluation/ grade

Sample test or evaluation method

*Videotape of your teaching

As performance assessment of students gains popularity (see Chapter 6), an increasing number of school districts are likely to ask teachers to engage in assessment on the same terms as their students. Portfolios are concrete products that illustrate what the teacher can actually do. Even if your district does not require portfolios, consider keeping one to capture what you do in the classroom and your knowledge and decision making as a professional. Sit down occasionally to review it, reflect on your growth, and pat yourself on the back because the evidence confirms that you are doing a great job.

Strategies for Success in Your First Year and Beyond

Throughout this book, I have emphasized that teaching and learning go hand in hand. The effectiveness of your teaching directly affects students' effectiveness as learners. Learning about learning and teaching becomes a lifelong commitment for successful teachers.

The important question is not "What am I doing?" but "What am I doing for my students?" You must constantly ask yourself if you are creating learning experiences that result in positive outcomes for children. As a beginning teacher, it is easy to get trapped in time and logistic pressures as you manage a myriad of details. One of the realities of school life is that resources are finite and that decisions involve compromises. As you allocate that most precious resource—the teacher's *time*—look to your students. Make decisions based on what happens to them. Will they be truly engaged in the learning tasks? Will your classroom provide rewarding social and personal experiences?

It's hard to imagine a more demanding job than teaching. You could easily spend fourteen hours a day preparing to teach and teaching. Please don't. Try to establish a point each day when schoolwork stops, even if it is not done. To survive and flourish at teaching, you must find some relaxation time. Enjoy the other important aspects of your life, too. You will have more of yourself to give to your students if you take care of yourself. Feelings of burnout are a prevalent and serious problem for new teachers. Realize that few things are ever totally completed in education. Pace yourself. Beware of allowing the pressures of teaching to outweigh its positive aspects.

Veteran teachers have developed ways to cope with the pressures of the job. See their suggestions in the box below.

Time-Saving Tips From Veteran Teachers

- Review your "to do" list every morning. Check off tasks as they are completed.

- Assign each student a partner. When a student is absent, the partner can gather assignments that the absent student has missed. Have partners exchange phone numbers.

- Have students use an answer column along the right margin of the paper when doing math or similar short-answer assignments from textbooks. Students transfer answers from the problem to the answer column. (Learning to copy answers into an answer column carefully is an important skill, especially for taking standardized tests.) You can correct half a dozen papers at a time by looking at several answer columns.

- When you ask students to check each other's papers, have checkers sign their names at the bottom. Students are more careful when their names are on the checked assignments.

- Train students to place assignments, right side up, with their names at the top, into the "Completed Work" basket or bin. Have a labeled basket for each subject so papers are sorted for you.

- When you put students' names into your grade book, number the names in consecutive order. Have students always write their name *and number* on their papers. You (or a student) can quickly put papers in order. You can easily see which papers are missing, and when they are corrected, they will be in numerical order to readily mark into your grade book.

- Ask for clerical help from parents. Choose tasks for parents to do at home on a weekly or monthly basis, such as typing newsletters, preparing teaching materials, and preparing book club orders.
- Teach students to do as many clerical tasks (attendance, lunch count, etc.) as possible.
- Put answers on an overhead projector transparency to have students check their homework while you deal with morning "administrivia."
- Designate one spot on the chalkboard on which you write what students should do as soon as they enter the classroom. Teach students to look there and begin without wasting time. It will give an orderly beginning to your class at the start of the day and after recess and lunch breaks (good time to use miniworksheets—see below).
- For short warm-up activities, cut worksheets into strips containing four or five items. These miniworksheets can be completed in a few minutes and help prepare students for the lesson to come.
- Write frequently used directions on a chart instead of the chalkboard. When needed, hang up the chart. This is a good idea for assignment guidelines, book report outline, paper heading, studying tips (e.g., survey, question, read, recite, review—SQ3R), and many other procedures or reminders.
- If your classroom is far away from the office or teacher workroom, keep a personal supply box hidden in your room. Include pens, pencils, scissors, paper, Post-it note pads, and tape.
- Save time by designing your own lesson plan book. Take a page from the standard book and write in times, subjects, morning routine, recess, lunch, special classes, and other constant features. Duplicate this page so when you make your weekly lesson plans, you need only add the specific lesson topics for that week.
- Place extra copies of student worksheets in a Homework Box. Students who lost or forgot their copies can easily take another. Also, students can help themselves for extra practice/extra credit.
- Identify your supplies (pencils, scissors, markers, etc.) with a masking or colored tape strip.
- Use an overhead projector transparency instead of chalkboard to write class notes or graphic organizers during presentations. This way you can date and save them, use them again, lend them to a struggling student, and/or review them on another day.
- Designate one day a week, usually Friday, to send student work home to parents.
- Refile your materials as soon as possible so you can find them later.

- Set up a permanent bulletin board that includes class schedule, announcements, lunch menu, and other important information you (or your substitute) need regularly.
- Use only *one* calendar to keep track of future important events (pocket calendar, desk calendar, or lesson plan book).
- Make two blank copies of each student worksheet for your own use—one to file for future reference and one to make an answer key.
- Laminate frequently used materials for reuse in subsequent years.
- Keep a personal care kit at school (include aspirin and needle and thread).
- Idea for "floating" teachers: Make a box or use an audiovisual cart to keep your desk materials with you as you travel from room to room.
- Introduce lessons with visuals—transparencies, posters, slides, or realia.
- Use the overhead projector—it allows you to face the class and helps focus students' attention.
- Visit your local educational supply store to get fresh ideas for your classroom.
- Keep your seating chart in a plastic sheet protector. You can write on it with an overhead marker to keep a tally of student participation and other observations.
- When you check out textbooks to older students, have them complete a colored book charge card with all the appropriate information except the return date. These are easily alphabetized, and you won't have to fill the cards out later.
- Stamp your name inside all the books you use, both class sets and personal books you lend to students. If a book is misplaced, it finds its way to your faculty mailbox.
- Laminate a piece of construction paper, and write your assignments for the week on it using an overhead marker. Absentees won't have to ask you about missed assignments, and you won't have to worry about accidentally erasing the list from the chalkboard.
- Maintain an index card file on your students. Keep a separate card on each student to make notations on behavior (both positive and troublesome) and to record parent contacts. These cards become a great resource in determining grades and when talking to parents.
- Suggest scheduling a minimum day to be used just for teacher sharing and brainstorming ideas to help with professional growth. You could meet in subject area groups or grade-level groups.

Teaching can be a wonderfully rewarding career. Take pride in being a professional. Enjoy your students. As the years go by, you will find self-respect and satisfaction in your special role of developing children's minds and hearts as you prepare them for success in future years.

I touch the future . . .
I teach.

Christa McAuliffe

Professional Associations for Teachers

American Educational Research Association (AERA)
  1230 17th Street NW
  Washington, DC 20036
  202-223-9485
  http://www.aera.net/

Association for Supervision and Curriculum Development (ASCD)
  1250 North Pitt Street
  Alexandria, VA 22314
  703-549-9110
  800-933-ASCD
  http://www.ascd.org/

International Reading Association (IRA)
  P.O. Box 8139
  800 Barksdale Road
  Newark, DE 19714-8139
  302-731-1600
  http://www.reading.org/

National Council for the Social Studies (NCSS)
  3501 Newark Street NW
  Washington, DC 20016
  202-966-7840
  http://www.ncss.org/

National Council of Teachers of English (NCTE)
  1111 Kenyon Road
  Urbana, IL 61801
  217-328-3870
  http://www.ncte.org/

National Council of Teachers of Mathematics (NCTM)
  1906 Association Drive
  Reston, VA 22091
  703-620-9840
  http://www.nctm.org/

National Science Teachers Association (NSTA)
  1742 Connecticut Avenue NW
  Washington, DC 20009
  202-328-5800
  http://www.nsta.org/

Phi Delta Kappa (PDK)
Eighth and Union
P.O. Box 789
Bloomington, IN 47401
812-339-1156
http://www.pdkintl.org/

Teachers of English to Speakers of Other Languages (TESOL)
1118 22nd Street NW
Washington, DC 20057
202-872-1271
http://www.tesol.org/

References and Suggested Readings

Canter, L., & Canter, M. (1992). *Assertive discipline: Positive behavior management for today's classroom.* Santa Monica, CA: Lee Canter & Associates.

Canter, L., & Canter, M. (1993). *Succeeding with difficult students.* Santa Monica, CA: Lee Canter & Associates.

Carroll, J. A., Beveridge, D., & McCune, D. (1987). *The welcome back to school book.* Carthage, IL: Good Apple.

Cohen, E. G. (1994). *Designing groupwork: Strategies for the heterogeneous classroom* (2nd ed.). New York: Teachers College Press.

Commission on Teacher Credentialing. (1995). Framework of expectations for beginning teachers. In *Beginning teaching in California: Expectations for teacher development* (pp. 9-24) [Draft document]. Sacramento: California Department of Education.

Costa, A. L. (Ed.). (1991). *Developing minds: A resource book for teaching thinking* (Rev. ed.). Alexandria, VA: Association for Supervision and Curriculum Development.

Developmental Studies Center, Child Development Project. (1995a). *That's my buddy! Friendship and learning across the grades.* Oakland, CA: Author.

Developmental Studies Center, Child Development Project. (1995b). *Ways we want our class to be: Class meetings that build commitment to kindness and learning.* Oakland, CA: Author.

DiGiulio, R. (1995). *Positive classroom management: A step-by-step guide to successfully running the show without destroying student dignity.* Thousand Oaks, CA: Corwin.

Farkas, S., Johnson, J., & Foleno, T. (2000). *A sense of calling: Who teaches and why.* New York: Public Agenda.

Federal Interagency Forum on Child and Family Statistics. (1998). *Federal Interagency Forum on Child and Family Statistics home page.* Retrieved July 2, 2001, from the World Wide Web: http://www.childstats.gov

Federal Interagency Forum on Child and Family Statistics. (2000). *America's Children: 2000.* Retrieved July 2, 2001, from the World Wide Web: http://www.childstats.gov/ac2000/ac00.asp

Fisher, C. W., Filby, N. N., Marliave, R., Cahen, L. S., Dishaw, M. M., Moore, J. E., & Berliner, D. C. (1978). Teaching behaviors, academic learning time, and student achievement: Final report of phase III-B: Beginning teacher evaluation study. In *Beginning teacher evaluation study technical report* (Tech. Rep. V-1). San Francisco: Far West Regional Educational Laboratory.

Good, T. L., & Brophy, J. E. (2000). *Looking in classrooms* (8th ed.). Boston: Allyn & Bacon.

Hunter, M. (1994). *Enhancing teaching.* Englewood Cliffs, NJ: Macmillan.

Jencks, C. (1972). *Inequality: A reassessment of the effects of family and schools in America.* New York: Basic Books.

Johnson, D., Johnson, R., & Holubec, E. (1994). *Cooperative learning in the classroom.* Alexandria, VA: Association for Supervision and Curriculum Development.

Kellough, R., & Roberts, P. (1994). *A resource guide for elementary school teaching: Planning for competence.* Englewood Cliffs, NJ: Macmillan.

Kendall, J., & Marzano, R. (1996). *Content knowledge: A compendium of standards and benchmarks for K-12 education.* Alexandria, VA: Association for Supervision and Curriculum Development. (Developed by Mid-Continent Regional Educational Laboratory)

Koenig, L. (1995). *Smart discipline in the classroom: Respect and cooperation restored* (Rev. ed.). Thousand Oaks, CA: Corwin.

Kronowitz, E. (1996). *Your first year of teaching and beyond* (2nd ed.). White Plains, NY: Longman.

Miller, W. H. (1996). *Alternative assessment techniques for reading and writing.* West Nyack, NY: Center for Applied Research in Education.

Mitchell, R. (1992). *Testing for learning: How new approaches to evaluation can improve American schools.* New York: Free Press/ Macmillan.

Moran, C., Stobbe, J., Baron, W., Miller, J., & Moir, E. (1992). *Keys to the classroom.* Newbury Park, CA: Corwin.

National Center for Education Statistics. (2001). *National Center for Education Statistics home page.* Retrieved July 2, 2001, from the World Wide Web: http://nces.ed.gov

North Central Regional Education Laboratory. (2001). *North Central Regional Education Laboratory professional development page.* Retrieved July 16, 2001, from the World Wide Web: http://www.ncrel. org/pd/

Northwest Regional Educational Laboratory. (1982). *How to increase learning time: A tool for teachers.* Portland, OR: Northwest Regional Educational Laboratory Technical Assistance Center.

Northwest Regional Educational Laboratory (developed by Pascarelli, J. T., Heisinger, D., Blum, R. E., Butterfield, R., & Crohn, L.). (1986). Module III: Instructional management. In *Training model for academic efficiency* (pp. 122-216). Portland, OR: Author. (Sponsored by Washington Office of the State Superintendent of Public Instruction)

Pearson, M. J., & Honig, B. (1992). *Success for beginning teachers: The California new teacher project.* Sacramento: California Department of Education, Commission on Teacher Credentialing.

Podesta, C. (1990). *Self-esteem and the six-second secret.* Newbury Park, CA: Corwin.

Porro, B. (1996). *Talk it out: Conflict resolution in the elementary classroom.* Alexandria, VA: Association for Supervision and Curriculum Development.

Sanders, W. T. (1997). Teacher and classroom context effects on student achievement: Implications for teacher evaluation. *Journal of Personnel Evaluation in Education.* Retrieved July 16, 2001, from the World Wide Web: http://www.mdk12.org/practices/ensure/tva/

Schell, L., & Burden, P. (1992). *Countdown to the first day* (NEA Checklist Series). Washington, DC: National Education Association.

Unger, H. G. (1996). Coleman report. In H. G. Unger (Ed.), *Encyclopedia of American education* (Vol. 1, p. 213). Washington, DC: Brookings Institution.

Warner, J., & Bryan, C. (1995). *The unauthorized teacher's survival guide.* Indianapolis, IN: Park Avenue.

Williamson, B. (1988). *A first-year teacher's guidebook for success: A step-by-step educational recipe book from September to June.* Sacramento, CA: Dynamic Teaching.

Wlodkowski, R., & Jaynes, J. (1990). *Eager to learn: Helping children become motivated and love learning.* San Francisco: Jossey-Bass.

Wolfe, P. (1988). *Catch them being good: Reinforcement in the classroom* [Video series and manual]. Alexandria, VA: Association for Supervision and Curriculum Development.

Wong, H., & Wong, R. (1991). *The first days of school: How to be an effective teacher.* Sunnyvale, CA: Harry R. Wong.

CORWIN
PRESS

The Corwin Press logo—a raven striding across an open book—represents the happy union of courage and learning. We are a professional-level publisher of books and journals for K-12 educators, and we are committed to creating and providing resources that embody these qualities. Corwin's motto is "Success for All Learners."